ARCHITECTURAL
SCIENCE
REVIEW

ARCHITECTURAL
SCIENCE
REVIEW

VOLUME 53 | **NUMBER 1** | 2010
SPECIAL ISSUE

Transforming markets in the built environment: adapting to climate change

Architectural Science Review 53(1) February 2010.
Published by Earthscan: Dunstan House,
14a St Cross Street, London EC1N 8XA, UK.

© 2010 Earthscan

ISSN: 0003-8628 (print), 1758-9622 (online)

CIP Data has been applied for.

SUBSCRIPTIONS

Subscription prices for Volume 53:

Institutions

Online only: £247 $494   €323
Online & print: £260 $520   €340 (airmail extra)

Personal

Online only: £99 $199   €130
Print only: £99 $199   €130 (airmail extra)

Orders can be placed online at www.earthscan.co.uk/journals/asre or sent to the journal's distributors, Portland Customer Services, using the contact details below.

Post: Portland Customer Services, Commerce Way,
        Colchester, CO2 8HP, UK
Fax: +44 (0)1206 799331
Tel: +44 (0)1206 796351
Email: sales@portland-services.com

Architectural Science Review is abstracted and indexed in over 30 services worldwide, including Architectural Publications Index and Architectural Database (RIBA), Cambridge Scientific Abstracts (CSA), Scopys and EBSCO. For a full list please visit the journal website: www.earthscan.co.uk/journals/asre

Earthscan journals are hosted online at www.ingenta.com

Printed in the UK by MPG Books Ltd on FSC certified paper.

Architectural Science Review is published quarterly. Periodicals Postage Paid at Rahway, NJ. US agent: Mercury International, 365 Blair Road, Avenel, NJ 07001. POSTMASTER: Address changes to ARCHITECTURAL SCIENCE REVIEW, 365 Blair Road, Avenel, NJ 07001.

CONTENTS

THE UNIVERSITY OF
SYDNEY

publishing for a sustainable future

Mixed Sources
Product group from well-managed forests and other controlled sources
www.fsc.org Cert no. SA-COC-1565
© 1996 Forest Stewardship Council

www.earthscan.co.uk/journals/asre

ARCHITECTURAL
SCIENCE
REVIEW

AIMS AND SCOPE

Published continuously since 1958, *Architectural Science Review* is the leading international peer-reviewed journal devoted to Architecture and Design Science, commonly called Architectural Science, which is the study of the physical aspects of architecture and design. The area encompasses studies of many of the built aspects of the environment that surrounds us with particular reference to the phenomena of heat, light and sound. It can also include studies into how people react to environments.

Architectural Science Review publishes original research papers, shorter research notes and abstracts of PhD dissertations and theses in all areas of architectural science, including:

- building science and technology

- environmental sustainability

- structures and materials

- audio and acoustics

- illumination

- thermal systems

- building physics

- building services

- building climatology

- building economics

- ergonomics

- history and theory of architectural science

- social sciences pertaining to architectural science

All research papers, research notes and review articles are double-blind refereed by a distinguished international Editorial Advisory Board and other experts in the field. *Architectural Science Review* also publishes occasional refereed special issues, invited review papers, case studies, editorials, and extensive book review.

The following criteria are used to assess submissions:

- Is the topic relevant to the journal's subject matter, i.e, to the science of architecture and the built environment?

- Is the research problem important and/or is the methodological approach innovative?

- Is the literature review comprehensive and reviewed in an integrative and critical manner?

- Are the research methods clearly stated and appropriate for the questions being addressed?

- Are the findings, interpretations and conclusions warranted from the research and data collected?

- Will the findings have applicability beyond the particular situation studied?

- Is the quality of presentation clear and along the guidelines laid out for potential authors in the journal and online?

- Overall rating: Does the paper contribute to new knowledge in the field?

Please refer to the submission guidelines at the back of the journal or please go to www.earthscan.co.uk/journals/asre for more information.

ARCHITECTURAL
SCIENCE
REVIEW

Transforming markets in the built environment and adapting to climate change: an introduction

Sue Roaf[1]*, Richard Hyde[2], Colin Campbell[3] and Martin Seigert[4]

[1]School of the Built Environment, Heriot Watt University, Edinburgh, EH14 4AS, UK
[2]Faculty of Architecture, Design and Planning, Wilkinson Building G04, University of Sydney, NSW 2006, Australia
[3]Association for the Study of Peak Oil and Gas, Staball Hill, Ballydehob, Co. Cork, Ireland
[4]School of GeoSciences, University of Edinburgh, Edinburgh, EH9 3JW, UK

INTRODUCTION

Adaptation is the process by which a population becomes better suited to its habitat over time in a bid to improve its chances of surviving. The speed at which the climate is currently changing means that if we are to weather the changes ahead with equanimity we must be clear about the characteristics we need to hone to do so, of which, perhaps, the most important is that of resilience.

Definition: Resilience is the property of a material to absorb energy when it is deformed elastically and then, upon unloading, to have this energy recovered (http://en.wikipedia.org/wiki/Resilience).

Definition: Resilience is the potential to sustain development by responding to, and shaping, change in a manner that does not lead to the loss of future options. Resilient systems also provide capacity for renewal and innovation in the face of rapid transformation and crisis (Berkes *et al.*, 2008).

To cope with the speed of changing circumstances around us, we need not only to adapt rapidly ourselves but also to ensure that the population in general is given the opportunity to understand why and how change is needed and to be given the opportunity to be part of that change. There is no gated community in the world that will keep a few safe while the majority is at risk. This volume deals with the nature of those necessary transformations.

Definition: Transforming markets is a direction now espoused by the WWF and others. Governments have supported policies of trade and economic growth, which have improved the quality of life for millions of people around the world, but it has come at a high cost to the environment (www.panda.org/what_we_do/how_we_work/businesses/transforming_markets).

Definition: Transforming industry is a 'process change' that is needed within industry groups to achieve sustainable buildings, arguably led by market incentives; transformation can occur and some of the myths and barriers to sustainable design will be addressed in the unfolding transformation (Hyde *et al.*, 2006).

The articles in this volume deal with some of the many challenges we face in trying to radically transform markets and strengthen the resilience of our buildings and populations against the growing impacts of resource depletion and degradation, in a rapidly changing climate. A range of philosophies, strategies, targets, tools and technologies are presented that may help steer as safe and focused a passage as possible through the difficult decades ahead. Buildings are particularly important in both mitigating the causes and adapting to the effects of a changing climate because we spend most of our lives in them, they are our first and last defence against an increasingly hostile environment and they are also the single biggest source of greenhouse gas (GHG) emissions on the planet.

The authors of the articles in this volume are drawn from a wide range of disciplines in the natural, social and physical sciences and the humanities and interrogate issues from very different perspectives, each lending weight and adding light to potential solutions in their own way. In some articles, the questions themselves are of paramount importance, in others their solutions. To our surprise, a number of authors appear to converge around a related range of core conclusions from very different starting points.

Underlying the notion of resilience as the ability to adapt, self-repair and evolve a system to survive change are three sets of questions:

- *Values*: What, fundamentally, are we now as a society? What do we hope to be? What, exactly, do we value? What values are we prepared to lose?

*Corresponding author: *Email*: s.roaf@sbe.hw.ac.uk

ARCHITECTURAL SCIENCE REVIEW 53 | 2010 | 3–11
doi:10.3763/asre.2009.0104 ©2010 Earthscan ISSN: 0003-8628 (print), 1758-9622 (online) www.earthscan.co.uk/journals/asre

earthscan

- *Risk*: What would it take to mortally wound the system so it could not self-repair? How likely is it that the system is mortally wounded?
- *Stratagems*: What are the risks we face in retaining those core values and related qualities of life in a changing world? How do we defuse potentially lethal risk?

Risk can be described as having three vectors (Crichton, 1999; Roaf *et al.*, 2009):

- *Hazard*: How bad is it going to get?
- *Exposure*: Where are people situated in relation to that risk?
- *Vulnerability*: How likely is the combination of the above going to prove lethal?

Risks ultimately do, or do not, translate into damage to an individual, livelihoods, systems, landscapes, countries or the planet. Risk is calculated by many as:

$$(possible) \text{ hazard} \times \text{vulnerability} \times \text{exposure}$$

$$= (possible) \text{ impact}$$

Where, within this static equation, the dynamic vector of resilience fits is not apparent. The connectedness and complexity of the social, physical, economic and environmental systems in the built environment are central to discussions in many of the articles that follow. The fundamental properties of resilience and adaptability are discussed, as are targets and objectives towards which designers may aim their efforts, and the tools and methods available for optimizing products and systems to meet the chosen targets.

It is difficult to see how to define and achieve resilience in the real world. In our current economic systems, the levels of emissions of GHGs are directly tied to pounds spent in economies (Scottish Government, 2009). In the debt-driven carnage of the global economic crisis of 2008/2009, the preferred solutions of most nations involved re-liquidating markets with government-owned debt. In Britain, a political tussle arose between the Conservatives who wanted to promptly pay off their debts and the Labour party whose successful attempts to breathe life into the markets required citizens to work more, spend more and achieve a market growth of 3% plus, year on year, for the foreseeable future. However, more money spent means greater GHG emissions with devastating environmental and external economic costs. Nicholas Stern (2006) and Ross Garnaut (2008) began to quantify the unprecedented scale of the economic impacts of climate change in the UK in 2006 and in Australia in 2008, respectively. Put in a nutshell, the conventional solution favoured by many to current economic instability is the very market growth that is threatening the future of the planet.

J.K. Galbraith (1999) quotes John Maynard Keynes as saying:

> Conventional wisdom protects the continuity in social thought and action. But there are also grave drawbacks and even dangers in a system of thought which by its very nature and design avoids accommodation to circumstances until change is dramatically forced upon it ... the rule of ideas is only powerful in a world that does not change. Ideas are inherently conservative. They yield not to attack of other ideas but to the massive onslaught of circumstances with which they cannot contend.

Colin Campbell and Martin Seigert, respectively, contribute the following sections on two of the potentially lethal features of the massive onslaught of circumstances that we now face: resource depletion, in relation to the peak oil phenomenon of fossil fuels; and climate change, characterized by the melting of the world's ice caps and glaciers and ensuing radical effects on biodiversity and the world's ecology.

PEAK OIL

The history of fossil fuel use reflects the rise of civilizations since the last ice age. About 300 million people occupied the planet at the time of Christ 2000 years ago and the number no more than doubled over the next 17 centuries as people lived sustainable lives within the limits of whatever their particular region could support. There were plenty of mainly local wars and conflicts as barons sought more power.

Coal had been used for centuries coming from outcropping seams and lumps washed up on beaches, but in the early 19th century people started deepening the pits into regular mines, which flooded when they hit the water table. This led to the most remarkable technological development ever; the hand pump which became the steam pump and soon the steam engine, which in turn opened new markets for transport and trade. Coal-based energy allowed the population to grow.

Then around 1860, a German engineer found a way of introducing the fuel directly into the cylinder of the steam engine, thus inventing the internal combustion engine, which was much more efficient. At first it relied on benzene distilled from coal, but that soon turned to petroleum refined from crude oil. It changed the world: the first tractor ploughed its furrow in 1907, and agriculture became a process that turned oil into food.

Oil had been known since antiquity, but the first oil wells were drilled in Pennsylvania and on the shores of the Caspian Sea in the 1850s. At first it supplied fuel for lamps, replacing whale oil that was becoming scarce from over-whaling. However, oil soon became a major energy source, allowing global populations to grow six-fold in parallel. Today, oil provides the energy equivalent of billions of slaves. It is a simple comparison. A slave could carry, say, a load of 25kg 30km in a day, but a truck can carry 100 times the load the same distance on a gallon of petrol. The world today produces around 29 billion barrels a year, each containing 42 gallons of oil.

However, oil and gas were formed in the geological past under most exceptional conditions, with most oil coming from two epochs of extreme global warming 90 and 150 million years ago. It did not take long for the pioneering geologists to work out the necessary conditions in terms of source, reservoir, trap and seal to locate the oil fields. During the 20th century the whole world was explored, with the more prospective areas, along with the major fields within them, being identified first. As onshore limits were breached, the industry turned offshore in the 1960s, adding another chapter to the oil story, with the help of remarkable technology. Attention currently turns to extremely deep water (>500m) areas, but only a few have the right geology, mainly on the margins of the South Atlantic and in the Gulf of Mexico, where prospective troughs had formed as the continents moved apart.

Oil and gas, being finite natural resources formed in the geological past, are clearly subject to depletion. Accordingly, production in any area starts and ends, passing a peak in between when about half the resource has been extracted. The sum of the individual profiles gives the world total. Oil and gas also have to be found before they can be produced. The peak of oil discovery was in the 1960s (a matter of historical fact) and must accordingly deliver a corresponding peak of production, regardless of recent large finds. A debate rages as to the precise date of peak but misses the point when what matters is the vision of the long decline on the other side of it.

Iain Reid, head of European oil and gas research at Australian investment bank Macquarie, produced a detailed report in September 2009 on when the peak of oil supply will be hit. His estimate is that the peak would be passed in 2009, after the economic crisis and the low prices of the first quarter of 2009 slashed much-needed investment in exploration and drilling. 'This is our view – capacity has pretty much peaked in the sense that declines equal new resources'.

Reid's report (2009) on 'The big oil picture: we're not running out, but that doesn't mean we'll have enough' sees global oil production capacity topping out at 89.6 million barrels per day (bpd) in 2009, a far more pessimistic view than most other banks or traditional forecasters. Underinvestment in mature fields, rising resource nationalism, and the cost and difficulty of retrieving oil from discoveries in ultra-deep water all play a part and could see global production capacity fall to 87.3 million bpd by 2015.

Colin Campbell, co-author of this article, now believes that the peak of conventional oil production was passed in 2005 and the resulting small shortfall was made up by expensive nonconventional oil (heavy oil from tar sands etc., deep water, polar and NGL (natural gas liquids)). Prices began to rise and shrewd traders spotted the trend, buying positions on the futures market; the industry kept its tanks full, watching them appreciate in value; and a flood of petrodollars moved to the Middle East, where oil still costs $10–20 a barrel to produce. This surplus was recycled to western banks who lent it out on ever less reliable terms. His estimates show that the peak of all categories of oil was passed in 2008, and the surge in oil price to almost $150 a barrel was not a coincidence (Campbell and Heapes, 2008).

However, the shrewd traders began to see the limit and started selling short on the futures market, and the industry started draining its tanks. The high prices triggered an economic downturn that cut demand, and prices fell back to about 2005 levels before again edging up to around $70 in 2009.

Governments reacting to the economic and financial crash have been engaged in 'quantitative easing', printing yet more 'new' money to stimulate consumption, which may indeed lead to a brief recovery. But if so, as mentioned above, it will stimulate not only the demand for oil, leading to another price surge, but also a deeper consequential economic crash and escalating GHG emissions globally.

Today, 29 billion barrels of oil (conventional + nonconventional) a year support 6.7 billion people, but by 2050, production, Campbell estimates, will be down to about 7.5 billion barrels, which is enough to support no more than about 2.7 billion people in the current way of life of the world's advanced societies and peoples.

Therefore, the challenge of adapting is monumental. Despite the flood of cheap energy replacing slave labour, the 20th century saw two wars of unparalleled severity, which at root were probably about rival quests for economic and financial empires, built on oil-based energy. The prime benefit of the British Empire was the use of the pound sterling for world trade that delivered massive control to the banks of London, a power base that was gradually passed to the USA after Woodrow Wilson consolidated US banking with the creation of the Federal Reserve Bank in 1913. The US Empire emerged supreme after the Second World War, with the Cold War helping it maintain its global hegemony. Its indigenous oil supply peaked in 1970 but the subsequent expansion of domestic credit meant that in effect it got its rising imports for free. Perhaps the last throw of the US imperial dice came with the invasions of Iraq and Afghanistan, in a vain attempt to control the export of Middle East and Caspian oil and gas.

While it is a brave person who will admit that they know what the future holds, past big system modellers with much cruder tools than we have today have been impressively close to the mark. M. King Hubbert first predicted approximately when oil production would peak (Hubbert, 1956), and his estimates were remarkably accurate. Similarly, Meadows *et al.* (1972) of the Club of Rome produced calculations on humanity's 'Limits to Growth' that have impressively stood the test of time. Graham Turner (2008) showed that 30 years of historical Limits to Growth data compared well with key features of a business-as-usual scenario called the 'standard run' scenario. The data he runs result in a collapse of the global system midway through the 21st century and indicates the particular importance of understanding and controlling global pollution. Indicators and impacts of that collapse are now being felt in the changing climates of the world.

CLIMATE CHANGE AND THE WORLD'S RISING SEAS AND DISAPPEARING ICE

Climate scientists have provided clear evidence for, and projections of, the growing threats posed by climate change, most recently at an international level through the mechanism of the Intergovernmental Panel on Climate Change reports (IPCC, 2007a, b). The fourth report, AR4 published in 2007, provided sound scientific proof of the link between anthropogenic emissions of GHGs and climate change, and detailed the impending step changes in the severity of the resulting impacts. It states that significant emissions reductions must occur by 2015 to prevent the world's temperature from rising more than 2°C over pre-industrialized temperatures. Until the Fourth Assessment Report of the IPCC (IPCC, 2007a, b) there appears to have been some leeway in terms of time available to achieve what were CO_2 emission reduction targets in the region of 450–550ppm. However, since then such targets are thought to be optimistic by many. James Hansen *et al.* (2008) have proposed that if the world is to avoid a catastrophic 'tipping point' in global climates from which in this geological age it will not recover, humanity should aim to return the global atmospheric CO_2 levels to 350ppm or lower.

What few credibly deny now is the growing evidence that carbon dioxide emissions are rising (ESRL, 2009) and that changes currently occurring in the climate also indicate the potential for runaway climate change. These points were brought home clearly in the October report of the UK Meteorological Office (2009), updating the Intergovernmental Panel on Climate Changes's Fourth Assessment Report data (IPCC, 2007a, b) and highlighting the potential for catastrophic rises of 4°C plus to occur by 2060, unless strong action on emissions is taken now.

Nowhere is the evidence of the rate of climate change more clearly written than in the science and the images of the world's rapidly disappearing ice from its glaciers and ice caps, that are causing sea levels to rise. It is these two facets alone of a myriad of climate change impacts and arguments that we have chosen to highlight in this introduction.

Global sea-level rises

Global sea level has been rising by 1.5mm/year for the past 100 years or so, giving a total rise over the century of approximately 15cm (Warrick *et al.*, 1993). Three main factors affect global sea levels on timescales of decades to centuries:

- Net loss of mass from land-based glaciers and ice sheets to the oceans. It is thought that a tenth or so of the observed annual rise in sea level could be a result of ablation from glaciers and ice sheets.
- Continued abstraction of groundwater aquifers, with the consequence that this water enters the global hydrological cycle and eventually the sea.
- The physical principle that the oceans will expand in a world that has warmed by about 0.5°C over the past century.

Although most glaciers on the Earth are melting, the total contribution they can make to the global sea level if they all melt is limited to less than 0.5 m. It currently appears

that a sea-level rise of several centimetres over the next few decades is likely to be derived from glacier melt.

Catastrophic sea-level rise, of the order of metres, could only come from ice sheet melting. Currently, there is sufficient ice on Greenland alone to raise sea levels by over 7m and more than 65m worth of sea-level rise stored in the ice sheets of Antarctica. Ice sheets react to climate changes much more slowly than glaciers, but because they release substantial volumes of ice to the ocean such changes are likely to be over several centuries rather than a few years. At present, estimates of Greenland and Antarctic mass balances are prone to uncertainties. What is certain is that Greenland is experiencing substantial melting during summertime, at an unprecedented rate. In Antarctica, several coastal zones are shrinking in height as a consequence of ice melting directly into the ocean.

Ice sheets are able to modify global sea level by tens of metres. Evidence comes from the last ice age 21,000 years ago. At its last maximum, the build-up of ice sheets across the northern hemisphere led to sea-level lowering of around 120m followed by an equivalent level of sea-level rise in the following 10,000 years, at an average rate of >1m/100 years (Siegert, 2001).

Taking this rate as indicative of the maximum potential of ice sheets to force sea-level rise and adding that to the effect of glacier decay, we may expect sea levels to rise globally by several tens of centimetres over the next century, given projections of global temperatures. It would be prudent now, in good time, to put in place processes for negotiating, funding and implementing retreats of populations from high-risk low-lying regions.

The ice volumes for Greenland and Antarctica are for ground ice only, and exclude ice shelves. As ice shelves are floating, they have already displaced their weight in water; hence if they melted, sea level would not change as a consequence. The potential rise in sea level from ice sheets is determined by calculating the isostatic uplift that would occur if the ice were taken off, and allowing for the volume of sea water that would replace the ice in some areas. The sea level is therefore less than its ice volume equivalent (Table 1).

Table 1 | Present day volume of glaciers and ice sheets

Geographic region	Volume (km³)	Percentage	Potential sea-level rise (m)
Ice caps, ice fields, glaciers, etc.	180,000	0.6	0.45
Greenland	2,850,000	10.0	7.2
Antarctica	25,710,000	89.4	61.1
Total	28,740,000	100	68.75

Source: Adapted from Swithinbank (1985) and Williams and Ferrigno (2002)

Patterns of glacier retreat

The short response times taken for glaciers to melt and retreat make it possible to assess their reaction to climate change by surveying them over a few decades. Net mass balance measurements from glaciers around the world show, for the most part, a consistent trend of negative mass balance over the past 30 years and, in some examples where records permit, over the past 100 years (Braithwaite, 2002). In the Svalbard archipelago in northern Norway, for example, only four of the 44 measurements ($<10\%$) of net mass balance show a positive annual increment. In the Canadian Arctic islands, more than 70% of balance years are negative. However, it should be noted that these mass balance datasets have a relatively high inter-annual variability, although a number of the time series are statistically different from zero and indicate a negative mass balance.

From the mass balance measurements of Arctic glaciers, distributed relatively widely across the polar North, it can be concluded that, during the past 30–40 years, glaciers from most areas of the High and the Low Arctic have shown no sign of building up, and have experienced either a negative or near-zero average mass balance. In Alaska, almost all the glaciers observed are in a state of negative mass balance but a few have mass balances close to zero over the period of observation (Arendt et al., 2002).

Glaciers in maritime western Norway, such as Nigardsbreen, have had a clearly positive mean mass balance since measurements started in 1962 (Laumann and Reeh, 1993). A recent shift towards more positive annual balances has also been observed over almost the whole of Scandinavia since 1988 (Braithwaite, 2002). This region is a noticeable exception to the global trend of glacier retreat. It is thought that the region is influenced strongly by warming in the North Atlantic, the positive phase of the North Atlantic oscillation and the northward deflection of winter storm tracks. Such conditions result in additional snowfall on neighbouring glaciers, which more than counters the negative effect of enhanced melting.

Glaciological investigations from a variety of glaciers within the tropics show that most of them are in a perilous state of decay (Thompson et al., 2002). In fact, the mass balance of glaciers such as those on Kilimanjaro in Tanzania is so negative that the glaciers could completely disappear entirely in as little as 20–30 years. In many regions, not least the Himalayas, this means that summer water supplies will no longer be available to downstream populations, and suggests that strategies for alleviating future related drought conditions for billions of the world population should now be developed. Water from the melting glaciers of the Himalayas alone supplies nearly a third of the world's human population, but also sustains the habitats of millions of other species. The disappearance of the summer melt waters of glacial ice fields will trigger a major disturbance in the ecological equilibrium of the planet.

Melting ice sheets

The long response times of ice sheets mean that it has traditionally been difficult to determine whether they are in positive or negative balance. For example, Jacobs et al. (1992) estimated a negative balance of 469Gt/year for Antarctica, based on measurements of accumulation, iceberg calving, sub ice shelf melting and run-off. However, the uncertainties associated with some of these measurements were between 20 and 50%.

There are three general ways of defining the mass balance of a large ice sheet. The first is by an assessment of the mass budget, as Jacobs et al. (1992) did for Antarctica. The second is from airborne and satellite measurements of the ice sheet surface elevation (Wingham et al., 1998), which, if data are acquired over a period of a few years, allow changes in ice thickness to be measured to centimetre accuracy. The third is by using satellite-based gravity measurements, since ice volume changes will have a measurable gravitational consequence (e.g. NASA's Gravity Recovery and Climate Experiment).

These techniques have been used to understand the current balance of large ice sheets. In Greenland, NASA's Program for Arctic Regional Climate Assessment (PARCA) provided unprecedented data about the ice sheet's state of health. This work showed that Greenland is melting, and thinning, across its southern margin. Importantly, the surface melt water finds its way to the ice base and acts as a lubricant to ice flow, thus encouraging the ice to move faster and resulting in further thinning (Zwally et al., 2002).

In Antarctica, the problem of mass balance remains hard to solve. Satellite altimeter data show that certain parts of West Antarctica are thinning (e.g. Pine Island and Thwaites glaciers). At the same time, the Siple Coast ice streams appear to be gaining mass. There is a connection between ice thickness changes and ice dynamics (i.e. as ice flow increases, ice thickness will decrease), and this could explain the difference in elevation changes observed from different parts of the ice sheet. In the Siple Coast, for example, Ice Stream C has stopped flowing rapidly and Whillans Ice Stream (formerly known as Ice Stream B) is slowing down (Joughin and Tulaczyk, 2002). Similarly, the ice loss across the Pine Island sector could be a result of increased velocities here rather than an alteration to the surface balance. The complexity of the systems involved require and are receiving massive research attention, commensurate with the scale of related impacts including escalating rates of sea-level rise and melting of the Himalayan glaciers.

IMPERATIVE FOR CHANGE

While scientists work hard to understand such complex and dynamically changing systems, new techniques and technologies are employed to measure and interpret the risks and realities of climate change. The results we have to date are 'good enough' to show that along with their hinterland eco-systems, human systems will have to change radically and rapidly to survive. We now have more people wanting and needing to do more work with less cheap fossil fuel energy. Emerging new burdens include the need to move our populations away from danger, to provide enough water for existing populations where existing supplies are drying up, and to continue to grow economies against the backdrop of rapid environmental change.

Our resilience in the near and further future will depend on the extent to which the buildings we occupy and the life-styles we live in them can cope with more extreme climates with dwindling stocks of fossil fuels and less money to go around. Some individuals and communities will be more able to survive than others, but for the global masses there must be a growing societal imperative to use combinations of persuasion, incentives, punishments and coercion to influence behaviour and effect real change.

The following articles begin to deal with the challenge of making those changes happen in the real world rather than merely in the theoretical models of academics alone. The following authors, from very different disciplines and directions, approach the common theme of making change happen by transforming the markets and mindsets of our citizens to embrace change in the difficult decades ahead. As a whole, the articles offer an important starting point for solutions and together they have the potential to initiate powerful alliances for innovation and real change.

WHAT THIS VOLUME CONTAINS

David Wadley, a social scientist involved with built environment disciplines, provides an overview of models from social theory and behavioural psychology that shed light on central drivers for social action from which many of the underpinning assumptions regarding notion of 'market transformation' may be garnered. As in climate science, significant research questions are emerging of what 'tipping points' exist, or are needed, to transform attitudes, values and to spur a behaviour change that leads to adoption of mitigation and adaptation strategies in buildings.

While Al Gore focuses our attention on images associated with catastrophes in the natural and human worlds arising from climate change, one could construe this as an attempt to simply create political capital from the science investigating the phenomena. The real question centres on whether this is sufficient to create a response or indeed bridle change within the dominant social paradigm. Climate change and its related biophysical effects are not something that just happens in the natural world but not in the human world. Unfortunately, socially greater impacts are experienced in the developing world with its escalating poverty and human suffering, while people in the developed world still largely maintain their quality of life. Significant dualities now exist between these four worlds, that is, the developed and the developing, the natural and the man-made; how can these be reconciled and translated into action to transform behaviour through market systems?

Simon Guy builds a theoretical case for flexibility and pragmatism in design located in the real world of actual projects and locations, as being essential for resilient and adaptive systems. He sets the scene for this issue by defining the need to fundamentally revise the focus and scope of the debate about sustainable architecture, to reconnect issues of technological change with the social and cultural contexts within which change occurs. He sees the challenge of engaging society in the solutions as crucial and points out that while both checklists and philosophical speculation can be helpful and even necessary to achieve certain objectives, they rarely provoke the wider 'public talk' necessary to engage community participation in sustainable design. That is, the 'work' of choosing how we want to live – with and in nature – in order to sustain life into the future. Exploration of diversity in design and development would encourage a deeper engagement with sustainable architecture, one that does not shy away from broader sociological or philosophical questions or merely indulge in the narrowly technical debates that characterize so much of the green architecture literature. He urges the move away from standardization and productification and argues the need to identify situationally specific challenges and address them in contextually viable solutions. As he highlights, a range of design solutions may provide appropriate solutions, one size definitely does not fit all.

Ted Trainer offers us an opposite view, with a very clear understanding of a system that in the coming decades is vulnerable to lethal 'overshoot', as system capacities are exceeded. He argues that the magnitude of the overshoot is so great that it is not plausible that technical advance or conservation effort could eliminate problems of global sustainability and injustice while the fundamental commitments of our consumer society remain, characterized by the pursuit of affluent living standards and economic growth within a market system. He offers a community living model, with simple, communal living standards, that he believes provides the best hope for resilience and survival over the long term. One very much gets the impression that the model he promotes may be an Australia solution and perhaps may not be so appropriate for the dense city dwellers of Beijing, New York or São Paulo. He contributes a radical vision of where we may eventually have to aim, to live within our means, within the finite capacities of our ecological systems in a post fossil fuel society.

This baton is taken up by Gatersleben et al., who study people's values and sustainable lifestyles. Their findings show that many people express both relatively high levels of environmental concern and relatively high levels of materialism simultaneously and that materialism and environmental concern appear to be related to different types of behaviour. This raises an interesting paradox: if markets are to be transformed rapidly to have lower consumer impacts, does this have to be met with the use of products that appeal to the general public as fashionable signals and symbols of a 'consumer society'?

Silva Larson also builds on this notion that changes in aspirations and consumer models will have to be better understood and sold to the public. Her article proposes that improved 'translation' of policy goals and actions into issues relevant to local stakeholders on the ground may play an important role in stakeholders' understanding and consequent acceptance of the principles of sustainability and adaptation. In turn, the policies themselves could be considerably improved by increasing their relevance and acceptability to that public. One way of doing this is to touch a profound cord with individuals, such as that it is the well-being of family and close friends that would benefit from actions taken. Her studies of perceptions of well-being help develop this theme and give an insight into effective motivational factors that may enhance adaptive actions and reduce vulnerability for individuals and communities alike.

Cândido et al. present a fascinating study on attitudes towards the use of air conditioning in Maceio, in northeastern Brazil. In a warm humid climate where the mean annual temperature is around 26°C and the annual thermal amplitude is 3.4°C, it was found that an occupant's thermal history has a large influence on their perception of indoor thermal environment. Two groups, one in air-conditioned buildings and the other in naturally ventilated buildings, both found their working environments to be in the 'neutral', 'slightly warm' and 'warm' categories. However, two-thirds of occupants exposed to air conditioning systems at their workplace preferred air conditioning systems, whereas the remaining third indicated a preference for natural ventilation or natural ventilation plus fans. In contrast, the results were completely the opposite for those occupants without exposure to air conditioning systems at their workplace. In this sample, two-thirds of cooling preference responses was for natural ventilation and fans whereas only one-third preferred air conditioning systems. This goes very much back to Gatersleben's points on technology as a symbol, and the importance of understanding its function as such.

Roaf et al. then set about to dismantle a key barrier to the execution of low carbon buildings, identified in Ward et al.'s article, that of rigid and inappropriate indoor air temperature standards that have evolved to promote the drive towards air conditioning, and at the same time prevent naturally ventilated buildings from being deemed acceptable by many current building regulation standards. The article by Cândido et al. demonstrates that for many climates in the world, virtually the same levels of comfort can be provided at no cost in a naturally ventilated building and at a very high energy cost in an air-conditioned building. Roaf et al. attempt to explain why this state of affairs has arisen starting with an overview of the evolution of thermal comfort standards and the two main approaches to the measurement and application of comfort standards. They are, first, that

of comfort as a product to be sold to people and, second, comfort as a perceived quality to be achieved by exploiting the adaptive opportunities provided by the building and the people in it, to improve experienced conditions or lower energy running costs. The article then goes on to propose two potentially better ways of regulating the control of indoor air temperatures in buildings. The first is that of using the adaptive method of thermal comfort relating the indoor air temperature preferences to running means of outdoor temperatures for adapted populations. The second is the blanket use of an annual maximum and minimum temperature range for a particular region, and allowing building owners and users to control their indoor air temperatures within, and outwith, that zone, relying on the negotiation by occupants of optimal agreed indoor temperatures. The article argues that in future, because of issues of peak oil and the need to reduce GHG emissions, building regulations will be reversed to favour and promote low-energy and low-emission buildings rather than the reverse that occurs today.

Tuohy et al. then take the three comfort approaches from Roaf et al.'s article and model iterations of an office building in London to determine what exactly are the energy penalties of the current regulations, the adaptive and the fixed zone approaches. If market transformations are to be driven by policy and regulation, then it is imperative that the regulations move markets in the right direction. Such studies are vital to promote an understanding of the physical limits of the adaptive capacity of people and buildings in different climates. The article shows what a great difference careful design of a building and its adaptive opportunities can make not only in reducing energy use but also in protecting occupants from extremes of climate. This pair of articles demonstrate the importance of understanding how people, buildings and climate interact, in contrast to the Newton and Tucker article and the Ward et al. article that deal more specifically with the relationship between technologies, buildings and management, or to the Cândido et al. article that sheds light on the values associated with building conditioning decisions.

Ward et al. at Australia's Commonwealth Scientific and Industrial Research Organisation (CSIRO) report on trials that are currently being conducted in Australian commercial office buildings to demonstrate the effectiveness of advanced heating, ventilation and air conditioning (HVAC) controls. In order to minimize energy use in, and GHG emissions from, the building, they include behaviour-reliant technologies to actively manage occupant expectations, influence comfort perception and promote thermal acceptability. To realize maximum reductions, the adoption of bioclimatic architectural principles and incorporation of renewable energy technologies are employed in conjunction with systems that enable indoor environments to move away from fixed indoor comfort conditions and towards adaptive comfort control and a wider range of acceptable indoor temperatures. They found that deep reductions can be achieved with occupant responsive strategies to automate and motivate opportunities for change. The study does provide a significant step towards radically lower impact buildings and again harks back to Gatersleben's understanding that people want to be 'modern' and Cândido's finding that people will choose and promote products that reflect a preferred self-image, and the values on which that image is based. Working with those value issues, while still creating low carbon products and services, may be possible but the total product must be understood if it is to be successfully marketed.

The Newton and Tucker article shows the power of technology to reduce emissions from homes with a detailed study of the technical opportunities available for the reduction of GHGs from Australian houses. A range of design strategies are modelled to explore ways of minimizing the carbon footprints of a range of house types (detached, medium density and high-rise) with different levels of construction and distributed or local energy generation. The study presents feasible, technical pathways to zero carbon housing, with quantified average energy and carbon emission savings per dwelling and technology type, comparing proposed improvements with new detached project homes designed to current 5 star energy standards. This study is useful in informing policy decisions on emission reduction investments in technologies. What it does not provide is a map of the social pathways/value systems that may be used to promote the technologies. Here the work of Gatersleben *et al.* and Larson could be combined to explore acceptable product packages that may lead to more rapid market transformations in this direction.

Gardner and Vieritz deal with that most vital of all resources, water. The change in rainfall patterns in most of Australia's urban water supply catchments under recent conditions of acute drought in many regions has focused the attention of water planners on the need for diversity and robustness of supply in a changing climate. This detailed study on the use of water storage tanks in Australia covers the many aspects of their use, regulation, cost and impacts. Using a range of models and covering a range of key issues, the study concludes that water tanks have a significant role to play in 21st century urban Australia but their long-term advantages will be more easily promoted if their benefits and constraints are better understood, particularly those of energy consumption for their pumps and filters, their microbiological safety and the success of various social ownership models for their uptake. This is an article that is as relevant to the communities of Nepal and Tanganyika as it is to Queensland. It deals with the challenge of surviving in so many regions of the world in a hotter and drier future.

In the final article, Hawasly *et al.* take a theoretical design study of a village of 20 new houses at Heriot Watt University in Scotland, and use an agent-based, complex, dynamic, simulation platform to provide a model that integrates the building performance with the occupant's 'fuzzy' behaviours, the intermittent stochastic contributions of a range of renewable energy generators, a dynamic climate model and any number of contributory dimensions in the search for new ways of reducing emissions from the built environment. This complex platform enables modellers to investigate the benefits of individual and community optimizations strategies, and the study revealed very large-scale benefits from communalizing energy saving activities, such as sharing fridges, washing machines or TVs, in ways that reflect the narrative of Trainer's article. Validated, behavioural dimensions of such models may offer the most promising way of asking 'what if' questions about complex social and physical systems and inform developing resilience measures, incorporating values and accounting costs and impacts within proposed solutions. The model also has the potential to help develop conversations with communities on the costs and impacts of their own choices, and provides a tool to inform and enable new enviro-social contracts to be written, taking inspiration from the hydro-social contracts of Gardner and Vieritz.

Just as Berkes *et al.* (2008) promoted the need for resilience in their seminal book on social-ecological systems, through better management of natural resources and the human capacity to deal with change, so we hope that this volume will shed new light on ways of building resilience for populations in the buildings and communities they occupy.

The severity of the issues we touched on above, of dwindling oil resources, rising seas and melting ice, gives us a glimpse of the scale of the risks we face in not acting in time. The virtual extinction of *Homo sapiens* this century, as proposed by Lovelock (2006, 2009) and others, would not be wholly illogical as there are many examples in the geological record of over-adapted species that died out when the environment on which they depended changed for climatic or other reasons. To be more optimistic, one could imagine a more benign life opening for the people and regions, as Ted Trainer does, where resilience has been built, communities have learnt to live in a sustainable way, in connected urban neighbourhoods, or suburbs and villages growing vegetables instead of lawns, sleeping at sundown, bicycling to the pub for a social evening free of screen or loudspeaker, and above all living in sustainable buildings and cities.

A key question that emerges from these articles is whether our salvation lies with technology or with behavioural change – or a well-orchestrated combination of the two?

It is our hope that the sensible integration and application of the type of research being developed and shared in this volume, aimed at finding solutions to even the gravest of global problems, will help to smooth the transformation of minds and markets, to adapt and build resilience, to teach us how to live within the capacity of our ecosystems and to find a new equilibrium with nature, so we can all live to enjoy such comfortable futures.

References

Arendt, A.A., Echelmeyer, K.A., Harrison, W.D., Lingle, C.S. and Valentine, V.B., 2002, 'Rapid wastage of Alaskan glaciers and their contribution to rising sea level', *Science* 297, 382–386.

Berkes, F., Colding, J. and Folke, C., 2008, *Navigating Social-Ecological Systems: Building Resilience for Complexity and Change*, Cambridge, UK, Cambridge University Press.

Braithwaite, R.J., 2002, 'Glacier mass balance: the first 50 years of international monitoring', *Progress in Physical Geography* 26, 76–95.

Campbell, C.J., 2005, *Oil Crisis*, Brentwood, UK, Multi-Science Publishing.

Campbell, C.J. and Heapes, S., 2008, *An Atlas of Oil and Gas Depletion*, Huddersfield, UK, Jeremy Mills Publishing

Crichton, D., 1999, 'The risk triangle', in J. Ingleton (ed), *Natural Disaster Management*, London, Tudor Rose.

ESRL (Earth System Research laboratory), 2009, 'Current trends in CO_2 at Mauna Loa Laboratory'. Available at: www.esrl.noaa.gov/gmd/ccgg/trends/

Galbraith, J.K., [1958]1999, *The Affluent Society*, Canada, Penguin Books, 17.

Garnaut, R., 2008, *The Garnaut Climate Change Review*, Cambridge, Cambridge University Press. Available at: www.garnautreview.org.au/index.htm

Hansen, J., Sato, M., Kharecha, P., Beerling, D., Berner, R., Masson-Delmotte, V., Pagani, M., Raymo, M., Royer, D.L. and Zacho, J.C., 2008, 'Target atmospheric CO_2: where should humanity aim?', *Science*, 6 August. Full paper available at: http://arxiv.org/ftp/arxiv/papers/0804/0804.1126.pdf

Hubbert, M.K., 1956, *Nuclear Energy and the Fossil Fuels*, Publication No. 95 of the Shell Oil Company, Exploration and Research Division, Huston, TX, Full text available at: www.hubbertpeak.com/hubbert/1956/1956.pdf

Hyde, R.A., Watson, S., Cheshire, W. and Thomson, M., 2006, *The Environmental Brief*, London, Taylor and Francis.

IPCC, 2007a, *Climate Change 2007: The Physical Science Basis. Summary for Policymakers, Contribution of Working Group I to the Fourth Assessment Report of the Intergovernmental Panel on Climate Change*, Geneva, IPCC.

IPCC, 2007b, *Mitigation. Contribution of Working Group III to the Fourth Assessment Report of the Intergovernmental Panel on Climate Change*, Geneva, IPCC. Available at: www.wmo.ch/web/Press/Press.html

Jacobs, S.S., Hellmer, H.H., Doake, C.S.M., Jenkins, A. and Frolich, R.M., 1992, 'Melting of ice shelves and the mass balance of Antarctica', *Journal of Glaciology* 38, 375–387.

Joughin, I. and Tulacyk, S., 2002, 'Positive mass balance of the Ross Ice Streams, West Antarctica', *Science* 295, 476–480.

Laumann, T. and Reeh, N., 1993, 'Sensitivity to climate change of the mass balance of glaciers in southern Norway', *Journal of Glaciology* 39, 656–665.

Lovelock, J., 2006, *The Revenge of Gaia*, London, Penguin Publications.

Lovelock, J., 2009, *The Vanishing Face of Gaia: A Final Warning*, London, Allen Lane.

Meadows, D.H., Meadows, D.L., Randers, J. and Behrens, W., 1972, *The Limits to Growth; A Report for the Club of Rome's Project on the Predicament of Mankind*, London, St Martins Press.

Reid, I., 2009, *The Big Oil Picture: We're Not Running Out, But That Doesn't Mean We'll Have Enough*, Sydney, Macquarie Bank. Available at: www.theglobeandmail.com/globe-investor/peak-oil-expected-in-2009-macquarie/article1289428/

Roaf, S., Crichton, D. and Nicol, F., 2009, *Adapting Buildings and Cities for Climate Change*, 2nd Edition, Oxford, Architectural Press.

Scottish Government, 2009, Carbon Assessment Report on the 2010–2011 draft budget of the Scottish Government. Available at: www.

scotland.gov.uk/Publications/2009/09/17102339/0

Siegert, M.J., 2001, *Ice Sheets and Late Quaternary Environmental Change*, John Wiley, Chichester, UK.

Stern, N., 2006, *The Stern Review Final Report*, HM Treasury, London. Available at: www.hm-treasury.gov.uk/sternreview_index.htm

Swithinbank, C.W.S., 1985, 'A distant look at the cryosphere', *Advances in Space Research* 5(6), 263–274.

Thompson, L.G., Mosely-Thompson, E., Davis, M.E., Henderson, K.A., Brecher, H.H., Zagorodnov, V.S., Mashiotta, T.A., Lin, P.-N., Mikhalenko, V.N., Hardy, D.R. and Beer, J., 2002, 'Kilimanjaro ice core records: evidence of Holocene climate change in tropical Africa', *Science* 298(5593), 589–593.

Turner, G., 2008, 'A comparison of "the limits to growth" with thirty years of reality', *Global Environmental Change* 18(3), 397–411.

UK Meteorological Office, 2009, *Avoiding Dangerous Climate Change*, Exeter, Met. Office. Available at: www.metoffice.gov.uk/publications/brochures/cop14.pdf

Warrick, R.A., Barrow, E.M. and Wigley, T.M.L. (eds), 1993, *Climate and Sea Level Change: Observations, Projections and Implications*, Cambridge, Cambridge University Press.

Williams, R.S. and Ferrigno, J.G., 2002, 'Estimates of present-day area and volume of glaciers and maximum sea level rise potentials', *Satellite Image Atlas of Glaciers of the World*, US Geological Survey professional paper 1386-A, Washington, US Geological Survey. Available at: http://pubs.usgs.gov/fs/fs133-99/gl_vol.html

Wingham, D.J., Ridout, A.J., Scharroo, R., Arthern, R.J. and Shum, C.K., 1998, 'Antarctic elevation change from 1992 to 1996', *Science* 282, 456–458.

Zwally, H.J., Abdalati, W., Herring, T., Larson, K., Saba, J. and Steffen, K., 2002, 'Surface melt-induced acceleration of Greenland ice-sheet flow', *Science* 297, 218–222.

ARCHITECTURAL
SCIENCE
REVIEW

Exploring a quality of life, self-determined

David Wadley*

School of Geography, Planning and Environmental Management, The University of Queensland, 4072, Queensland, Australia

Built capital combines with social, personal and natural capital to contextualize people's quality of life. Although this last concept has strongly tested academic reasoning, it is often presented simply and as a *fait accompli* in strategic planning documents. This article questions these pragmatic 'top-down' scripts by engaging the self-determination theory of motivation. It argues the transience of hedonic or material reward and posits a much higher plane of eudemonic fulfilment. The key to self-determination and, thus, an agreeable quality of life lies in an individual's acquisition of competence, autonomy and relatedness. From this bridgehead and via a macro-level analysis, the article identifies contemporary economic, environmental and social challenges to the achievement of quality of life, ones that are likely to need individual resourcefulness and resilience to overcome. The account concludes that, instead of proffering cookie-cutter or one-size-fits-all formulae, authorities may consider ways of helping individuals help themselves to a better quality of life based on a precept that life is, in part, what you make it and does not rely on material wealth alone. In this way, it could be possible to substitute other forms for material capital to improve environmental and social sustainability.

Keywords: Hedonic and eudemonic welfare; hierarchy of needs; quality of life; self-determination theory; strategic planning

INTRODUCTION

Strategic planning schemes regularly posit liveability, lifestyle or quality of life as part of their vision for urban development. In Australia, for example, the recent South East Queensland Regional Plan (SEQRP) aims for sustainability, affordability, prosperity and liveability (Queensland Government, 2009). The last term is associated with safety, health, accessibility and inclusivity, provision of infrastructure and services, integration of urban and rural areas, retention of significant landscapes and availability of open space. These elements are mainly macro in scale, reflecting what the public sector or society as a whole can provide.

Such plans, conceived by bureaucrats, politicians or both, represent top-down models of how people may or should live. In its methodology, the SEQRP regards liveability as a desirable dependent variable, allegedly produced by interactions among the aforementioned independent variables. As Haggett and Chorley (1967, p24) have underlined, models are to be judged not in terms of 'true' or 'false' but, rather, through their utility in understanding, or otherwise achieving, human objectives. Fair questions are therefore the following:

- Has a plan correctly interpreted the interactions of independent variables and their role in producing the dependent variable (i.e. internal validity)?
- Are there duplicating or confounding independent variables among those proposed (efficiency)?

- Are there any other variables not included that could either greatly assist or hinder achievement of the dependent variable, liveability (external validity)?

Yet, while such interrogation addresses the construction of quality of life, it remains partial. The scripting is that of a policy elite. It sits oddly with the individualism behind the neoliberal wave that has swept the Anglo West since the 1980s. Collaborative planning theory generally elevates the views of those for whom plans are made above those of the planners. Thus, it is possible that people on the street in southeast Queensland, or anywhere else, may be disinterested in a discussion of quality of life based on their perception in the process of an unfavourable benefit-to-cost ratio, or they may propose a different definition from that officially forwarded and, consequently, a different set of variables to achieve it.

Overall, these deliberations question the relationship between ends and means and the sense of 'quality' in life. This article tackles these problems in a series of steps. First, as background, some conventional research into the precepts of quality of life is recounted. Thereafter, several foundational models are explored to assist our logical positioning in a move from the governmental line to one that admits an individual approach. They enable subsequent discussion of the economic, environmental and social contexts that people face and how they may respond to them in attempting to improve their lot. A set of conclusions rounds off the discussion.

*Email: d.wadley@uq.edu.au

doi:10.3763/asre.2009.0SI1 ⓒ2010 Earthscan ISSN: 0003-8628 (print), 1758-9622 (online) www.earthscan.co.uk/journals/asre

earthscan

QUALITY OF LIFE AND SUBJECTIVE WELL-BEING RESEARCH

Quality of life

Almost everyone is surrounded by different sorts of capital (Mulder *et al.*, 2006). Social capital connotes interpersonal relations and is allied with human capital as represented in people's growth and development. Connection with nature provides natural capital, whereas the urban and rural environments we have created contribute built capital. Given all these wellsprings of capital, whence comes our quality of life?

Addressing this matter in terms of satisfaction outcomes, Sirgy and Cornwell (2002) tested three models, each of which sees life satisfaction proceeding from an interaction among different components. It could be alternatively that:

- Satisfaction with social, economic and physical features contributes to a person's satisfaction with a neighbourhood (neighbourhood satisfaction), which, in turn, bears positively on overall satisfaction with life (life satisfaction).
- Neighbourhood satisfaction, as defined, exercises a hierarchy of satisfaction effects, influencing both community and housing satisfaction. Housing satisfaction determines home satisfaction. Both home and community satisfaction go on to govern life satisfaction.
- Physical features affect both neighbourhood and housing satisfaction. Neighbourhood satisfaction plays a role in community satisfaction whereas housing satisfaction influences home satisfaction. Both community and home satisfaction then feed into life satisfaction.

Although these qualify of life elements appear quite empirical, their pathways are evidently complex. Survey findings incline the authors to the third of the satisfaction models. They argue that satisfaction with social features of a neighbourhood (type of residents, interactions generated, level of crime, race relations, play areas and privacy considerations) is mediated through community satisfaction to determine life satisfaction. Simultaneously, the physical and economic characteristics of a neighbourhood affect residents' feelings, but housing satisfaction, twinned with home satisfaction, plays a more vital role in life satisfaction.

This line of enquiry is positive and proceeds from the grass roots (i.e. bottom up) but its efficacy must be compared with that offered in broader theorizing about subjective well-being.

Subjective well-being

As ably summarized by Mulder *et al.* (2006), macro-level research into well-being has relied on certain models in psychology and economics. In psychology, 'set point' theory holds that, as established by genetics and personality, each individual has a fixed level of happiness, around which she or he will fluctuate according to the eventualities of life.

When scaled up, the primary influence in determining the subjective well-being of communities is therefore nature, exemplified in genetics, rather than nurture as in income, health, education and infrastructure.

By comparison, neo-classical economists have argued that, for normal as opposed to inferior goods, more is better and that the chief factor behind subjective well-being is income.

Richard Easterlin (2003), a leading scholar within the burgeoning 'happiness literature',[1] has rejected both these standpoints. No doubt reflecting the insight of the political philosopher John Rawls (1971) that envy is ever present in human affairs, he suggests that people often regard positional goods as signposting the road to happiness. Yet, these artefacts and the income needed to purchase them facilitate hedonic adaptation and easy social comparison. Easterlin observes that people spend a disproportionate amount of time working to make money to the detriment of health and family life, even though these latter domains contribute strongly to the attainment of individual goals. In this regard, he underscores the importance of non-pecuniary concerns in creating happiness (as opposed to mere economic 'utility').

With this footing in the conventional literature, we can turn to a less orthodox approach that reinterprets quality of life issues not from planning pronouncements but from the standpoint of the ordinary person, acknowledging his or her 'patch' in physical space and position in life.

FOUNDATIONAL MODELS

Daly's means–ends spectrum

A useful orientation can be had in a model devised by the environmental economist Herman Daly (1977), who arranges the disciplines in a linear (Aristotelian) sequence (Figure 1). By this reckoning, we have ultimate means in matter and energy that are converted into intermediate means, 'usable resources', through change from a lower to a higher entropy state as per the second law of thermodynamics. Physics, chemistry, engineering and architecture are lead disciplines in this arena. With intermediate means, we are able to satisfy intermediate ends, assisted by studies in economics, planning and sociology. Beyond these disciplines, however, lie others within the humanities and arts that are concerned with the ultimate ends of human existence. They include conventional philosophy, ethics and religion. Many facets of architecture and city building in the past have aspired to embody these ultimate ends, so they should not be overlooked today.

Maslow's hierarchy of needs

Daly's comprehensive means–ends spectrum can be interpreted in the model of human motivation created by the psychologist Abraham Maslow in 1954 (Figure 2) (Maslow, 1987). His hierarchy of needs starts with the ultimate means of survival – the physiological necessities of food, shelter

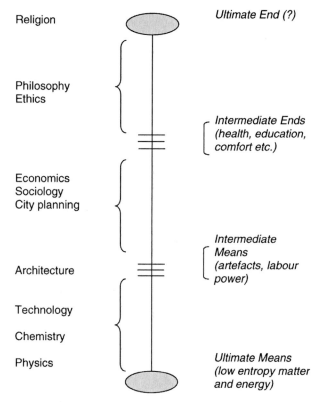

Religion — Ultimate End (?)

Philosophy
Ethics

Intermediate Ends
(health, education,
comfort etc.)

Economics
Sociology
City planning

Intermediate
Means
(artefacts, labour
power)

Architecture

Technology

Chemistry

Physics — Ultimate Means
(low entropy matter
and energy)

Figure 1 | A means–ends spectrum of disciplines
Source: Daly (1977, p19), reproduced and adapted with the
permission of Herman E. Daly

and so on. It progresses to needs for safety, involving the self and its property, which also contribute to survival. Further up the hierarchy, we move from the tangible realm of economic artefacts to intangible or non-pecuniary needs.

Next is the level of belonging, involving partners, family, friends and associates. Getting involved with people, rather than looking after the self, promotes needs for esteem and recognition among one's peers. It involves reputation that can assist personal development or, instead, create self-indulgence. Finally comes the highest ('being') plane of self-actualization, the locus of elements such as morality, acceptance, problem-solving and conceptual skills. Their integration and reconciliation point the way to fulfilment. We have gone beyond needs to satisfy wants or, alternatively, have overcome the need for wants. Assuming a reasonable material standard of living, we will most likely have achieved a high personal quality of life.

Self-determination theory

Maslow's work has been advanced by two American psychologists via a self-determination theory of human motivation. They concur that people have basic physical demands such as those for food, shelter and security (Deci and Ryan, 2000; Ryan and Deci, 2000a, b). Without basic

satisfaction, life would not go on. Assuming that these physical requirements are met, conceptualization can concentrate on psychological issues leading to mental health and, on a higher plane, well-being. Hence, human behaviour and experience are seen in terms of the meaning of events to people in their attempts to satisfy three basic psychological needs, those for competence, autonomy and relatedness.

As a variable dependent on the achievement of competence, autonomy and relatedness, 'well-being' must surely constitute a key, higher level, pre-condition for a satisfactory quality of life. Yet, Ryan and Deci point out that there are two views of well-being – hedonic and eudemonic. The hedonic angle is of well-being as happiness or possession of a positive mood. By contrast, eudemonic well-being is more complex and involves the Aristotelian concept of a fully functioning person within society.

Self-determination theory asserts that success under external regulation results in hedonic, but not eudemonic, well-being. The hedonic route involves extrinsic aspirations such as wealth and fame, but the happiness it delivers is often only transitory and not associated with feelings of fulfilment. In this sense, hedonism would effectively short-change intelligent people's appreciation of a quality of life. The pursuit and attainment of meaningful relationships, personal growth and community contributions are more closely aligned with competence, autonomy and relatedness, which promote the deeper sense of well-being represented in eudemonia. The condition is associated with vitality and self-actualization represented in personal growth, life purpose and self-acceptance. It would also connote the absence of anxiety, depression and somatic symptoms.

Ryan and Deci suggest that the three personal needs are seminal, fundamental and interrelated. They are true needs that everyone has, notwithstanding their degree of self-awareness or cultural context. The proactive well-being that they can promote will be customarily reflected in secure, high-level self-esteem. Unlike envy, it depends on anchored positive feelings of worth that do not involve promoting oneself or feeling superior to others.

An important part of eudemonic functioning is experience, which involves acquisition of senses of coherence, integrity and congruence within the self. However, meaning is equally a function of connectedness to important others, ability to negotiate the territory of life, experiencing potency in one's actions, and a feeling of personal agency in relating to people and accomplishing goals that reflect one's core values.

Also significant is the concept of autonomy, which implies self-governance within a social context. It denotes the extent to which people actually concur with the forces that influence their behaviour. People can see themselves as pawns in someone else's larger game or, instead, regard external forces as being conducive and congruent influences that support their initiatives. Intrinsic motivation and integration rather than extrinsic motivation and introjection are the basis of autonomy and they contribute to the

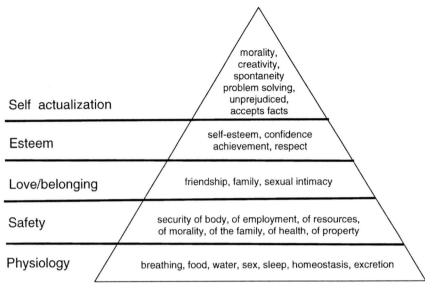

morality,
creativity,
spontaneity
problem solving,
unprejudiced,
accepts facts

Self actualization

self-esteem, confidence
achievement, respect

Esteem

Love/belonging

friendship, family, sexual intimacy

Safety

security of body, of employment, of resources,
of morality, of the family, of health, of property

Physiology

breathing, food, water, sex, sleep, homeostasis, excretion

Figure 2 | A typical representation of Maslow's hierarchy of human needs
Source: Derived from various worldwide web images of Maslow's hierarchy

development of the self, in society. In this way, different forms of internalization support cultural adherence.

Social, cultural and economic structures contextualize needs for competence, autonomy and relatedness and they can nurture or inhibit them. The social setting can sponsor all three needs in a complementary fashion or it can separate them and pit one against another. People may experience a differing strength in their needs or claim at times that they have no psychological requirements at all. Ryan and Deci (2000a, p328) counter that 'even if they say that they do not *want* autonomy, competence, or relatedness, their well being will be diminished if they do not get [them]'. Conscious or unconscious and possibly dysfunctional 'deficit motives' are likely to emerge when such needs are not met.

These writers thus 'place value on knowledge that has implications for structuring social circumstances to facilitate well being or prevent illness' (Ryan and Deci, 2000b, p336). Self-determination theory can be applied in many governmental or social settings to specify the necessary conditions for promoting growth (read as intrinsic motivation), integrity (integration) and well-being. It is directed to the explication of conditions that optimally support human development, whether or not this aim is value-laden or political in nature.

APPLICATION TO QUALITY OF LIFE

In combination with more orthodox 'happiness' research, the three foundational models offer new insights on quality of life issues. They follow the logic of the layperson, rather than of planning or political figures. Daly apprises us of the interrelations of means and ends among the disciplines but, more importantly, of their gradation to the upper bounds of existential purpose. His work implies that what is professionally recognized as elements of quality of life could represent the lower or middle rungs of the Maslovian hierarchy. People with marked ethical and philosophical leanings may find that the provisions of planning authorities were, at best, hedonic, offering an intellectual, moral or spiritual milieu lacking eudemonic virtue.

What, then, could create the conditions for eudemonic reward? Is it possible, as Mulder *et al.* (2006) suggest from survey results, that social capital (interpersonal relations) could be substituted for built capital in order to improve sustainability outcomes? Initially, there appear to be a couple of necessary considerations. First, the literature is unanimous that normal human activity involves interaction. It can have both positive and negative impacts on other people and, more widely, the environment. Logically, it is unlikely that a person could attain eudemonic well-being knowing that, in the process, he/she had disadvantaged others or impacted the environment. In this Paretian sense, a precursor of attainment of the highest levels of quality of life is a measure of self-reflection, consideration or temperance.

Second, any individual's experience is, to some extent, dependent on his/her surroundings. Macro conditions will affect people in different ways. The attempt to aggregate individual desires from the ground up to enable broader quality of life statements is thus difficult and subject to ideographic influences. It represents the same problem that economists face in conceiving maximization within utilitarian models of well-being. For such reasons, quality of life is much more readily dispensed in broad and often undefined categories that assume general social acceptance (i.e. as in planning pronouncements). One way around the conceptual problem is to set out some general conditions – economic, environmental and social – characterizing a milieu and suggest how individuals may respond to them to achieve self-determination and, thereby, the quality of life to which they aspire.

Economic aspects

Economically, to achieve material comfort, a person or community would need sufficient means to reach the mid levels of Daly's and Maslow's schemata. The work of Ryan and Deci suggests that over-provision of economic goods is neither necessary nor sufficient in creating a high quality of life, since it leads mainly to hedonic satisfaction. So, too, would the pursuit of economic outcomes designed to demonstrate superiority relative to others, a syndrome that the popular philosopher Alain de Botton (2004) has termed 'status anxiety'. On another front, psychologist Barry Schwartz (2005) observes that excessive freedom and choice may actually exert negative effects on people, with the potential to frustrate, disorient and paralyse decision-making processes. The economic message thus appears to be one of moderation, hinting that recourse to non-material elements is required to create happiness or eudemonic well-being (Diwan, 2000).

From the Ryan and Deci interpretation, an important way in which economic endeavour can influence individual quality is by allowing people to meet or exceed their own expectations of themselves. They would thereby experience feelings of competence, autonomy and possibly also relatedness. As in the 'satisficing' of Herbert Simon, (1955, 1957, 1959) and allied behavioural economists, the key is to establish realistic aspirations, attain them and then nominate further or higher goals. For employees, the drive to ascend organizational hierarchies has been eroded, since lean, flexible firms often adopt matrix or other forms of management. Transition from one job to another offers a replacement means to economic aspiration and social mobility. It is important for workers to recognize points of pecuniary or material sufficiency, after which a transition to Daly's higher-order existential elements would ideally occur.

Advanced capitalism will provide a challenging macro-economic environment for the individual seeking not only a high but also a consistent quality of life. Wadley (2008, pp664–668) has speculated on the future of work in advanced societies, attended as it is by outsourcing, offshoring and increasing efficiencies in production processes. Labour rationalization is proceeding from agriculture and manufacturing to the service sector, traditionally the largest absolute and relative employer of labour. Bowring (2002, p162) writes ominously that 'the product of work in the most productive enterprises is ultimately the abolition of work'. The world already has a significant excess of labour and it will only increase with technological advance, unless a host of new goods and services can be imagined and commercialized.

Aside from any official planning rhetoric about 'strong' or 'resilient' economies, individual quality of life will depend in future on acquisition of relatively stable, gainful employment. What is needed is a completely new equilibrium of labour and capital, which is unlikely to appear under deregulated globalization. It will, more likely, produce critical divides between the haves and have-nots. There is no reason to be ebullient about the stability of a production system developed during the Industrial Revolution or the Fordist era. For the individual, the best option is to seek an occupation that has high barriers to entry, involves considerable competence, is regulated with respect to standards of quality delivery, has an inelastic demand function, and can achieve quasi or real monopolies in supply. Specialized medicine offers a good example and that is why it is a vocation of choice for capable realists and the upwardly mobile from advanced and developing countries. The other, riskier, course for the more entrepreneurially minded is to seek a future in innovation in products or services. Technologically advanced building design may provide an example of this type of inelastic skill set, which incurs significant risk if the core product becomes obsolete due, for instance, to excessive running costs, changes in consumer tastes or costs, and patterns of energy use.

High-level individual vocational choices of this nature would obviously benefit communities as a whole. Society's most obvious means to facilitate a reasonable quality of life for members is to maintain full employment with adequate wage levels. This provision involves recognizing the present and likely future state of the economic drivers mediating between labour and capital. There is little public or political acknowledgement of any foreseeable disjunction and the scholarly literature investigating the nexus is sparse, deferring to business advocates and cosmopolitan idealists who would promote a borderless world. Wadley (2008, p668) has brought together some of the key components: the level of demographic growth; differentiation in a labour force; the length of new product life cycles; technological change in output and in production processes and the rate of productivity growth. Topping this list is the extent of global protection of intellectual property, since many goods and services are now information-intensive and represent essentially an assembly of concepts and ideas. The mix is dynamic and any solution presently elusive.

Environmental aspects

Apart from their roles outlined above, economic elements exert powerful influences over environmental and social aspects of the quality of life. Principles of sustainability and environmental stewardship have been amply enunciated (Kao, 2007). They are sufficiently understood to be popularized as maxims that tell individuals what to do (e.g. 'live simply so that others may simply live'). For present purposes, a half century of environmental literature can be summed up in a single identity of human impact, namely,

$EI = f(P, A, C, T)$. It posits that environmental impact (EI) is a function of population numbers (P), people's attitudes (A), consumption aspirations and habits (C), and the state of technology (T). The dependent variable in this identity, environmental impact, is biophysical. We have to accept that humans inevitably cause environmental damage, and if too much is occasioned, a highly entropic state will ensue in which life on Earth is at least degraded if not eliminated.

Presently, all the independent elements are trending upwards. The world population is increasing by some 80 million or 1.2% per annum. By 2050, it is projected to exceed 9 billion, about a third more people than today. Will the world, seen as individuals or a collective, be better off for the extra numbers? Despite any environmental epiphany in the West, there are currently around 5 billion people who may prefer hedonic material advance to conservation standards preached by well-heeled foreigners. Consumption will rise absolutely with population growth, but also relatively as a result of per capita increases. Capitalism is characterized by excess production capacity, so profitability depends on the creation of positive attitudes among consumers to purchase the abundance of goods and services available. Given the finiteness of the Earth's resources, the stranglehold of these first three variables (P, A and C) can, some say, be broken only by greater application of technology leading to improved resource management and productivity of the four microeconomic factor inputs: land, labour, capital and management.

Authors like Herman Kahn and Thomas Pepper (1980) thus argued that humanity would overcome its problems by ever more efficient technological fixes. Likewise, the expansionary demographer Julian Simon broadly maintained that the more brains that exist on Earth, the greater the chance of finding solutions to human problems (Simon, 1990). Apart from the sceptical environmentalist Bjørn Lomborg (2001, 2007), such optimism now appears muted. Indeed, in respect of the greenhouse effect, Birrell and Healy (2008) have advanced a compelling case that relentless population expansion (libertarian as it is) cancels out the best-intentioned attempts to moderate human impact by way of technological remediation. Technology must proceed at a rate of around 1.5% per annum just to keep up with the demographic growth.

The elephant in the room or, more particularly, in the environmental impact identity is the P term, population. Capitalists free-ride on this variable in the expectation that the demographic size of markets will undergo an annual 1–2% enlargement, hopefully with spending power to match. Such expansion can underwrite profits and avoid recourse to the much more difficult path to economic growth which lies in meaningful technological advance. Alternatively, preaching the virtues of technology in environmental affairs obviates the need to analyse and judge population as the underlying impellor. Business lobbies lock political elites into pro-natalist and unconstrained demographic policies and any who question the process are usually derided. Although demography is a strong driver, the manner in which density or sheer weight of numbers adds to, or detracts from, liveability is not adequately canvassed. Although the notion exists of diseconomies of scale in city size, few studies are willing or able to nominate the onset of disutility in liveability as population rises in different settlement contexts. Yet even the layperson blocked on the M25 around London would have time to develop a vague idea of what is meant.

Discussions on environment and quality of life should thus be predicated on the fact that a degraded environment will do little for anyone's well-being, offering neither hedonic nor eudemonic satisfaction. While it is plain how deleterious impacts are created, it is far less clear that technology can either match demographic growth or make progress over and above it to offset effects of human occupation. For quality of life and environmental sustainability, the most rational and efficacious course for both individuals and societies would be to apply the precautionary principle and check population growth via a more positive variant of the Chinese experience (cf. Daly, 2005). The first steps to these ends should be taken by green parties and non-government organizations, many of which currently adopt ostrich-like postures to the issue (Sloan and Lines, 2003).

Only thereafter, individuals could moderate their aspirations relating to A (attitude) and C (consumption) in line with the usual green protocols and look for ways actually to make a difference. Social and political organizations could take the matter more seriously to promote incentives for energy and resource efficiency. They could sponsor innovative research producing environmentally friendly technologies, one current example being that of photovoltaic solar cells for domestic electricity production. In the longer term, of course, such measures would become unnecessary if demographic profligacy were curtailed. The discussion here is not of extreme Malthusian scenarios or the lifeboat ethics of eco-philosopher Garrett Hardin (1974), although, given human hubris and folly, they should not be discounted. Rather, the need is for a fundamental rebalancing of resources with population, consumption and technology, which regards sustainability as a reality rather than throw-away rhetoric (or, as Herman Daly has said, treating the Earth as a 'business in liquidation'). It would ensure a reasonable quality of life for the presently unborn. They are arguably the most disadvantaged, arriving through no choice of their own. Potentially, they inherit a world burdened with a compounding legacy of 'wicked' problems as originally defined in a 10-point framework by Rittel and Webber (1973, pp160–167). To improve equity, the best inheritance we can leave for coming generations could be to underwrite their wealth and well-being by reducing their overall size.

Social aspects

From the passages above, it appears complicated to construct quality of life precepts from the individual viewpoint upwards. The quick response would therefore be that: someone needs to lead society; planning agencies are not theoreticians; they have a practical job to do, and they must cater for the majority. The most cerebral of the population presumably have the means to seek remaining nirvanas that can cater fully for their requirements.

Logicians or proceduralists would counter that this position is insufficient, since democracy and planning are intended to apply to, or service the needs of, everyone in society, not just the masses. In attempting to provide a quality of life, a focus by officials on easier-to-deliver hedonic and material elements sets the bar too low.

To the philosopher, if the bar is to be lowered, it may as well be dropped altogether to reveal a base from which exegesis, revelation or enlightenment can proceed. Writing around this line was John Stuart Mill (Mill, 1929), a classical economist or 'moral philosopher' of the 19th century. In *On Liberty*, he put forward the (libertarian) concept that people in a free society can do what they like as long as no one else is affected in the process (i.e. productive or consumptive activity contains its externalities, certainly creating no negative spinoffs and, presumably, no positive ones either). However, the post-modern corollaries to this proposition are that 'anyone can do what s/he likes as long as it does not affect me' and that, being immediately unaffected, 'I do nothing to relieve the situation of anyone else' (Wadley, 2008, p661). These maxims tap an ethical nadir of human nature – 'sufficient unto the day, sufficient unto him/herself'.

So, while a route towards evaluating quality of life from an individual perspective has been developed, which can offer self-actualization and account for the highest ideals, we now find that it can also plumb the depths of human self-interest, discouraging people from having regard for anyone or anything else. So, is this approach likely to be more efficacious than the top-down ones concocted by planning and other authorities? Recognizing its potential downsides, along with the prevailing neoliberal ethos, can an individual perspective on quality of life be up-scaled to form a viable, social one?

Responding positively, it is necessary to examine contemporary 'turns' and 'moments' in the West and elsewhere. It is common to hear expressed assumptions like 'change is inevitable'. Few take the trouble to ask whether, for the bulk of the population, such remarks posit improvement or regression. Globalization is presently a very cogent force that falls into this category. It poses both positive and negative social aspects but, so far worldwide, only a few observers appear to have expressed strong opposition. Even fewer have asked where, *in extensio*, the movement may lead.

Globalization is not new, having commenced with increased trade in goods and services from early in the Industrial Revolution. During the 20th century, it saw the internationalization of capital via direct and portfolio investment. After the oil price shocks of the 1970s, a new international division of labour commenced with the offshoring of manufacturing production from western countries and the establishment of economic unions and free trade blocs. Today, new frontiers are being crossed with relaxed labour movement, which can influence wage rates in both advanced and emerging countries. It is this last development that will most significantly influence individuals' quality of life in the West.

Wadley (2008, pp671–675) has thus pictured a world of economism, founded on cosmopolitan secular materialism as the most facilitative precept abetting globalization. It involves dismantling particularistic national, cultural and religious structures to ensure social focus and harmony. This formula may edge more people up the lower rungs of Maslow's hierarchy and achieve some hedonic welfare, but could neglect the need argued by Ryan and Deci for relatedness as a requirement for eudemonic well-being. In a scenario that extends beyond the world's currently global cities, notably London and New York, the issue will be the difference between constructive cosmopolitan identification and the sort of transience and lack of rootedness foreseen by Toffler (1970). Hanging in the balance are any conventional concepts of social capital and the nature and meaning of place, all ideas that have in the past helped people locate themselves socially and spatially.

As part of globalization, western populations will in future have to adjust to increasing *in situ* and imported labour competition. It will erode the current 20:1 differential in hourly wage rates experienced between advanced and poor developing nations (Faux, 2006, p47). Following historical practice, hedonistic capitalists will do what they can to reduce real wages, now assisted by the opening of world factor markets. Personal competence will obviously count for much in such an environment which, without regulation, could tend towards Darwinism and the subsistence characterizing parts of the Third World.

Social sustainability could thus become a major challenge in achieving quality of life in years to come. Apart from the systemic changes outlined, a further consideration is the disposition of western societies. In an insufficiently noted book on *The Lost City*, Alan Ehrenhalt (1995, preface) talks of the baby boomers' relativism in America in this way:

> The worship of choice has brought us a world of restless dissatisfaction, in which nothing we choose seems good enough to be permanent and we are unable to resist the endless pursuit of new selections – in work, in marriage, in front of the television set. The suspicion of authority has meant the erosion of standards of conduct and civility, visible most clearly in schools where teachers who dare to discipline pupils risk a profane response. The repudiation of sin has given us a collection of wrongdoers who insist that they are not responsible for their actions because they have been dealt bad cards in life. When we declare that there are no sinners, we are a step away from deciding that there is no such thing as right and wrong.

This excerpt would be enough for progressives and liberals to dismiss Ehrenhalt as a paleo-conservative. But what if he were even half right? Globalization and cosmopolitanism would be adding unprecedented mixing of, and competition among, people to what appear to be shifting sands and slippery slopes in western societal mores and philosophy. It is said that if you have no principles or precepts or, alternatively, profess to believe in everything, you actually believe in nothing. Absent in the portrayal above is any sense of attachment, responsibility or community. It reflects Margaret Thatcher's claim that 'there is no such thing as society'. The only problem is that ideological and power vacuums are inevitably filled by raffish parties determined to use whatever it takes to force their ideas on people.

Those in the market for eudemonic well-being would do well to consider the possibility that the social context develops along lines posited here. It would provide few macro-level anchors – things like shared and consensual morality, outlooks, *modi operandi*, heritage, future visions and beliefs about what constitute fairness and justice. Without such props, rational people may well turn inward and seek out those of like mind and values. Society would fragment as a series of mosaics, rather than the mixing pot beloved of cosmopolitans.

A progression of this type suggests that individuals, to build a quality of life, would have to work on their social relationships far more intensely than has been normal to this point. This orientation would not only provide prolonged associations but, by creation of networks, would also act to reduce the risk envisaged in the emerging economic environment, especially if demographic growth continues unabated. A time would be coming in which people would have to decide not only what, if anything, but also whom they valued for the long term. If properly used, modern mobile communications could provide some viable conduits towards meaningful relatedness as a component of liveability. Outward orientation may also take care of the other critical social need of the future – that individuals curtail their negative externalities to achieve the harmony necessary for a decent quality of life.

CONCLUSIONS

This article has eschewed the published orthodoxies and received wisdoms surrounding contemporary statements of quality of life.[2] It turned instead to the complementary contribution that individuals can make by themselves to access desired levels of liveability. Despite the assistance of positioning and developmental models, the contrarian domain proved challenging and was found to be most easily tapped through an exposition of contexts and responses to them. Accordingly, economic, environmental and social settings were canvassed and suggestions outlined as to how people could respond to produce both hedonic and eudemonic well-being.

From this preliminary appraisal, it appears that self-determined individuals could theoretically achieve what, in their own terms, could be a worthwhile quality of life. Although facing mounting problems, born of insouciant economic development and compliant public policy, they would primarily concentrate on maintaining stable employment or gainful occupation, harbouring realistic and expanded environmental awareness, and undertaking greater social liaison to create at least a small-scale version of civil society. To these ends, they may not engage the same independent variables as do policymakers and bureaucrats in their generic formulations. The individual evaluation of quality of life need not approximate any accepted social mean but could lie above or below it. There seems not to have been much official consideration of how authorities could assist individuals, as opposed to the mass, to achieve self-determination and eudemonic well-being.[3] However, there is some sign that actualizing individuals, mindful of each other, could collectively achieve better lifestyle outcomes. In this way, the approach outlined could be scaled up to a societal level. In the process, non-pecuniary could be substituted for material outcomes, providing a fillip to environmental sustainability.

It is in the nature of philosophers and futurists to be bearish. Given overarching demographic pressures and worries about system capacity, the view here of quality of life has been measured, if not problematic. With luck, some elements will be discounted as the years roll by. Enabled by advanced technologies, particularly in information handling and communications, the West has been led by its business and political elites into a series of massive experiments, some overt and some not. People are prodded into behaviour of which they may only dimly appreciate the consequences. Climate change is admittedly a major environmental impact but other changes could be more thoroughgoing and even less reversible. Since, in the future, counterintuitive outcomes will certainly occur, it behoves the world's Cassandras to scrutinize the claims of progressives, the naive, the chattering classes, and the proselytizers, apologists and deniers who inhabit the fringes of serious discussion. With unbridled demographic expansion, the margin for error this century could shrink. Before there are too many thoughts of elevated quality of life, widespread, lower-level Maslovian sustainability is the first prerequisite.

After the global financial crisis, few would be under the illusion that the world owes them a living. Rather, they may heed the clear message of self-determination theory that quality of life is, in part, what you make it and that it does not rely on material wealth alone. The flipside is the argument put forward in this article that, rather than assuring anyone a living, the global society at least owes its members the hope that collective action will improve rather than worsen current contexts. The 20th century, sponsoring two world wars and one cold war, rather failed the test. Only through application of human rationality and restraint will prospects for the 21st century be markedly better.

ACKNOWLEDGEMENTS

The author acknowledges the research assistance of Ralph Lengler and Anir Upadhyay, both of The University of Sydney, in providing references central to the development of this article.

NOTES

1 The torchbearer for this field of research is the *Journal of Happiness Studies*, now in its 10th year.

2 Based on empirical observation, it has not been difficult to take this position. Despite their best intentions, how many planning authorities effect their liveability models by actually, within a given time period, *delivering* the promised levels of infrastructure, open space and other capital investment to offset the demands of increasing populations? In most places, it seems that reality falls behind the rhetoric.

3 Arguably, some settings that politicians and officials favour work directly *against* the quality of life calculus held by certain individuals. Freeway building and airport expansion characteristically offer good examples.

References

Birrell, B. and Healy, E., 2008, 'Labor's greenhouse aspirations', *People and Place* 16(2), 1–14.

Bowring, F., 2002, 'Post-Fordism and the end of work', *Futures* 34, 159–172.

Daly, H.E., 1977, *Steady State Economics: The Economics of Biophysical Equilibrium and Moral Growth*, San Francisco, CA, Freeman.

Daly, H.E., 2005, 'Economics in a full world', *Scientific American* 293(3), 100–107.

de Botton, A., 2004, *Status Anxiety*, London, Hamish Hamilton.

Deci, E.L. and Ryan, R.M., 2000, "The "what" and "why" of goal pursuits: human needs and the self-determination of behaviour', *Psychological Inquiry* 11(4), 227–268.

Diwan, R., 2000, 'Relational wealth and quality of life', *Journal of Socio Economics* 29(4), 305–340.

Easterlin, R., 2003, 'Explaining happiness', *Proceedings of the National Academy of Sciences* 100, 11176–11183.

Ehrenhalt, A., 1995, *The Lost City: The Forgotten Virtues of Community in America*, New York, NY, Basic Books.

Faux, J., 2006, *The Global Class War: How America's Bipartisan Elite Lost Our Future – And What It Will Take to Win It Back*, Hoboken, NJ, Wiley.

Haggett, P. and Chorley, R.J., 1967, 'Models, paradigms and the new geography', in R.J. Chorley and P. Haggett (eds) *Models in Geography*, London, Methuen, 20–41.

Hardin, G., 1974, 'Living on a lifeboat', *BioScience* 24(10), 561–568.

Kahn, H. and Pepper, T., 1980, *Will She be Right?: The Future of Australia*, St Lucia, University of Queensland Press.

Kao, R.W.Y., 2007, *Stewardship Based Economics*, Hackensack, NJ, World Scientific.

Lomborg, B., 2001, *The Skeptical Environmentalist: Measuring the Real State of the World*, Cambridge, Cambridge University Press.

Lomborg, B. (ed), 2007, *Solutions for the World's Biggest Problems: Costs and Benefits*, Cambridge, Cambridge University Press.

Maslow, A.H., [1954] 1987, Motivation and Personality, 3rd edition, New York, NY, Harper and Row.

Mill, J.S., [1859] 1929, *On Liberty*, London, Watts.

Mulder, K., Constanza, R. and Erickson, J., 2006, 'The contribution of built, human, social and natural capital to quality of life in intentional and unintentional communities', *Ecological Economics* 59, 13–23.

Queensland Government, 2009, *South East Queensland Regional Plan 2009–2031*. Available at: www.dip.qld.gov.au/regional-planning/regional-plan-2009-2031.html [accessed November 2009].

Rawls, J., 1971, *A Theory of Justice*, Cambridge, MA, Harvard University Press.

Rittel, H.W.J. and Webber, M.M., 1973, 'Dilemmas in a general theory of planning', *Policy Sciences* 4(2), 155–169.

Ryan, R.M. and Deci, E.L., 2000a, 'Self-determination theory and the facilitation of intrinsic motivation, social development, and well-being', *American Psychologist* 55(1), 68–78.

Ryan, R.M. and Deci, E.L., 2000b, 'The darker and brighter sides of human existence: basic psychological needs as a unifying concept', *Psychological Enquiry* 11(4), 319–338.

Schwartz, B., 2005, *The Paradox of Choice: Why More is Less*, New York, NY, Harper Collins.

Simon, H.A., 1955, 'A behavioral model of rational choice', *Quarterly Journal of Economics* 69, 99–118.

Simon, H.A., 1957, *Models of Man*, New York, NY, Wiley.

Simon, H.A., 1959, 'Theories of decision-making in economics and behavioral science', *American Economic Review* 49, 253–283.

Simon, J., 1990, *Population Matters: People, Resources, Environment and Immigration*, New Brunswick, NJ, Transaction Publishers.

Sirgy, M.J. and Cornwell, T., 2002, 'How neighbourhood features affect quality of life', *Social Indicators Research* 59, 79–114.

Sloan, N. and Lines, W., 2003, 'Party of principle: the Greens and population policy', *People and Place* 11(2), 16–23.

Toffler, A., 1970, *Future Shock*, London, Bodley Head.

Wadley, D., 2008, 'The garden of peace', *Annals of the Association of American Geographers* 98(3), 650–685.

ARCHITECTURAL
SCIENCE
REVIEW

Pragmatic ecologies: situating sustainable building

Simon Guy*

Manchester Architecture Research Centre (MARC), School of Environment and Development, The University of Manchester, Humanities, Bridgeford Street, Oxford Road, Manchester, M13 9PL, UK

Debates about sustainable architecture and cities are shaped by different social interests and diverse agendas, based on different interpretations of the environmental challenge and characterized by different pathways, each pointing towards a range of sustainable futures. The related analytical framework of sociotechnical theory presented here responds to the contingent and contextual nature of technological innovation and building design. This analysis recognizes both the contested nature of the sustainability concept and the need to encompass the differing contextual values of the design process across cultures when understanding buildings. In order to more fully understand the heterogeneity of sustainable architecture we therefore have to account for the multiple ways environmental problems are identified, defined, translated, valued and then embodied in built forms through diverse design and development pathways. Exploring debates and mapping practices of sustainable architecture involves tracing the interplay of competing environmental values and practices through the enactment of alternative design logics as they shape the technonatural profiles of green building development. While acknowledging how a technical, performance-based approach to understanding environmental design has brought undoubted benefits in terms of highlighting the issues of energy efficiency in buildings, the article argues that we must fundamentally revise the focus and scope of the debate about sustainable architecture and reconnect issues of appropriate technological change to the social and cultural processes and practices within which a specific design is situated. Drawing upon more critical, interpretative, participative and pragmatic approaches to sustainable design would involve researchers both in defining the nature of the environmental challenge while encouraging a wider range of context-specific responses. By exploring sustainable architectures, in the plural, as competing interpretations of our environmental futures, we can begin to ask new questions, introduce some fresh thinking, and find new 'socially viable' solutions to the mounting challenges associated with climate change.

Keywords: Architecture; cities; pragmatism; sociotechnical; sustainability

INTRODUCTION: MODELS AND PRACTICES

'Uncertainty, ambiguity, and a constantly evolving vision of just what nature is will guide architecture as long as there are buildings.' (Jodidio, 2006, p28)

Debates about sustainable architecture and cities are shaped by different social interests and diverse agendas, based on different interpretations of the environmental challenge and characterized by different pathways, each pointing towards a range of sustainable futures (Guy and Farmer, 2001; Guy and Marvin, 2001). These competing environmental debates are the result, not of uncertainty, but of the existence of 'contradictory certainties: severely divergent and mutually irreconcilable sets of convictions both about the environmental problems we face and the solutions that are available to us' (Hannigan, 1995, p30). The related

analytical framework of sociotechnical theory developed here responds to the contingent and contextual nature of technological innovation and building design. It is further argued that the most fundamental issue, understandably marginalized in the policy debate about industry standards and replicable building codes, is that the environment is a contested terrain, and that implicit within alternative technological strategies are distinct philosophies of environmental place-making and futures (Guy and Marvin, 2001). Individual models of the sustainable city, even the boundaries of the city-region, are prefigured by the particular environmental problem presented. Seen this way, environmental concerns are both time and space specific and are framed by the identification of specific and dynamic models of nature, which delimits the selection of design and development responses.

This same logic of selectivity can be applied to technology and to sustainable cities more generally, that is, they are characterized by an 'interpretative flexibility'. This

*Email: simon.guy@manchester.ac.uk

ARCHITECTURAL SCIENCE REVIEW 53 | 2010 | 21–28
doi:10.3763/asre.2009.0102 ©2010 Earthscan ISSN: 0003-8628 (print), 1758-9622 (online) www.earthscan.co.uk/journals/asre

earthscan

perspective points towards the need for research and policy to acknowledge how certain development pathways fade away, while others are 'economically reinforced as members of a society come to share a set of meanings or benefits' attached to it (Moore, 2007, p25). Adopting a sociotechnical perspective then has critical implications for sustainable architectural practice, education and research. Rather than searching for a singular optimal technological pathway, this perspective encourages us to recognize and listen to the number of voices striving to frame the debate, and the visions they express of alternative environmental place-making. The search for consensus that has hitherto character-ized (and often still does characterize) sustainable design and policymaking must be translated into the search for an enlarged context in which a more heterogeneous coalition of practices can be developed. In this sense, rather than viewing sustainable design practice as the 'implementation of a plan for action, it should be viewed as an on-going trans-formational process in which different actor interests and struggles are located' (Long and Long, 1992, p9). In an edu-cational context, there is an opportunity to encourage greater reflectivity in the teaching of environmental studies by chal-lenging the search for a true or incontestable, consensual definition of, for instance, green infrastructures and spaces.

If the future direction and success of sustainable city strat-egies rely on the abilities of urban professionals to act as moral citizens, by engaging in an open process of negotiation, criticism and debate, then it is vital that students are encour-aged to become more sensitive to the range of possible logics of innovation that may surface in design practice. This requires critical methods for understanding technological innovation which transcend both instrumental and determinis-tic interpretations and which can begin to open 'the discourse of technology to future designers in the hopes of engendering a more humane and multi-vocal world' (Allen, 1997, p2). Here, multiple opinions and perspectives are not only valid, but highly desirable. Further, once a diversity of possible approaches have been exposed 'they might lead to a more reflective attitude towards certain environmental constructs and perhaps even the formulation of alternative scenarios' (Hajer, 1995, p298). But before turning to the development of this perspective it is instructive to explore some of the paradoxes of the debate about sustainable building.

THE PARADOX OF SUSTAINABLE BUILDING

'There is no compelling, immediately identifiable formal language on which to pin the cause of environmenta-lism.'
(Hagen, 2008, p25)

The idea that there is contestation over the meaning or prac-tice of sustainable design is not novel. Neither is the sugges-tion that context is important or that a geographically

comparative perspective may be important and productive. There have been numerous projects and initiatives to explore the variability of sustainable ideas, practices and standards. Typical was a series of regional conferences to promote sustainable building held in 2004–2005 promoted by the International Council for Research and Innovation in Building and Construction (http://cibworld.xs4all.nl/dl/ib/0302/SB01.pdf). A major debate running through all the events was the contested nature of sustainability and the search for some sort of stable knowledge base upon which to act. Of course, variability is not a surprise when we are facing such diverse contexts of development as can be found across Asia, South America, Africa and Europe. Marteen Hajer has pertinently argued that, if examined closely, environmental discourse is fragmented and contra-dictory. That is, environmental discourse is an astonishing collection of claims and concerns brought together by a great variety of actors (Hajer, 1995). Debate about what the priorities of sustainability are have become very politi-cally charged with some economists even urging us to forget climate change as the least of our worries, and to instead focus on aids, water and hunger (Vidal, 2004). Although the authors were united in opposing this view and urging strategies to engage with sustainability, they were uncertain about what such an agenda may mean. In particular, many authors called for the development of common assessment methods and models and advocated the use of environmental tools and assessment methods, that communication and training should be intensified and sustainable building construction concepts be spread to improve performance and demystify incorrect perceptions. Of course, there is a key role to be played by such approaches and models but as Cole points out (Cole, 2005), perhaps we should ask whether 'too great an expectation is now placed on their ability to create the desired change at the expense of their relationship with other potential change mechan-isms'. The critical concern here is that we start to avoid the contingent complexities of sustainability by focusing our attention on apparently universalized systems of measure-ment as a guide through cultural diversity. 'Until a consensus is attained, the ability of the architectural community to adopt a coherent environmental strategy, across all building types and styles of development, will remain elusive' (Brennan, 1997). As has been suggested elsewhere (Guy and Farmer, 2001), such 'environmental realism' is founded on the notion that 'rational science can and will provide the understanding of the environment and the assess-ment of those measures which are necessary to rectify environmental bads' (Macnaghton and Urry, 1998). Further implicit in this model of consensus is a 'process of standardisation', which means that 'particular local con-ditions' and competing 'forms of local knowledge' tend to be ignored (Macnaghton and Urry, 1998). While some of the researchers also warn against this tendency and call for a recalibration of assessment methods to account for local cultures, there is an inherent danger that the science of assessment may encourage a convergence of priorities that precludes the diversity explored through these conferences.

SEARCHING FOR PLURALISM: BEYOND STANDARDIZATION

'There may well be as many types of relationship between nature and architecture as there are architects and buildings.'
(Jodidio, 2006)

There is a growing body of literature now that rejects both these calls for standardization. Brian Edwards, for example, celebrates the fact that the agenda of sustainability is not 'leading to a single universal style but to a rich and complex architectural order around the world', arguing that this diversity of interpretation can be too easily 'overwhelmed by the internationalisation of sustainability as evidenced by scientific literature' (Edwards, 2001). Here we find clear recognition that there is 'no class or style of design which is unequivocally sustainable architecture, and no fixed set of rules which will guarantee success if followed' (Williamson *et al.*, 2003). Unfortunately, Edwards appears to look for a form of cultural essentialism to explain the alternative formation of sustainability between 'west' and 'east', suggesting that:

'The West tends to 'measure' sustainability whilst the South and East simply 'feel' it. Asia and Africa act out good green practices by instinct, and their point of reference is not Newton or Einstein but the local shaman or wisdom keeper ... As a general statement, the spiritual approach to green design is found in the underdeveloped world and the low-energy, high-material approach in the developed.'
(Edwards, 2001)

This analysis usefully recognizes both the contested nature of the sustainability concept and the need to encompass the differing contextual values of the design process across cultures when understanding buildings. However, the result is a relatively limited dualistic categorization of values in which the dilemma of environmentalism is often portrayed as an expression of two distinct and unbridgeable world views. Taking another stance, Williamson *et al.* ask, 'How, then, should we look at a building, at architecture as a cultural product that needs to be judged as an integrated entity while recognizing that it is simultaneously "coming from" multiple origins and objectives?' (Williamson *et al.*, 2003). They point to the importance of integrating social, economic and environmental sustainability in what is often termed the 'triple bottom line'. They draw upon the planner Scott Campbell's (Campbell, 1996) triangular model of sustainable development, with its tripartite structure of equity, economy and ecology, and conflicts between these goals over property, development and resources. The aim of the model is then to mediate these competing priorities and conflicts in the search for a resolution represented by the centre of the triangle. Williamson *et al.* reinterpret Campbell's model with their own emphasis on the coexistence, parity and optimization of nature, culture and technology.

This theme is developed in a collection of essays appropriately titled *The Green Braid*, which seek to flesh out this new paradigm in relation to the three key stands of the 'green braid': ecology, equity and economy (Tanzer and Longoria, 2007). David Orr starts by arguing for design to look beyond the art and science of building design towards a more expansive, three-fold role. First, the "aesthetic standards for design" have to be broadened beyond appearance towards the goal of reducing human or ecological 'ugliness', both now and in the future. Second, design should 'instruct us' in relation to our 'mindfulness' about nature, or as Orr puts it, the 'ultimate object of design is not artefacts, buildings, or landscapes, but human minds'. Third, design should encompass health, healing and spirituality. Rejecting the 'default setting' of faith in science and technology to meet the environmental challenge, Orr calls for an 'ecological design revolution' to convert our 'pre-ecological' mind, to 'calibrate human behaviour' and to 'educate people'. Strangely, this is a revolution that looks not forwards but backwards, in a 'rediscovery of old and forgotten things' (Orr, 2007). Orr strongly equates this design revolution not with any particular approach or strategy, but with a break from the 'addictive quality' of modernity and reconnection with a more 'sensuous' relationship to nature. Design here is a romantic gesture that locates the 'beginning of design' with a 'generosity of spirit'.

Thomas Fischer (2007) develops this theme by invoking Native American practices of living sustainably with each other and with nature. By contrast he argues that architects have become complicit with a system dedicated to providing material surrogates for happiness. Fischer argues that we need a new social contract between architects, communities and nature to produce a 'modern-day version of how Native Americans lived before Europeans arrived'. Illustrating by reference to the disaster relief work of 'Architects for Humanity', Fischer suggests that this would mean a new kind of practice for architects based on 'advocacy, activism, and attention to what the rest of the world wastes'. Again, what is key here is an ethical frame for design that involves commitment to a socially progressive agenda focused on community and spiritual development.

Turning to the third element of the green braid, the economic, Ellen Dunham-Jones further reinforces this critique of modernization, through a critical exploration of architecture's role in treating buildings and places as disposable assets and the concomitant 'sprawlscapes' that result. Singling out the work of Frank Gehry, Dunham-Jones (2007) equates the representational obsessions of contemporary architectural production with the branding of commodities. Given this complicity, she asks how architecture can promote 'even' rather than 'uneven' development? The answer, it seems, is in looking beyond the building unit and in embracing the values of a 'new urbanism', which again looks backwards, although not as far as Native American society, and echoes a slower, smaller scale, pre-industrial model of development. While working within existing market structures, the objective is to revalue and reconfigure the sprawl of suburbia through design-led place-making. Less radical in its intent than chapters by Orr and Fischer, the aim here is not to transform the system but to stretch its boundaries and possibilities.

Taken together, these three authors attempt to articulate the green braid as a coherent systemic framework for articulating a new contract between architecture, nature and society that is co-constitutive and dynamic. However, the tensions are glaring. To work with the market or against it? To look backwards or forwards historically and if so how far? To centralize, decentralize or suburbanize? To pursue technological complexity or to simplify? And so on. Perhaps the key problem is, as Steven Moore puts it in his chapter, the idea of the 'green braid' as an abstract model that balances and optimizes what are actually often competing conceptualizations of sustainability (Moore, 2007). For Moore, any attempt to model sustainability in this way is bound to fail to represent 'the nuance or contingency of history, past or future'. That is, such abstract models tend to obscure local, placed-based histories of sustainability that serve to reinterpret the environmental challenge and in doing so add to or develop our understanding of a more pluralistic vision of sustainability. For Moore, the danger in such models is in the premature fixing of definitions resulting in the closing down of debate, or rather the squeezing out of alternative stories of sustainability.

Paradoxically, this metaphor of stories or 'environmental talk' provides a rather better frame for what follows in the collection than the 'green braid':

> 'We can look at this as the construction of a reasoned argument that weaves together the ethical, human, scientific, aesthetic and other aspects of these three contexts. If an architect can do this, taking into account all the stakeholders, she or he is performing a beautiful act.' (Williamson *et al.*, 2003)

This emphasis on the participation of stakeholders in the rebalancing of priorities points the way towards an alternative conception of sustainable design. Rather than seek the certainties of standardized solutions and universal objectives, Cole (2005) describes an approach that emphasizes 'process over product' in which 'assessment methods . . . facilitate dialogue between stakeholders in formulating and pursuing a design project'. Kaatz *et al.* write similarly of a participative process that considers 'biophysical, social and economic issues' and 'reflects the different value sets that are at play in a given project context'. This emphasis on 'conversation' may help to open up a debate about sustainable architecture, to ask 'what alternative ways of seeing we can envisage?; how do we analyse environmental problems?; how do we want to live both in and with nature?', and to 'appreciate the ways in which we culturally interpret rather than objectively reflect the relationship of society to nature' (Fischer and Hajer, 1999).

BUILDING HYBRIDITY

> 'What is clear is that there is no still point of the turning world as far as green is concerned. Variations are thrown up by social, political, cultural and economic factors, as well as by individual preferences.' (Castle, 2001, p5)

In sum, exploring debates and mapping practices of sustainable architecture involves tracing the interplay of competing environmental values and practices through the enactment of alternative design logics as they shape the technonatural profiles of green building development (Guy and Farmer, 2001; Guy and Moore, 2005). As Noel Castree has put it, and as practices of sustainable architecture make clear, 'ideas about nature' do not:

> '. . . somehow touch down uniformly across time and space. Rather they are produced by myriad knowledge-communities who possess similar (and sometimes different) outlooks on nature.' (Castree, 2005, pxiv)

Seen this way, alternative design strategies are the result not simply of contestation over technological optimization or expression of the environmental sublime, but of distinct philosophies and practices rooted in differing accounts of the nature/culture relationship. In order to fully understand the heterogeneity of sustainable architecture, we therefore have to account for the multiple ways environmental problems are identified, defined, translated, valued and then embodied in built forms through diverse design and development pathways. The current 'society–nature dualism', which we have shown to structure the debate about sustainable architecture, is, as Castree again suggests, blinding us to the 'need for a new vocabulary to describe the world we inhabit' (Castree, 2005, p224). For Castree, this would not be a 'vocabulary of pure forms' – in architectural terms, the performative or the iconic – but one that 'captures the hybrid, chimeric, mixed-up world in which we are embedded' (Castree, 2005, p224). From this perspective, it is clear that we need to open up and explore the language we use to talk about sustainable architecture. As Andrew Jamison has suggested, 'More fluid terms are needed: dialectical, open-ended terms to characterize the ebbs and flows, nuances and subtleties and the ambiguities of environmental politics' (Jamison, 2001, p178). Similarly, David Schlosberg has called for 'statements that are open rather than doctrinaire', that 'conscript' rather than alienate, and that encourage a debate in which 'discourse is never-ending, and solidarity is forever creating new networks and mosaics' (Schlosberg, 1999). Seen this way, we need more 'fluid' interpretations of sustainable architecture. This does not mean to suggest that buildings are infinitely flexible, subject only to the whims of designers. The obduracy of certain materials and contingencies of particular technologies are part of the story of building design and development as Annique Hommels has shown (Hommels, 2005). Rather, fluidity here suggests an interpretative flexibility and plasticity of design and technology, or as Steven Moore puts it, it could have been designed in a different way (Moore, 2001). Following the fluidity of design, we would ask: How and why are designers pursuing environmentalism in very particular ways, with very different notions of nature and culture, and with highly variable technological strategies? Critically, our use of the term 'technology' here is an expansive one. We mean by it not only the artefacts associated with sustainable architecture – solar collectors, wind generators, biomass boilers and the like – but the knowledge required to construct and use these artefacts, as well as the practices that engage them. This stance echoes that of Andrew Feenberg who has similarly explored these approaches and emphasized the need to avoid the essentialist fallacy of splitting technology and meaning, and to focus instead on the 'struggle between different types of actors differently engaged with technology and meaning' (Feenberg, 1999). Seen this way, the contexts of technology include such diverse factors as 'relation to vocations, to responsibility, initiative, and authority, to ethics and aesthetics, in sum, to the realm of meaning'. Wrapped up in each technological artefact, or in the case of our architectural interests, each building, is a set of ideologies, calculations, dreams, political compromises and so on. Eric Swyngedouw has similarly pointed to the 'combined metabolic transformations of socio-natures' in the construction of a skyscraper which testifies:

> ' . . . to the particular associational power relations through which socio-natural metabolisms are organized (in terms of property ownership regimes, production or assemblaging activities, distributional arrangements and consumption patterns.' (Swyngedouw, 2006)

Tracing these networks would mean looking beyond the polemical debates about architectural visions and sustainable futures to the often messy ways in which architectural artefacts are assembled on local sites, funded by particular financial regimes, utilize specific expertise (or lack of), connect to technical networks, are argued over by a restricted or enlarged community of users, are placed within a planning framework (or not). Again, looking beyond the ideological choice between employing the technical disciplines of energy management to produce new forms of 'smart buildings', or simply mimicking of organic nature in architectural form, dialogue about sustainability may come to inhabit what Amerigo Marras has termed an 'architecture of the inbetween' (Marras, 1999). For Marras, design involves a weaving of ecology and technology in a 'transformative flux . . . a catalytic fusion . . . intentionally generating some hybrid transgendering paradigms' (Ref). Rejecting the 'extreme positions of being either-or', Marras urges the 'fluid process of in-between' (Ref). Adopting this way of seeing and describing building design as 'fluid', we may better recognize both the hybrid nature of the green building and competing pathways towards sustainable futures.

TRACING FLUID ARCHITECTURES

Tracing these fluid hybrids means looking beyond fixed definitions and dualistic typologies, while at the same time resisting the temptation to either abandon the environmental project or simply swimming along in an ocean of free-flowing design options with no fixed reference points. It also means neither accepting the status quo – familiar buildings symbolically retrofitted with wind turbines and solar collectors – nor exclusively searching for radically new typologies. Looking back across the competing definitions of sustainability offered by leading architects reviewed above, we may be unable to identify any semantic solutions to what sustainability really means in architectural terms, but we can find a convincing and workable tool-box of design innovations, technological options and creative practices. The question is less whether any combination of these might provide a universal blueprint (they won't), but more importantly how may they contribute to meeting specific environmental challenges? Seen this way, we may begin to sketch out some general principles of 'fluidity' in order to frame diverse sustainable design approaches which may aspire to be: flexible, situated, pragmatic and participative. We can very briefly (and tentatively) explore what we may call these design frames and illustrate them with examples of architecture beyond the fold of what is conventionally thought of as sustainable architecture.

First, we should develop 'flexibility' to a range of technological options – whether high-tech or low-tech – and an appetite to mix these where it makes sense. Second, we need to look beyond contested league tables of environmental performance in terms of materials (wood vs concrete), height (skyscrapers vs ground-scrapers vs underground architecture), location (cities vs suburbs vs rural villages) and be willing to be open to heterogeneous combinations of purpose and programme, from 'mixed' to 'mixed-up' uses. Echoing the emphasis on 'interpretative flexibility' found in science and technology studies (cf. Bijker, 1995), the point here is not to abandon judgement but to avoid closing down the evaluative process prematurely, to always be open to other design possibilities.

One exemplar here is the work of Atelier Bow-Wow in Japan who focus their work on the narrow, inbetween spaces of Tokyo where uses are continually shifting. Bow-Wow have made a study of what they term Tokyo's

'Pet Architecture', buildings that appear monstrous in their rejection of standardized design and purpose and which instead celebrate wild juxtapositions of use: temples and shops, laundries and saunas, shrines and restaurants, pachinko parlours and banks, taxi company with golf driving range (Kaijima *et al.*, 2001). Bow-Wow use these pet architectures as an inspiration for their own design practice, which is characterized by strategic interventions into the existing fabric, responding to new demands through creative conversion and adaptation of the built fabric of Tokyo. While not overtly a 'green practice', the work of Bow-Wow is dedicated to satisfying changing human needs, intensifying the use of urban space with great economy and efficiency and focusing on recycling and reusing space.

Second, a frame is necessary to give shape to this fluidity, to enable a design to be 'situated'. This is a familiar theme in architecture, often promoted in terms of 'regionalism' (Frampton, 2001) and familiar to environmentalists in discourses of 'bio-regionalism'. But here the emphasis is away from fixed spatial containers defined in concepts like local, city, region, characterized by their cultural and/or physical attributes, and more on creating unique solutions to local challenges defined according to a specific attribute. These local attributes may vary hugely, from comfort to community and from energy security to emergency shelter to flood prevention. To take this latter example, with climatologists predicting that precipitation in The Netherlands could increase as much as 25% in the next few years, Dutch architects are now designing built environments that can float and which could grow in the future into 'waterproof' towns. In a recent example, the Dutch architecture practice company Dura Vermeer has built 26 amphibious homes in Massbommel in The Netherlands, each built on a hollow concrete cube base that is anchored to the land by a single vertical pile. All utilities, including electricity and water, are brought into the house through flexible pipes that allows each house to adapt to a 13-foot rise in the water table. While this is a response to a perennial challenge for Dutch urbanism, it is not difficult to think of further applications of this 'situated' response to environmental change across the world from New Orleans to Bangladesh.

Third, although environmental change may affect and be effected by us all, our strategies for ameliorating and coping with its causes and symptoms could vary dramatically. And this brings us to 'pragmatism'. Here we may follow Richard Rorty, in the footsteps of John Dewey, when he calls on us to abandon 'the attempt to find a (*single*) theoretical frame of reference within which to evaluate proposals for the human future' (Rorty, 1998). Instead, the pragmatic imperative is to deal with the particular challenge at hand. This is well illustrated in the work of Architects for Humanity, a charity-based practice with its HQ in California but operating as a worldwide volunteer network. A declared principle for this work is 'pragmatism', providing shelter after disaster and to communities in need (Architecture for Humanity, 2006). A typical

project was the provision of global village shelters in Grenada after Hurricane Ivan in 2004. Made from recycled corrugated cardboard impregnated with fire retardant and laminated for water resistance, the structures provided speedy transitional shelter that could be distributed and erected easily and quickly. Refinements made from evaluation of the Grenada project led to implementation of almost 500 shelters in Pakistan following the Kashmir earthquake of 2005.

The pragmatic perspective would emphasize, finally, a 'participative' approach to design in which voices beyond the architect/developer/investor nexus are heard and make a difference. This frame takes in notions of participatory politics (Barber, 1984), but also takes inspiration from Bruno Latour's concern in his *Politics of Nature* to multiply the number of representations of any specific issue (Latour, 2004). More specifically in design terms, it means building with the participation of the community you are building for. Sam Mockbee's Rural Studio practice personifies this approach. They talk about 'sharing the sweat' with the community, preferring to see themselves as 'citizens' rather than experts (http://cadc.auburn.edu/soa/rural%2Dstudio/). Refusing to abstract architect from their context of work, they aim for low-cost, sustainable 'workable solutions', in one scheme made of discarded carpet tiles, for their economically disadvantaged local community in Alabama in the heart of Tornado Alley. The approach of Rural Studio brings together the flexible, situated, pragmatic and participative principles of fluid architecture into an adaptive assembly fit for a purpose and a community, both low cost and low impact.

A 'fluid' perspective on sustainable architecture does not mean rejecting one particular typology (skyscrapers) and celebrating another (vernacular). It may mean valuing different aspects of the design. While the examples above are deliberately chosen to stretch our conception of what green architecture may represent, we can equally well re-read some of our current icons of eco-design within this different interpretative frame. Take the celebrated Commerzbank, an ecological skyscraper by Norman Foster in Frankfurt. The designers were able, through a process of public dialogue, to mediate a dispute between images of American (high-rise) and European (low-rise) style urbanism that encouraged both business groups and environmental campaigners to collectively embrace a more sustainable development pathway for Frankfurt (Guy and Moore, 2007).

Our search for flexible, situated and pragmatic solutions requires us to revise our ideas of what constitutes progress. Returning to Rorty we may argue that 'instead of seeing progress as a matter of getting closer to something specifiable in advance, we see it as a matter of solving more [local] problems' (Rorty, 1998). For designers, this may mean reducing dependency on pre-packaged, universalized design solutions and beginning each project with a process of identifying and prioritizing the key challenges to be tackled for the specific time and place (Guy and Moore, 2007).

CONCLUSIONS: TOWARDS PRAGMATIC ECOLOGIES

'A fundamental feature of the new environmental politics is that there is no one true, or trusted, form of expertise, no single path to the truth.'　　　　　(Jamison, 2001, p27)

To conclude, while acknowledging how a technical, performance-based approach to understanding environmental design has brought undoubted benefits in terms of highlighting the issues of energy efficiency in buildings, we must fundamentally revise the focus and scope of the debate about sustainable architecture and to reconnect issues of appropriate technological change to the social and cultural processes and practices within which a specific design is situated. Drawing upon more critical, interpretative, participative approaches to sustainable design would involve researchers both in defining the nature of the environmental challenge while encouraging a wider range of context-specific responses. While both checklists and philosophical speculation can be helpful and even necessary to achieve certain objectives, they rarely provoke the wider 'public talk' (Barber, 1984) necessary to engage community participation in sustainable design – that is, the 'work' of choosing how we want to live, with and in nature, in order to sustain life into the future.

This is not an idle debate. Exploration of diversity in design and development would encourage a deeper engagement with sustainable architecture, one that does not shy away from broader sociological or philosophical questions or merely indulge in the narrowly instrumental debates that characterize so much of the green architecture literature (Guy and Shove, 2000). By exploring sustainable architectures, in the plural, as competing interpretations of our environmental futures, we can begin to ask new questions, introduce some fresh thinking, and find new 'socially viable' solutions to the mounting challenges associated with climate change.

References

Allen, B.L., 1997, 'Rethinking architectural technology: History, theory, and practice', *Journal of Architectural Education* 51(1), 2–4.

Architecture for Humanity (eds), 2006, *Design Like you Give a Damn: Architectural Responses to Humanitarian Crises*, London, Thames and Hudson.

Barber, B. 1984, *Strong Democracy: Participatory Politics for a New Age*, Berkeley, CA, University of California Press.

Bijker, W.E., 1995, *Of Bicycles, Bakelites and Bulbs. Toward a Theory of Sociotechnical Change*, Cambridge, MA, MIT Press.

Brennan, J., 1997, 'Green architecture: Style over content', *Architectural Design* 67(1–2), 23–25.

Campbell, S., 1996, 'Green cities, growing cities, just cities? Urban planning and the contradictions of sustainable development', *Journal of the American Planning Association* 62(3), 296–312.

Castle, H., 2001, 'Editorial-Green Architecture', *in Architectural design* 71(4), 5.

Castree, N., 2005, *Nature*, London, Routledge.

Cole, R., 2005, 'Building environmental assessment methods: redefining intentions and roles', *Building Research & Information*, 33(5), 455–467.

Dunham-Jones, E., 2007, 'Economic sustainability in the post-industrial landscape', in K. Tanzer and R. Longoria (eds), *The Green Braid: Towards an Architecture of Ecology, Economy, and Equity*, London, Routledge, 44–59.

Edwards, B., 2001 (Guest Editor) 'Green architecture', *Architectural Design*, London, Wiley-Academy.

Feenberg, A., 1999, *Questioning Technology*, London, Routledge.

Fischer, T., 2007, 'A new social contract: equity and sustainable development', in K. Tanzer and R. Longoria (eds), *The Green Braid: Towards an Architecture of Ecology, Economy, and Equity*, London, Routledge 34–43.

Fischer, F. and Hajer, M.A., 1999, *Living with Nature: Environmental Politics as Cultural Discourse*, Oxford, Oxford University Press.

Frampton, K., 2001, 'Technoscience and environmental culture: a provisional critique', *Journal of Architectural Education* 54(3), 123–129.

Guy, S. and Farmer, G., 2001, 'Re-interpreting sustainable architecture: the place of technology', *Journal of Architectural Education*, 54(3), 140–148.

Guy, S. and Marvin, S., 2001, 'Constructing sustainable urban futures: from models to competing pathways', *Impact Assessment and Project Appraisal: Journal of the International Association for Impact Assessment* 19(2), 131–139.

Guy, S. and Moore, S. (eds), 2005, *Sustainable Architectures: Cultures and Natures in Europe and North America*, Oxford, Spon.

Guy, S. and Moore, S., 2007, 'Sustainable architecture and the pluralist imagination', *Journal of Architectural Education*, 60(4), 15–23.

Guy, S. and Shove, E., 2000, *A Sociology of Energy, Buildings and the Environment*, London, Routledge.

Hagen, S., 2008, *Digitalia, Architecture and the digital, the environment and the avant-garde*, London, Routledge.

Hajer, M., 1995, *The Politics of Environmental Discourse: Ecological Modernisation and the Policy Process*, London, Oxford University Press.

Hannigan, J., 1995, *Environmental Sociology: A Social Constructivist Perspec-tive*, London, Routledge.

Hommels, A., 2005, *Unbuilding Cities: Obduracy in Urban Sociotechnical Change*, Cambridge, US, MIT Press.

Jamison, A., 2001, *The Making of Green Knowledge: Environmental Politics and Cultural Transformation*, Cambridge, UK and New York, NY, Cambridge University Press.

Jodidio, P., 2006, *Architecture: Nature*, London, Prestel.

Kaijima, M., Kuroda, J. and Tsukamoto, Y., 2001, *Made in Tokyo*, Tokyo, Japan, Kajima-Publishing Co.

Kaatz, E., Root, D. and Bowen, P., 2005, 'Broadening project participation through a modified building sustainability assessment', *Building Research and Information* 33(5), 441–454.

Latour, B., 2004, *Politics of Nature: How to Bring the Sciences into Democracy*, Harvard, Harvard University Press.

Long, N. and Long, A., 1992, *Battlefields of Knowledge: The Interlocking of Theory and Practice in Social Research and Development*, London, Routlege.

Macnaghton, P. and Urry, J., 1998, *Contested Natures*, London, Sage.

Marras, A. (ed), 1999, *ECO-TEC: Architecture of the Inbetween*, New York, NY, Princeton Architectural Press.

Moore, S.A., 2001, *Technology and Place: Sustainable Architecture and the Blueprint Farm*, Austin, TX, The University of Texas Press.

28 Guy

Moore, S., 2007, *Models, lists, and the evolution of sustainable architecture*, in K. Tanzer and R. Longoria (eds), *The Green Braid: Towards an Architecture of Ecology, Economy, and Equity*, London, Routledge, 60–76.

Orr, D., 2007, *Architecture, ecological design, and human ecology*, in K. Tanzer and R. Longoria (eds), *The Green Braid: Towards an Architecture of Ecology, Economy, and Equity*, London, Routledge, 15–33.

Rorty, R., 1998, *Achieving Our Country: Leftist Thought in Twentieth Century America*, Cambridge, Harvard University Press.

Schlosberg, D., 1999, *Environmental Justice and the New Pluralism: the Challenge of Difference for Environmentalism*, Oxford, Oxford University Press.

Swyngedouw, E., 2006, 'Circulations and metabolisms: (hybrid) natures and (cyborg) cities', *Science as Culture* 15(2), 105–122.

Tanzer, K. and Longoria, R., 2007, *The Green Braid: Towards an Architecture of Ecology, Economy, and Equity*, London, Routledge.

Vidal, J., 2004, 'Forget climate change, that's the least of our worries, say Nobel winners', *The Guardian*, Thursday, 21 October, p. 3.

Williamson, T., Radford, A. and Bennetts, H., 2003, *Understanding Sustainable Architecture*, Oxford, Spon.

ARCHITECTURAL
SCIENCE
REVIEW

The global predicament: radical implications for design

Ted Trainer*

Faculty of Arts, University of NSW, Kensington, Sydney, Australia

Although there has been a rapid increase in awareness that the world is running into major problems, the magnitude and significance of this are not well understood by officials or the general public. When some commonly available facts and estimates are examined, it becomes clear that rich world per capita rates of resource consumption and ecological impacts are far beyond those that could be sustained when generalized to all people. It is argued here that the magnitude of the overshoot is so great that it is not plausible that technical advances, or conservation efforts, could eliminate problems of global sustainability and justice while the fundamental commitments of the current consumer society remain, that is, the pursuit of affluent living standards and economic growth within a market system. If this perspective on our global situation is valid, then radical implications for a range of concerns to do with the design of a sustainable and just society follow.

Keywords: Alternative society; design; global problems; limits to growth; settlements; sustainability

INTRODUCTION: THE GLOBAL PREDICAMENT

There are two major faults built into the foundations of our society. Both faults derive from the fundamental structures and commitments of consumer-capitalist society. A brief examination of some of the relevant issues and solutions indicates that these problems cannot be solved within such a society.

Rich countries, with about one-fifth of the world's people, are consuming about three-quarters of the world's resource production. Rich world per capita consumption is about 15–20 times that of the poorest half of the world's people. The global population is estimated to stabilize at above 9 billion, after 2060. If all those people were to have the present Australian per capita resource consumption, then the world production of all resources would have to be about eight times as great as it is now. If we tried to raise present world production to that level by 2060, we would by then have completely exhausted all probably recoverable resources of around one-third of the mineral items we use. All probably recoverable resources of coal, oil, gas, tar sand and shale oil, and uranium (via burner reactors) would have been exhausted by 2045 (Trainer, 1985).

Petroleum appears to be especially limited. A number of geologists have concluded that the world oil supply will probably peak by 2010 and to half that level by 2025–30. Colin Campbell, in the introductory chapter of this volume, posits that the peak of conventional oil production occurred globally in 2005. Yet if in 2050, 9 billion people were to consume petroleum in line with current Australian trends, the available petroleum supply would have to be about 10 times as great as it is now.

Recent 'footprint' analysis estimates that it probably takes 8ha of productive land to provide water, energy settlement area and food for one person living in a rich country. Therefore if 9 billion people were to live as we do in Sydney, we would need about 72 billion ha of productive land. But that is about nine times all the available productive land on the planet.

After the publication of the IPCC Fourth Assessment Report (IPCC, 2007) atmospheric scientists tend to indicate that the amount of carbon dioxide in the atmosphere has to be kept below 450ppm, and probably 400ppm, to prevent global temperature rising above the critical 2°C limit. That would require an 80% reduction in global CO_2 emissions, to less than 0.6 tonnes per capita. The present Australian emission rate is 26 tonnes per capita. However, in the past two or three years, global warming has been occurring faster than the IPCC anticipated, and James Hansen of NASA and others have argued that emissions must be reduced to below 350ppm to prevent climate chaos (Hansen et al., 2008; Climate Action Summit, 2009). Geosequestration of CO_2 cannot solve this problem because it can easily extract only 20–30% of CO_2 emissions from stationary sources such as power stations, as distinct from vehicles. It therefore cannot deal with the bulk of our current emissions.

*Email: F.Trainer@unsw.edu.au

doi:10.3763/asre.2009.0049 ©2010 Earthscan ISSN: 0003-8628 (print), 1758-9622 (online) www.earthscan.co.uk/journals/asre

earthscan

These are some of the main 'limits to growth' arguments that lead to the conclusion that there is no possibility of all people rising to the living standards we take for granted today in rich countries like Australia. Note the magnitude of the overshoot. Over-population is a core element in the predicament, but there is a far more important problem – over-consumption.

Impossible implications of economic growth

The foregoing argument has only been that *present* levels of production and consumption are unsustainable. Yet the consumer-capitalist society is predicted to continue to increase living standards and levels of output and consumption, as fast as possible in perpetuity. The economic goal of most nations is growth, with few apparently recognizing the impossible consequences of its pursuit.

A 3% p.a. increase in economic output would produce eight times as much every year by 2070. If by then the predicted 9 billion people have risen to the living standards Australians now enjoy, then the total world economic output would be more than 60 times as great as it is today. Yet even the present levels of consumption are unsustainable.

But can't technical advance solve the problems?

Most people assume that the development of better technology will enable us to go on enjoying affluent lifestyles and pursuing limitless economic growth, for example, by reducing the energy and resource intensity of products. However, the magnitude of our over-consumption makes this highly implausible.

Perhaps the best known 'technical fix' optimist, Amory Lovins (von Weizacker and Lovins, 1997) claims that we could at least double global output while halving the resource and environmental impacts, so producing a 'factor 4' reduction. However, this would not solve the problems.

Let us assume that the present global resource and ecological impacts only need to be halved. If we in rich countries average 3% growth and 9 billion people rose to Australian living standards, we would then have by 2070 a total world output of 60 times that of today. Technical advances would have to make it possible to multiply total world economic output by 60 while halving impacts, that is, a factor 120 reduction. A factor 4 or 10 reduction would be insignificant.

A common assumption held by those espousing technical fixes is that we can decarbonize energy sources by moving from fossil fuels to renewable energy use, but the validity of this view is being questioned (Hayden, 2004; Mackay, 2008; Trainer, 2007, 2008). For instance, consider the liquid fuel problem. It is possible now to produce around 7GJ of ethanol per tonne of biomass (Fulton, 2005) and to grow biomass at no more than 7 tonnes per hectare, with large-scale production. To provide the 128GJ of oil and gas that each Australian now consumes a year, on average, would require about 2.56ha of biomass plantation. To provide this amount of energy to over 9 billion people would require 25 billion ha of plantations, on a planet with only 13 billion hectares of land. The consumption figure for Australians is estimated to double by 2050 (ABARE, 2008). It is therefore implausible that all people could consume liquid fuels derived from biomass at a rate taken for granted in Australia today.

The estimation of future electricity provision is more complex, and problematic, primarily due to the variability of sun and wind and the difficulty of storing large quantities of electricity.

GLOBAL ECONOMIC INJUSTICE

The second major reason why the consumer-capitalist model of society is flawed is because it promotes economic injustice. It is a market system, and although markets do some things well it is easily shown that the market system is responsible for widespread deprivation and suffering in the world, as currently evidenced in many parts of the Third World (Trainer, 2006).

The enormous amount of poverty and suffering in the Third World is not due to lack of resources; there is for instance sufficient food and land to provide for all. The problem is that these resources are not distributed well. The way the market economy works is by ensuring that scarce products go first to the rich, to those who can pay most for them. Rich countries consume most oil for instance, and more than 500 million tonnes of grain are fed to animals in rich countries every year, over one-third of the total world grain production, while 850 million people go hungry.

Even more important is the fact that the market system inevitably brings about 'inappropriate' development in the Third World, that is, development of the wrong industries. It will lead to the development of the most profitable industries, as distinct from those that are most necessary or appropriate. As a result, there has been much development of plantations and factories in the Third World that will produce things for local rich people or for export to rich countries, but there is little or no development of the industries that are most needed by the poorest 80% of their people. Thus the Third World's productive capacity, its land and labour have been drawn into producing for the benefit of others, especially rich world corporations and consumers. This is most disturbing, where most of the best land is devoted to export crops.

Consider the situation of the people in Bangladesh who produce shirts for export, being paid 15 Australian cents an hour. Obviously, it would be far better for them if they could be putting all their work time into little local farms and firms that used local land, labour and skill to produce for themselves the basic things they need. But in capitalist development this is deliberately prevented. Third World ruling classes and rich world governments will only support development that is led by whatever will maximize profits for an investor. The conditions of the structural adjustment packages imposed by the World Bank on indebted countries prohibit any other kind of development, and force poorer countries to open their economies more to market forces and corporate investment. The poorest 1–2 billion people live in countries where corporations cannot make much, if any, profit so there is almost no 'development' in them, when those countries could be solving their basic problems via appropriate development quickly and without much capital or dependence on the global economy. The Third World problem cannot be solved as long as we allow these economic principles to determine development and to deliver most of the world's wealth to the rich (Mander and Goldsmith, 1997).

The orthodox argument is that conventional development is reducing poverty, for instance in China. However, China's success has involved taking the export markets many others once had and this is not a path all can follow. Most Chinese remain very poor, and even at the Chinese rate of 'trickle down' it would take more than 100 years for the Third World rise to present rich world income levels. In any case, it has been shown that those above are not sustainable or generalizable to all. Most importantly, conventional growth and trickle-down development cannot solve the Third World problem, if only because there are far too few resources for all to rise to rich world ways.

Satisfactory Third World development cannot take place until rich countries stop taking far more than their fair share of the world's resources, until development and distribution begin to be determined by need and not by market forces and profit, and therefore until we develop a very different global economic system. Again this must mean huge and radical structural change, to simpler living standards and to an economy that focuses on the meeting of needs rather than the maximizing of profits.

Loss of cohesion and quality of life

In addition to the foregoing sustainability and justice problems, in the richest countries we are experiencing accelerating social breakdown and a decreasing quality of life (Eckersley, 1997, 2004). This is the result of the triumph of neo-liberalism. Many are not given a satisfactory share of the wealth, jobs and resources, and therefore people have to work harder, in more insecure circumstances, and many are being dumped into 'exclusion'. It is not surprising that there is much drug abuse, crime, stress and depression. Public institutions such as hospitals, universities and public transport systems are deprived of sufficient funds. Social attitudes harden towards others. Increasing numbers of people believe the future will be worse than the present. Popular political doctrines advocate that all compete against each other for as much wealth as possible rather than more sensibly cooperating in collective ways. The stigmatization of 'socialism' in America can be seen as evidence of these trends.

Conclusions on the global situation

The foregoing sections demonstrate the problems faced by humanity resulting from a rapidly expanding population and over-consumption, and the futility of planning to give all people rich world 'living standards'. National governments around the world are beginning to discuss 80% carbon emission reduction targets by 2050 and per capita reductions in resource consumption by 90% or more. Meeting such targets will be impossible without huge and radical changes and new systems. Mere reform of a society that continues to pursue increasingly affluent living standards and economic growth cannot solve the problems. It is not difficult to conclude that the problems cannot be fixed in consumer-capitalist society, because they are the result of some of the fundamental tenets and systems of such a society. However, the need for such radical change is almost universally ignored.

THE ALTERNATIVE: THE SIMPLER WAY

Building on the notion that the foregoing arguments are basically valid, the following sections propose a new social, political and economic system, The Simpler Way, that is actually capable of meeting such radical targets for consumption reduction. It is based on the following premises:

Material living standards must be far less affluent. In a sustainable society, per capita rates of use of resources must be a small fraction of those in Australia today.

Small-scale highly self-sufficient local economies offer the greatest potential for radical reductions in consumption.

Cooperative and participatory local governance systems in which small communities control their own affairs, independent of the much-reduced international and global governance systems, offer a potentially effective model to decouple local and global economies. Systems of governance and economic control are inevitably interlinked.

A very different economic system must be developed that is geared to meeting needs, as distinct from maximizing profits, not driven by market forces, and decoupled from a growth model.

None of this is possible without a radical change in values, away from competition, self-interest and acquisitiveness.

Implications for design: The Simpler Way model

The following is an elaboration on some of the radical, practical visions for 'design', defined and developed by an Australian group and called The Simpler Way, resulting from these premises. The Simpler Way envisions the design of a new society, including economic, political, social, geographical, technical and cultural elements. The description of this vision begins with the more obvious assumptions about buildings that are likely to appear extreme to many. It should be kept in mind that in general the goal is to design systems and structures that are capable of achieving at least a 10-fold reduction in per capita resource use and environmental impact.

Housing and settlements

Given the magnitude of the reductions required in rich world per capita resource use, implications for housing go well beyond the standard 'light green' prescriptions to focus on features such as very small houses, built from earth. A satisfactory dwelling may be built for a small family for $10,000 (these claims derive from my own building experience; see also Bee, 1997). Ideally, owners would do the building, mostly by hand, at a leisurely pace, with advice and assistance from their community, repaid in kind. Passive solar principles would cut lifetime energy costs. Simple rainwater tanks, for instance made of cement plastered over chicken wire, can be made for about one-twentieth of the cost of commercially available plastic tanks, excluding labour cost. All 'waste' water would run to neighbourhood garbage gas units and then to gardens and orchards. Houses would typically have spacious backyards containing sheds and workshops, vegetable gardens, fruit trees and poultry pens, and here and there fish tanks. Households would contain extended family members. The household economy would be an important source of production, purpose and life satisfaction, more so than career and paid work for many.

Buildings would not have escalators or lifts, and therefore settlements would have few high-rise constructions. Fittings and furniture would be made to last, mostly from wood and there would be little use of aluminium or plastic. Because neighbourhoods would be abundant sources of fresh food, there would be little need for refrigeration and neighbourhood or block fridges may suffice. In a zero-growth economy, there would be no increase in housing stock. Designs would be mostly very simple and 'home-made'. Therefore few architects would be needed.

The most notable feature of a sustainable settlement will be its geography. Towns and city suburbs would be highly self-sufficient economically, producing within cycling distance most of the basic necessities for everyday life. The landscape would include many small firms and farms, mostly at family scale, some private and some cooperative along with many community ponds, forests, orchards, dairies, etc. There would be few roads and vehicles. Most people would be able to get to work on foot or bicycle, and most would only need to work a few days a week for monetary income.

Suburbs and towns would be crammed with permaculture in 'edible landscapes' (Mollison, 1989), with most streets dug up and replaced by plants producing food and fibres, bamboo, craft materials and timber. Most of these areas would be commons, developed and maintained by community cooperatives and working bees. The neighbourhood workshop would be a central institution, containing many community facilities such as machinery, a tool library, craft and art rooms, recycling areas, an art gallery, library, computers, storage space, perhaps freezers, meeting rooms, a restaurant and concert space. This is where citizen assemblies will govern the town.

The design of settlements would be intended to maximize self-sufficiency in food, energy, water, simple manufacture, repairs, services, education, health services, mutual support and community, education, entertainment and cultural activities. Thus the scale of these operations would be quite small, enabling face-to-face informal relations and the almost complete elimination of bureaucracy and professional government, that is, paid officials and politicians. There would probably be remnant state and federal governments. Committees and working bees would organize and maintain many operations and services on a voluntary basis. Remember that systems, for instance for water recycling or energy provision, would be very small in scale and geared to meet frugal demand, and therefore technically relatively uncomplicated, as was the case in many pre-industrial societies.

It is understandable that in an era of passive consumerism it is not believed that ordinary people have the ability and willingness to come together spontaneously to provide such public services or to govern themselves. In the 1930s the Spanish anarchist workers' collectives governed Barcelona and regions containing 8 million people through citizen assemblies and committees and without any paid or professional bureaucracy or politicians (Dolgoff, 1973).

Cities would be few and very small, given that there would be far less concern with centralized administration by corporations and states. Their main functions may be to do with arts, research, higher education, etc. Large towns may occur within an hour's travel from each other along railway lines connecting many small towns.

The new economy

There is no chance of making these changes while we retain the present economic system. The fundamental concern in a satisfactory economy would simply be to 'apply the available productive capacity to producing what all people need for a good life', with as little bother, resource use and waste, and work as possible, but with a high level of purpose and satisfaction from their livelihoods.

Most obviously in the required new economy there would have to be far less production and consumption going on, and there would have to be no growth. Market forces and the profit motive may have a place in an acceptable alternative economy, but they cannot be allowed to continue as major determinants of economic affairs. The basic economic priorities must be decided according to what is socially desirable (democratically decided), mostly at the local level via participatory local assemblies and not dictated by huge and distant state bureaucracies. Centralized, bureaucratic, authoritarian, big-state 'socialism' cannot enable The Simpler Way. However, much of the economy could remain as a form of private enterprise carried on by small firms, households and cooperatives whose goals would be to provide their owners and workers with satisfying livelihoods, and to provide things the town needs. Market forces may operate within regulated sectors. For example, there could be local market days enabling individuals and families to sell small amounts of garden and craft produce from private 'entrepreneurs'.

We must develop as much self-sufficiency as we reasonably can at the national level, meaning less international trade, at the household level, and especially at the neighbourhood, suburban, town and local regional level. We need to convert our presently barren suburbs into thriving economies that produce most of what they need from local resources. They would contain many small enterprises, such as the local bakery, enabling most of us to get to work by bicycle or on foot. Much of our honey, eggs, crockery, vegetables, furniture, fruit, fish and poultry production could come from households and backyard businesses engaged in craft and hobby production. It is much more satisfying to produce most things in craft ways than in industrial factories. There would be many small firms throughout and close to settlements, and some cooperatives but many could be private firms. They would mostly produce for local use, not export from the region. Many surpluses, for example from home gardens, would be given away.

Very few items, such as steel, would be moved long distances, and very little (perhaps items such as high-tech medical equipment) would be transported from overseas. Many market gardens could be located throughout the suburbs and cities, for example on derelict factory sites and beside railway lines. Having food produced close to where people live would enable all nutrients to be recycled back to the soil through compost heaps and garbage gas units and reduce the need for packaging and storage.

There would also be many varieties of animals living in our neighbourhoods, including a fishing industry based on tanks and ponds. In addition, many materials and chemicals can come from communal woodlots, fruit trees, bamboo clumps, ponds, meadows, etc. These would provide many free goods. Thus we will develop the 'commons', the community land and resources from which all can take food and materials. All the furniture-making wood needed could come from those forests, via one small saw-bench located in what used to be a car port. Small clay pits would provide clay for pottery and earth for mud bricks.

It would be a leisure-rich environment. Suburbs at present are leisure deserts; there is not much to do. The alternative neighbourhood would be full of familiar people, small businesses, common projects, drama clubs, farms and animals, gardens, forests and alternative technologies, and therefore full of interesting things to observe and do. Any neighbourhood has abundant unused potential resources, including comedians, actors, artists, musicians, play writers, acrobats, jugglers and dancers. Thus vast but presently unused productive capacity will be harnessed to enrich our dormitory suburbs. Dolgoff (1973) describes the way in which output surged when the Spanish anarchist collectives put unused village resources to work. Consequently, people would be less inclined to go away at weekends and holidays, which would reduce the national per capita footprint and energy consumption greatly.

We would also share more things. We could have a few stepladders, electric drills, etc., in the neighbourhood workshop, as distinct from one in most houses. We would be on various voluntary rosters, committees and working bees to carry out most of the child minding, nursing, basic educating, and care of the aged and disabled in our area. We would also perform most of the functions that councils now carry out for us, such as maintaining our own parks and streets. We would therefore need far fewer bureaucrats and professionals, reducing the amount of income we would need to earn to pay for services and to pay taxes. Especially important would be the regular voluntary community working bees to build and maintain the commons, edible landscape, and energy and water systems.

Much of the new economy would not involve money. Many goods and services would be acquired via the commons, informal barter arrangements, the giving away of surpluses, and mutual aid and friendship networks. In other words, there would be an important gift sector of the economy. There would also be the use of local currencies, to keep track of inputs to co-ops and subsequent shares of output.

When we eliminate the huge amount of unnecessary production, and shift much of the remainder to backyards and local small businesses and cooperatives and into the non-cash sector of the economy, most of us will need to go to work for money in an office or a mass production factory only 1 or 2 days a week. In other words, it will become possible to live well on a very low cash income. We could spend the other 5 or 6 days working/playing around the neighbourhood doing many varied and interesting and useful things everyday, and in community-enhancing activities.

Unemployment and poverty could easily be eliminated, just as in the Israeli Kibbutz settlements. We would have neighbourhood work coordination committees who would make sure that all who wanted work had a share of the work that needed doing. Far less work would need to be done than at present. It can be argued that in our present society we work three times too hard. We would not tolerate anyone being left without a livelihood or a worthwhile contribution. There would be many cooperatives serving groups of people with common needs, for example, childminding, house building, care of the aged and bee keeping, who come together to share ideas, labour and goodwill to develop and run things. In general, co-ops are far more efficient and productive than private firms. The town would assist cooperatives in providing the necessary goods, using working bee labour and interest-free loans.

Town banks and business incubators would be central institutions in the new economy, enabling the establishment of desirable but conventionally unprofitable enterprises. In a zero-growth economy there can be no interest paid on loans, meaning a radically reduced 'finance' industry. Communities would take most of the responsibility for care of their aged and invalid members, partly via working bees, rosters and local voluntary taxes. Superannuation systems based on interest from investments would not be possible in a zero-growth economy.

Therefore, central to The Simpler Way is the need for ordinary people of the town or suburb to collectively take control over the development and operation of our own local economy, which we will run via participatory processes and rational decision making to meet our needs. Every one of these elements contradicts the normal economy of consumer-capitalist society.

It would of course not be possible to go straight to such an economy. It will have to be developed slowly from humble initiatives by small groups within existing settlements. What we will be doing is creating Economy B, the one which will guarantee we can all have a good and secure way of life because it enables us to provide for ourselves irrespective of what happens in the national and international economies. The remnants of the present normal economy may still provide many desirable but secondary items, via market forces, production for profit and international trade.

Government and politics

The required settlements also have coercive and radical implications for the design of political systems. These again are not optional; they must be implemented or the new communities cannot work effectively.

The political situation would be very different from what it is today. There would have to be genuine participatory democracy. This would be made possible by the smallness of scale, and it would be vitally necessary because big centralized governments could not run our small local economies. That could only be done by the people who live in them because they are the only ones who would understand the local conditions, know what will grow best there, how often frosts occur, how people there think and what they want, what the traditions are, what strategies will and will not work there, etc. They have to do the planning, make the decisions, run the systems and do the work. Above all, only they can develop the customs and procedures they are comfortable with and will lead to willing contributions. In any case, in an era of intense scarcity we will not be able to afford much centralized or professional government.

Most of our local policies and programmes could be worked out, administered and conducted by elected unpaid committees, and we could all vote on important decisions concerning our small area at regular town meetings. There would still be some functions for state and national governments, but relatively few, and there would be a role for some international agencies and arrangements.

The core governing institutions will (have to) be voluntary committees, town meetings, direct votes on issues and especially informal public discussion in everyday situations. In a sound self-governing community, fundamental political processes take place through discussions in cafes, kitchens and town squares, because this is where issues can be slowly thrashed out until the best solutions for all come to be generally recognized. The chances of a policy working out well depend on how content everyone is with it. Consensus and commitment are best achieved through a slow and sometimes clumsy process in which the real decision-making work is done long before the meeting when the vote is taken. Therefore, voting will probably be relatively unimportant compared with the processes designed to move us towards consensus on what is best for all. Politics will again become participatory and part of everyday life, as was the case in ancient Greece. This is not optional; we will have to do things in these participatory, cooperative ways or the right decisions for the town will not be found and the motivation and goodwill to achieve them will not be forthcoming.

Thus the advent of serious and insoluble scarcity will enable the realization of the classic anarchist vision of political life. If material abundance can be assumed, then technical sophistication inevitably leads to highly complex, integrated, centralized systems, especially for governing, and therefore to the need for a tiny elite to be elected to govern us, that is, to representative democracy. But if material conditions contradict this world view, then most governing has to be carried out at the local level by participatory systems, meaning that the anarchist vision has to be adopted.

Marxist hostility to this vision derives from faith in the possibility of material abundance and technical/industrial sophistication, and belief that ordinary people are not capable of self-government. Therefore, Marxists assert the need for centralized and authoritarian rule to achieve revolution and to run things, at least for some time, if necessary using force. This is a plausible case, but the coming conditions of scarcity and localism will give us no choice but to try to make such radical visions work. It could be argued that they are the only form of government that is ideologically acceptable in terms of the long-term history of human relations.

New values and world view

The most difficult changes will have to be in values. The present fierce commitment to individualistic competition for affluent-consumer 'living standards' and endless increases in wealth must be replaced by a strong desire to live simply, cooperatively and self-sufficiently. In view of the current domination of neo-liberal doctrine, it hardly needs to be pointed out that a sustainable and just society has to be highly collectivist, in the sense that the common good must be the primary concern of individuals. Only if these alternative values and sources of satisfaction, which contradict those of consumer society, become the main factors motivating people can The Simpler Way be achieved.

All this requires the contradiction of some of the fundamental drivers of western culture, so it is not obvious that we can achieve such huge and radical change in values and world view. However, the conditions we will experience in the new communities will provide the right incentives and will reinforce the required motivation. They will require and reward these better values and behaviours. It will be obvious to everyone from their everyday experience that their quality of life, indeed their chances of survival, will suffer if they do not cooperate for the common good. More importantly, it will be evident that giving, working for the public good, being generous, etc. are more satisfying orientations than competing as individuals. This understanding will be reinforced by the fact that well-being will derive primarily from public wealth, such as edible landscapes, rich cultural activities, and the security and peace of mind that a well-organized community provides.

Higher quality of life

People currently working for The Simpler Way have no doubt that the quality of life would be much higher than it is now. We would have fewer material things and much lower monetary incomes, but there would be many powerful alternative sources of life satisfaction. These would include a much more relaxed pace, having to spend relatively little time working for money, having varied, enjoyable and worthwhile work to do, a supportive community, experiencing giving and receiving, growing some of one's own food, keeping old clothes and devices in use, running a resource-cheap and efficient household, practising many arts and crafts alongside experts, participating in community activities, having a rich cultural experience involving local festivals, performances, arts and celebrations, being involved in governing one's area, living in a beautifully landscaped environment including farms and gardens, and being totally free from the insecurity of unemployment and poverty or of old age or illness. Especially valuable would be the peace of mind that would come from knowing that you are not contributing to global problems through over-consumption. Note again that the main sources of our quality of life would be public. Our private wealth and possessions would be of little significance. What would matter is whether we lived in a culturally and ecologically rich community.

Abandon modern technology?

It should be stressed that The Simpler Way would enable retention of all the high tech and modern ways that made sense, that is, in medicine, windmill design, electronics and IT, public transport and household appliances. We would still have national systems for some things, such as railways and telecommunications, but on nothing like the present scale. We would have far more resources for socially useful science and research, and for education and the arts than we do now because we would have ceased wasting so many resources on unnecessary research and production, including arms, advertising, commercial entertainment, most cars, aircraft and ships, and roads.

CONCLUSIONS: WORKING FOR THE TRANSITION

Our chances of making the radical transition required are not at all promising. The dominant world view is deeply entrenched and unquestioned, and there is not much time left. The foregoing arguments constitute such a fundamental challenge to the dominant ideology of consumer society that it is not surprising they have been almost completely ignored.

These kinds of changes will not be led by governments, whose top priorities today are driven by the apparent need to maximize business turnover and promote growth in an attempt to respond to public demand for rising 'living standards'. Changes of the magnitude outlined above can only come via a slow process of grass-roots public education aimed at getting people in general to see the sense of moving to radical new systems. There will be no significant change while the supermarket shelves remain well stocked. It will only be when people are jolted by something like a major petroleum shortage that they will start to doubt the consumer-capitalist society.

Many like-minded community groups now see it as their task to pioneer such new models for society, so that when the era of scarcity really bites, people will have viable, sensible alternative ways of living close at hand. These groups include the Global Eco-village Network (GEN, 2009), which pioneered new models, and was followed by the rapidly spreading Transition Towns movement (Transition Towns, 2009). The fate of the planet will depend on how effective these movements become in the next two decades.

References

ABARE (Australian Bureau of Agricultural and Energy Economics), 2008, *Energy in Australia*, Canberra, ABARE (Australian Bureau of Agricultural and Energy Economics).

Bee, B., 1997, *The Cob Builder's Handbook*, Oregon, USA, Groundworks Publishing.

Climate Action Summit, 2009, Canberra, *Arena Journal*, 99, 2.

Dolgoff, S. (ed) 1973, *The Anarchists Collectives: Workers Self-Management in the Spanish Revolution 1936–1939*, Montreal, Canada, Black Rose Books.

Eckersley, R., 1997, *Perspectives on Progress: Is Life Getting Better?* Canberra, CSIRO.

Eckersley, R., 2004, *Well and Good: How We Feel and Why it Matters*, Melbourne, Text Publishing.

Fulton, L., 2005, *Biofuels for Transport: An International Perspective*, Paris, International Energy Agency.

GEN (Global Eco-village Network), 2009, Available at: http://gen.ecovillage.org/about/index.html [accessed 22 August 2009].

Hansen, J., Sato, M., Kharecha, P., Beerling, D., Masson-Delmotte, V., Pagani, M., Raymo, M., Royer, D.L. and Zachos, J.C., 2008, 'Target atmospheric CO_2; where should humanity aim?', *Climate Progress*. Available at: http://climateprogress.org/2008/03/17/hansen-et-al-must-read-back-to-350-ppm-or-risk-an-ice-free-planet/

Hayden, H., 2004, *The Solar Fraud*, Pueblo West, CO., Vales Lake Publishing.

IPCC (Intergovernmental Panel on Climate Change), 2007, *Climate Change 2007*, Fourth Assessment.

Mackay, D., 2008, *Energy – Without the Hot Air*. Available at: www.withoutho-tair.com/download.html [accessed 5 October 2009].

Mander, J. and Goldsmith, E., 1997, *The Case Against the Global Economy*, San Francisco, Sierra.

Mollison, B., 1989, *Permaculture: A Designers Manual*, Tyalgum, Tagari.

Trainer, F.E., 1985, *Abandon Affluence*, London, Zed Books.

Trainer, T., 2006, *Third World Development*. Available at: http://ssis.arts. unsw.edu.au/tsw/08b-Third-World-Lng.html [accessed 25 May 2009].

Trainer, T., 2007, *Renewable Energy Cannot Sustain a Consumer Society*, Dordrecht, Springer.

Trainer, T., 2008, *Renewable Energy – Cannot Sustain an Energy-intensive Society*. Available at: http://ssis.arts. unsw.edu.au/tsw/RE.html [accessed 25 May 2009].

Transition Towns, 2009, Available at: www. transitiontowns.org/ [accessed 23 August 2009].

von Weizacker, E. and Lovins, A.B., 1997, *Factor Four: Doubling Wealth – Halving Resource Use: A New Report to the Club of Rome*, St. Leondards, Allen & Unwin.

ARCHITECTURAL
SCIENCE
REVIEW

Values and sustainable lifestyles

Birgitta Gatersleben[1]*, Emma White[1], Wokje Abrahamse[1], Tim Jackson[2] and David Uzzell[1]
[1]Department of Psychology, University of Surrey, Guildford, Surrey, GU2 7XH, UK
[2]Centre for Environmental Strategies, University of Surrey, Guildford, Surrey, GU2 7XH, UK

With ever-increasing concerns about the consequences of climate change, households are an important focus for change. There is increasing pressure on households to change lifestyles and adopt behaviours that require less energy and natural resources. At the same time, retailers and producers of consumer goods aim to persuade people to consume more through commercial advertisements. Social science research examining sustainable behaviours often fails to examine the relative influence of both environmental concern and materialism simultaneously. Moreover, most of this research focuses on explaining or promoting behaviours with pro-environmental intent, thereby ignoring many consumer behaviours that may have a significant environmental impact. This article aims to address some of these shortcomings by examining the relationships between materialistic and environmental values and different consumer behaviours. Survey data from 194 individuals from 99 households were analysed. The findings show that quite a number of people express both relatively high levels of environmental concern and relatively high levels of materialism simultaneously. Moreover, materialism and environmental concern appear to be related to different types of behaviours. This raises important questions for the promotion of sustainable lifestyles, which may need to address not only environmental concerns but also materialistic concerns.

Keywords: Environmental concern; household consumption; materialism; sustainability; values

INTRODUCTION

The environment has come to the forefront of the political agenda in recent years, with increasing concerns over the threats posed by climate change and finite natural resources. If current global carbon emissions are not reduced substantially we risk irreversible climate change, resulting in 'major disruption to economic and social activity, on a scale similar to that associated with the great wars and the economic depression of the first half of the 20th century' (Stern, 2007, pvi). The UK Climate Change Act, passed into law during 2008, commits the nation to reduce CO_2 emissions by at least 80% by 2050 (DEFRA, 2008). Around 27% of UK carbon emissions arise directly from households (Office of Climate Change, 2007). Moreover, when indirect (upstream) emissions are taken into account, households are responsible for more than 70% of UK carbon emissions (Druckman and Jackson, 2009). Likewise, 25% of all the water abstracted in England and Wales is used directly in households (DEFRA, 2008).

As in other Western societies, household energy use, water consumption and waste production account for a substantial proportion of UK resource use and carbon emissions, and consumer behaviour change can play an important role in helping to meet reduction targets. Many policymakers have urged the need to develop more sustainable lifestyles.

Most social science research in this area focuses on the relationship between environmental values and attitudes and behaviours with pro-environmental intent, thereby ignoring other values and behaviours, which may have a significant environmental impact. The few studies that do exist suggest that different behaviours may be related to different variables (e.g. Stern and Oskamp, 1987; Axelrod and Lehman, 1993; McKenzie-Mohr et al., 1995; Pepper et al., 2009).

The current article aims to provide a broader perspective on the relationship between values and lifestyles. It explores the relationship between values, materialism and environmental concern and a range of consumer attitudes and behaviours, including intentional pro-environmental behaviours.

Lifestyles

The need to develop more sustainable lifestyles is generally accepted (Jackson, 2008). However, in the social science literature, it is not always clear what lifestyles are and whether different lifestyles can or should be distinguished (Heijs et al., 2005). What is clear though is that lifestyle changes suggest not only the adoption of intentional pro-environmental behaviour but also changes in behaviours that people do not necessarily link to the environment. Any research that seeks to elicit beliefs about the environment and environmental change must investigate those beliefs within a

*Corresponding author: *Email*: bgatersleben@surrey.ac.uk

ARCHITECTURAL SCIENCE REVIEW 53 | 2010 | 37–50
doi:10.3763/asre.2009.0101 ©2010 Earthscan ISSN: 0003-8628 (print), 1758-9622 (online) www.earthscan.co.uk/journals/asre

larger context (Räthzel and Uzzell, 2009). Understandings and beliefs about environmental change have to be seen as intermeshing within a wider set of understandings and beliefs, and it is this inter-relationship that enables the prediction of pro-environmental behaviour.

Existing research on environmental behaviour often only focuses on self-reports of intentional pro-environmental behaviours. The focus of this research is on explaining or changing behaviours that people adopt because they wish to be environmentally sound: for example, recycling products, using public transport instead of a car, turning down their thermostats. However, decisions to adopt these behaviours are not only linked to environmental concerns. Moreover, there are many consumer behaviours where environmental concerns rarely play a significant role, for example, buying audiovisual equipment or going on holiday. Some existing research has shown that although environmental concern is related to intentional pro-environmental behaviour, it is not necessarily related to the actual environmental impact (direct and indirect energy use) of households (e.g. Stern, 1992; Gatersleben et al., 2002). If the aim of our research is to help reduce the environmental impact of households or individual consumers, it is essential, therefore, to examine a wide range of consumer behaviours.

In this article we examine the relationship between values and a range of consumer behaviours. The article examines intentional pro-environmental behaviours as well as behaviours that people may not necessarily directly associate with environmental issues but which may vary significantly in energy requirements and therefore environmental impact. These are behaviours such as time spent watching television (TV) or reading a book. It also examines the possession of consumer products associated with different levels of direct (related to the use of a product) and indirect (related to the production of a product) energy use. And finally, it examines the relative importance people attach to these products as an indicator of consumer intentions.

Values

In the social sciences, values are usually defined as 'concepts or beliefs about end states or behaviours that transcend specific situations, guide selection or evaluation of behaviours and events, and are ordered by relative importance' (Schwartz and Bilsky, 1990; see Dietz et al. (2005) for an overview of values and environmental concern literature). Most of the research on values in the social sciences is rooted in the work of Rokeach (1973), who developed a list of 18 instrumental and 18 terminal values. Schwartz built on this list and developed a list of 56 'guiding principles in life' (e.g. Schwartz, 1992). A large number of studies, including populations from all over the world, have been conducted using the Schwartz value inventory. This research suggests that human values can be grouped into 10 motivational clusters: benevolence, universalism, self-direction, stimulation, hedonism, achievement, power, security, conformity and tradition. These value clusters can be plotted along two dimensions: self-enhancement (e.g. power) versus self-transcendence (e.g. universalism) and conservation (e.g. tradition) versus openness to change (e.g. stimulation).

Stern and colleagues have suggested that there are three values that underlie environmental concern: egoism, altruism and biospherism (Stern and Dietz, 1994; Stern et al., 1999). They adopted the Schwartz values inventory to test this hypothesis and found support for it. De Groot and Steg (2007, 2008) have since further developed this scale and created and tested a short rating scale that aims to measure these three value orientations. Their research has shown that biospherism and to some extent altruism are positively related to environmental concern and behaviour (De Groot and Steg, 2007, 2008).

MATERIALISM AND ENVIRONMENTAL CONCERN

A range of studies have shown that general values are related to consumer-related attitudes such as environmental concern and materialism. Materialism can be defined as 'the importance ascribed to the ownership and acquisition of material goods in achieving major life goals or desired states' (Richins, 2004, p210). Materialistic individuals place more value on becoming wealthy, owning possessions and conveying status with possessions. Environmental concern, in this study, is defined as the extent to which people place value on environmental protection and limited industrial growth as opposed to human control and management of the environment, limitless natural resources and unlimited industrial growth (Dunlap and Van Liere, 1978). The most common way to measure this environmental concern is by means of the New Environmental Paradigm (NEP) scale developed by Dunlap and colleagues (Dunlap and Van Liere, 1978; Dunlap et al., 2000). Materialism tends to be negatively related to pro-environmental behaviour (Richins and Dawson, 1992; Cohen and Cohen, 1996; Kasser, 2005). Environmental concern, on the other hand, is positively related to pro-environmental behaviour (e.g. Stern, 2000; De Groot and Steg, 2008), although relationships are generally weak. We know little, however, about the relationship between these values and consumer lifestyles beyond intentional pro-environmental behaviours.

There is an implicit assumption in the literature that materialism and environmental concern are simple opposites. The hypothesis that materialism and environmental concern should be negatively correlated originates in the Inglehart tradition (e.g. Inglehart, 1990, 1995). Inglehart's hypothesis is based on Maslow's (1954) insight that individuals pursue certain goals in hierarchical order: from materialism to postmaterialism. Inglehart (1990) showed that (political) values in Western societies have shifted from materialism (e.g. giving high priority to maintaining order in nations and fighting rising prices) to postmaterialism (e.g. giving higher priority to participation in government decision and freedom of speech; Inglehart, 1990; Abramson and Inglehart, 1995). Inglehart explains this by suggesting that in Western countries the basic need for food, shelter, safety and comfort has been satisfied; therefore, people can be more concerned with higher-order values such as personal freedom and development (see Maslow, 1954).

Kempton *et al.* (1996) suggest that materialism and environmental concern are incompatible, finding in their survey that more materialistic American individuals value environmental protection less. Similarly, Saunders (2007) found a significant negative correlation between materialism and attitudes towards environmentalism in an Australian sample. Other studies also find a negative correlation between materialism and environmental concern, although these correlations are not strong (e.g. Burroughs and Rindfleish, 2002; Clump *et al.*, 2002). The idea that materialism and environmental concern are opposites is also supported by research examining general values based on the Schwartz values inventory (e.g. Schwartz and Bilsky, 1990; Schwartz, 1992; Schwartz and Boehnke, 2004), which suggests that environmental concern and materialism are often inversely related to the same values. A range of studies have shown that materialism is strongly related to self-enhancement whereas environmental concern is strongly related to self-transcendence (Stern and Dietz, 1994; Schultz and Zelezny, 1999; Richins, 2004; Kilbourne *et al.*, 2005; De Groot and Steg, 2008). Richins (2004) used the Schwartz value survey (e.g. Schwartz and Bilsky, 1990; Schwartz, 1992, 2006) to test the external validity of her scale and found strong positive correlations between materialism and power, achievement, hedonism and stimulation and negative relations with self-direction, universalism, benevolence, tradition and conformity. Kilbourne *et al.* (2005) showed in a study among university students in Canada, Germany and the USA that materialism was positively related to self-enhancement and negatively to self-transcendence. Stern *et al.* (1995, 1999) found that general values are related to environmental concern (NEP), which is in turn related to specific environmental norms and self-reported pro-environmental behaviours. Several studies have supported this model (e.g. Schultz, 2001; De Boer *et al.*, 2007; De Groot and Steg 2007, 2008). De Groot and Steg (2008) have demonstrated that egoism is negatively related to NEP and pro-environmental behaviour whereas biospherism is positively related. Others have also shown that environmental concern is negatively related to tradition (tradition, conformity, security; e.g. Schultz and Zelezny, 1999; De Groot and Steg, 2008).

These studies suggest that materialism and environmental concern may be perceived as opposite ends on a self-enhancement versus self-transcendence dimension. However, most of these studies report small relationships between the relevant concepts and few studies find strong negative correlations between materialism and environmental concern, suggesting that many people may hold both, potentially conflicting values simultaneously. Some more recent literature rejects the hypothesis that materialism and environmental concern are incompatible by showing that environmentalism is rising not only in the developed world but also in developing countries (Brechin and Kempton, 1994). Indeed in later work, Maslow himself suggested that his earlier hierarchical ordering of needs was flawed (Maslow, 1968). Moreover, cross-cultural research by Ger and Belk (1996) suggests that individuals in more affluent societies (e.g. USA) are more materialistic than those who live in less affluent societies. Pepper *et al.* (2009) found that socially conscious behaviour was related to social values but frugal behaviour was not; this instead was more strongly related to materialism. Steger *et al.* (2005) showed in a survey among US and Canadian citizens and activists that the Inglehart postmaterialist value measure and the Dunlap and Van Liere NEP index are separate constructs and do not reflect a singular larger dimension.

This article will examine how materialism and environmental concern are related, how they are related to general values and specifically how they are related to different consumer behaviours. The study examines to what extent people may hold two potentially conflicting values simultaneously, one driving consumption up and the other potentially driving consumption down, and examines what this may mean for consumer behaviour, the environment and well-being.

Well-being

High levels of materialism have been linked to lower levels of well-being (Burroughs and Rindfleish, 2002; Kasser, 2002; Tatzel, 2002; Vansteenekiste *et al.*, 2006). This has been found for adults and adolescents (Cohen and Cohen, 1996; Sheldon and McGregor, 2000; Kasser, 2005). The negative correlation between materialism and well-being is often explained in terms of psychological and personality factors, which may underlie materialism (e.g. Kasser, 2002; Arndt *et al.*, 2004; Chaplin and John, 2007). Solberg *et al.* (2004), however, suggest that this relationship is determined by a range of factors. They did not find support for the hypothesis that it can be explained by personality factors. Burroughs and Rindfleish (2002) argue that the often found negative correlation between materialism and psychological well-being may actually be because of a value conflict that people experience. Their research in the USA showed that the extent to which people hold both materialistic values and conflicting social altruistic values (family values, religious values) at the same time is indeed related to psychological tension and well-being. In this research we will explore the relationship between values and well-being. We examine whether the extent to which respondents hold different values is related to their reported well-being.

RESEARCH QUESTIONS

This article explores how values are related to environmental concern and materialism and consumer behaviours. Specifically, it examines whether people with more altruistic and biospheric values are more likely to express values indicative of stronger environmental concern and weaker materialism. It also explores how values and attitudes are related to a range of consumer behaviours, including time spent on various activities, possession and perceived importance of consumer products, pro-environmental intentions and household communication about environmental issues. The article aims to shed more light on the relationship between materialism and environmental concern and to explore the extent to which these concepts can be perceived as extremes of one underlying dimension or as distinct concepts, which are related to different behaviours in different ways.

METHOD

Procedure and respondents

The data presented in this article are part of a one-year longitudinal study that aims to examine the values and behaviours of UK households and in particular how attitudes and behaviours of these households may change in response to a range of interventions aiming to reduce household energy use. The data reported here were all collected before the interventions took place. This article will focus on the relationship between values and behaviours. The effect of the interventions will be discussed elsewhere.

Participants for the study were recruited from a sample of UK households who own a store card of a major DIY chain in the UK. The context of the study may have affected participant responses, which should be considered when interpreting the findings.

After invitation letters were sent to all potential respondents, participants were selected from the initial responses ($N \approx$ 3000) using information on the database to select those who could be used to represent the current UK national composition of social grades. Care was taken to select households from all demographic groups, but some lower socio-economic status groups proved difficult to recruit and are therefore underrepresented in the project. The type and age of the home, and participant age were also considered. Questionnaires were sent to all household members 16 years and above in each of the participating households in July/August 2008. The respondents were asked to complete the questionnaire before they were visited by an interviewer who would assess the environmental impact of each household by means of a range of questions on home water and energy use and waste production. The interviewer collected the questionnaires from the householders and presented each household with a 'goodie bag' (including a range of eco-products) and energy advice. A £500 grant was given to each household participating in the study to spend on environmental improvements. They received this after the first interview together with the first information pack and some feedback information. All interviews were conducted in August and September 2008.

A total of 194 respondents from 99 households completed and returned the questionnaires. One participant (from a single household) was removed from the data file as too many questions were unanswered. Respondents' ages ranged from 16 to 73 years, with an average age of 43 years; 51% of respondents were female and 49% were male. The average number of people living in a household was 2.8. Around 20% of participants lived in three person households and 28% in four person households, with less than 5% each living in single, five person and six person households. The majority of households consisted of a couple with children (47%) or a couple with no children (32%). Around 36% of the respondents said they had plans for changing their household environmental impact in the coming year. They were most likely to refer to buying new products or technologies (mentioned by 73%) and less likely to report behavioural changes that aimed at reducing energy use (mentioned by 22%). The most often mentioned plan was to buy and install more insulation. Of the given reasons for participation, trying to live in a more environmentally friendly way was rated as most important, followed by saving money and learning about environmental issues. The £500 grant was rated lowest in contributing to their decision.

Questionnaire

The questionnaire comprised ten sections; only those relevant for this article are discussed here. Questions on household conflict will be reported elsewhere.

Activities: The first section examined how often respondents participated in 21 activities (1 = almost every day, 7 = I never do this), such as watching TV for 3 hours or more, eating meat and working as an environmental volunteer. For the analysis this was reversed so that 1 = I never do this and 7 = almost every day. Activities were chosen to reflect a range of activities that require the use of energy and materials (e.g. watching TV, playing computer games) as well as activities that do not necessarily require the use of energy and materials (e.g. gardening, going for a walk, volunteering).

Possessions: Respondents were asked to rate various items (e.g. TV, car, books) according to their personal importance (1 = totally unimportant, 5 = very important) and to indicate whether they owned that item. The list included things that require materials and resources to produce and use (e.g. TV, computer) and things that do not (e.g. a membership to a British conservation charity: National Trust) as well as things that were assumed to be clearly identifiable as environmentally friendly products (e.g. solar panels, water butts). A factor analysis was conducted to examine whether there is any underlying pattern in the respondents' perceptions of how important different consumer goods are to them. This analysis could not be conducted for all 23 consumer goods as there was very little variation in perceived importance for eight of them. The factor analysis with the 15 remaining items revealed two new scales. Two new variables were computed on the basis of these factors by calculating the mean importance ratings of items within each of these two groups: low-energy possessions, possessions associated with relatively low energy use or energy conservation (e.g. arts and crafts materials, solar panels, CF light

Table 1 | Relationship between different values

	Environmental concern	Materialism	Altruism/biospherism	Egoism
Concern	1.00			
Materialism	−0.20**	1.00		
Socio/bio	0.37**	−0.21**	1.00	
Egoism	−0.17*	0.50**	0.01	1.00

*Correlation is significant at the 0.05 level (two-tailed).
**Correlation is significant at the 0.01 level (two-tailed).

bulbs; $\alpha = 0.73$); and high-energy possessions, possessions associated with relatively high direct and indirect (embodied) energy use (e.g. DVD players, TVs, mobile phones and microwave ovens; $\alpha = 0.63$). On average, respondents found low-energy possessions slightly less important ($M = 3.14$, stddev $= 0.62$) than high-energy possessions ($M = 3.46$, stddev $= 0.67$; $t = 5.35$ (192), $p < 0.001$; $1 =$ not at all important, $5 =$ very important).

Participation in the project: Section three explored reasons for participation in the research product using

open-ended questions, asking about their motivations to take part in the project, whether they were planning any changes because of their participation, and on what they were thinking of spending the £500.

Pro-environmental intentions: In section four, respondents were asked to indicate which lifestyle changes they planned to try during the following 12 months. Questions were asked about intentions to save gas and electricity in the home, to change transport behaviours and to change food consumption (e.g. eat more organic produce) ($1 = $ I

Table 2 | Relationships between values and time spent on various activities

	Environmental concern	Materialism	Altruism/biospherism	Egoism
Watch more than 3 h TV	0.09	0.11	−0.12	−0.03
Sport/exercise	−0.06	0.02	0.09	−0.03
Arts and crafts	0.01	−0.08	−0.12	0.04
Env. volunteering	−0.08	0.10	0.06	−0.01
Community work	0.02	−0.06	−0.16*	−0.00
Attending church	−0.13	−0.13	−0.10	−0.03
Fun shopping	0.06	0.27**	−0.08	0.05
Read books	0.13	−0.08	−0.04	−0.10
Play computer games	0.01	0.20**	−0.11	0.09
Gardening	0.03	−0.31**	0.04	−0.14
Cook meals at home	0.10	−0.08	−0.07	0.19**
Go out for meals	0.05	0.14	−0.07	0.10
Go for a walk	−0.12	−0.17*	0.06	−0.07
Go cycling	−0.00	0.09	0.08	0.13
Meet up with friends	−0.01	0.15*	0.10	−0.05
Eat meat	−0.10	0.14	0.00	−0.11
Go to farmers' market	−0.01	−0.22**	0.11	−0.14*
Go to pub	0.04	0.16*	−0.08	0.03
Go to cinema	0.19**	0.14	0.03	−0.02
Surf the internet	0.05	0.19**	0.04	−0.08

*Correlation is significant at the 0.05 level (two-tailed).
**Correlation is significant at the 0.01 level (two-tailed).

will definitely not try, 5 = I will definitely try). To develop a robust scale indicating the average pro-environmental intention of each respondent, one scale was computed measuring the average pro-environmental intention of the respondents across all these behaviours. The scale had high internal consistency ($\alpha = 0.83$). On average, respondents reported relatively high intentions to adopt pro-environmental behaviours ($M = 3.59$, stddev = 0.52; 1 = no intention, 5 = strong intention).

Perceived difficulty: Section five examined how easy/difficult participants anticipated that these changes would be (1 = very difficult, 5 = very easy). On average, respondents believed it would be relatively easy to change their behaviour ($M = 3.14$, stddev = 0.54; 1 = very difficult, 5 = very easy; $\alpha = 0.78$).

NEP: The next section consisted of the NEP scale (Dunlap *et al.*, 2000), which was originally developed by Dunlap and Van Liere (1978). It involved respondents indicating how much they agreed (1 = strongly disagree, 5 = strongly agree) with a set of 12 statements concerning the environment (e.g. plants and animals exist primarily to be used by humans). A new scale was created by calculating the average score of each respondent across all items. A high internal consistency was found for this scale ($\alpha = 0.80$). On average, respondents indicated that they had strong environmental concern ($M = 3.86$; stddev = 0.79; 1 = totally disagree, 5 = totally agree).

Materialism (MVS): Section seven focused on respondent views of money and possessions with the materialism scale developed by Richins (2004). Respondents were presented with statements such as 'I admire people who own expensive homes, cars, and clothes' and asked to rate how much they agreed with each (1 = strongly disagree, 5 = strongly agree). One new variable was created representing the relative importance respondents attach to materialistic aspects in life, by calculating the average score for each respondent across the items. The internal consistency of this scale was high ($\alpha = 0.88$). On average, respondents indicated that they are moderately materialistic ($M = 2.58$; stddev = 0.55; 1 = totally disagree, 5 = totally agree).

General values: In section eight respondents were asked to report how important a set of 13 values were in their lives (-1 = opposed to my values, 0 = not important, 1 = somewhat important, 7 = of supreme importance), based on the value orientations scale of De Groot and Steg (2007, 2008). For each respondent, the mean score was calculated across the items belonging to the relevant scale: egoism (social power, wealth, being influential, authority, ambitious), biospherism (respecting the Earth, unity with nature, protecting the environment, preventing pollution) and altruism (equality, being helpful, a world at peace, social justice) (see De Groot and Steg, 2007). The internal consistency for the egoism scale was good ($\alpha = 0.78$). The internal consistency for the biospheric scale was very good ($\alpha = 0.87$). The internal consistency for the altruism scale was unsatisfactory ($\alpha = 0.50$). Further analyses suggested

that there was significant overlap between the biospheric and altruistic values. It was therefore decided to develop two scales, one reflecting the relative importance respondents attach to egoistic values ($M = 2.14$, stddev = 1.33) and the other reflecting the relative importance respondents attach to biospheric and altruistic (or self-transcendent) aspects ($\alpha = 0.79$; $M = 4.83$, stddev = 1.06).

Demographics and well-being: The final section included questions to assess demographic characteristics and well-being. One variable was calculated to represent the reported well-being of the respondents by calculating the mean score, for each respondent, across the five relevant times. On average, the respondents tended to report they were quite satisfied with their lives ($\alpha = 0.82$; $M = 5.13$; 1 = strongly disagree, 7 = strongly agree).

RESULTS

Values, materialism and environmental concern

Table 1 shows that, as expected, materialism is negatively related to biospherism and altruism. Materialism is positively related to egoism. Environmental concern is also negatively related to materialism and egoism. However, these correlations are not strong and suggest that a significant number of respondents express both relatively strong (i.e. above the mean) environmental concern and relatively strong materialism. Further analysis revealed that this was the case for around 25% of the respondents. Table 1 also

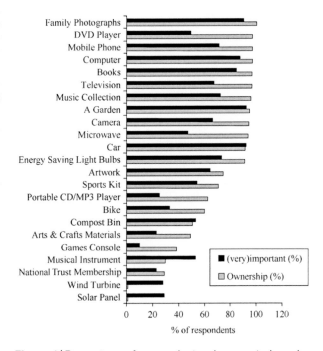

Figure 1 | Percentage of respondents who reported owning each of the possessions and percentage of respondents who rated it as important or very important

shows that there is no significant relationship between egoism and biospherism/altruism, suggesting that these are unrelated factors. This again supports the idea that materialism (and egoism) and environmental concern (biospherism) do not reflect one singular underlying dimension (e.g. self-enhancement versus self-transcendence).

Values and behaviour

Activities: The most popular activities undertaken by respondents on an almost daily basis included cooking meals at home (50% of respondents), reading books (37%), surfing the internet (36%) and watching TV for 3 hours or more (28%). Activities that most respondents conducted only a few times a week included eating meat (42%), playing sports/exercise (39%) and getting together with friends and family (27%). Activities that most respondents said they

rarely or never conducted included working as an environmental volunteer (93% respondents), spending time on collections (e.g. a stamp collection) (80%) and attending church or religious gatherings (60%).

Table 2 shows that neither general values nor environmental concern are strongly related to activities. Materialism does appear to be moderately related to a range of activities. Those who express stronger materialism spent more time fun shopping, playing computer games, meeting up with friends, eating meat, going to the pub and surfing the internet and less time gardening, going for a walk and going to a farmers' market. However, there may be an age and gender dimension underlying this finding. In this study, older respondents were significantly less likely to be materialistic ($r = -0.38$) and egoistic ($r = -0.30$) than younger people. Women had significant lower scores on egoism ($M = 1.96$) and materialism

Table 3 | Relationship between values and importance attached to consumer products

	Environmental concern	Materialism	Altruism/ biospherism	Egoism
Television	−0.18*	0.32**	−0.06	0.20**
Microwave	−0.29**	0.19*	−0.10	0.13
Computer	−0.17*	0.14	0.06	0.14
Mobile phone	−0.05	0.35**	0.01	0.22**
Music instrument	0.10	−0.05	0.12	−0.03
Arts and crafts	0.12	−0.20**	0.16*	−0.02
Camera	0.09	−0.03	0.02	0.10
National Trust membership	0.17*	−0.28**	0.18*	−0.05
Compost bin	0.34**	−0.35**	0.36**	−0.11
Car	−0.13	0.21**	−0.03	0.18*
Bike	0.10	0.11	−0.01	0.11
Solar panel	0.24**	−0.23**	0.24**	−0.06
Music collection	0.13	0.11	0.22**	0.03
Wind turbine	0.21**	−0.18*	0.30**	0.02
CF light bulbs	0.17*	−0.14	0.28**	0.16*
Sports goods	0.00	0.22**	−0.04	0.20**
Garden	0.13	−0.21**	0.15*	0.02
Books	0.07	−0.22**	0.23**	−0.02
CD player	0.12	0.22**	0.05	0.16*
DVD player	−0.08	0.22**	−0.02	0.13
Photos	0.00	0.01	0.18*	0.14*
Games console	0.00	0.34**	−0.02	0.35**
Artwork	0.22**	−0.15*	0.14	−0.07

*Correlation is significant at the 0.05 level (two-tailed).
**Correlation is significant at the 0.01 level (two-tailed).

($M = 2.49$) than men (M egoism $= 2.45$; $t = 3.18$ (192), $p < 0.01$; M materialism $= 2.66$; $t = 2.16$ (189), $p < 0.05$). Partial correlations were therefore computed to control for age. To control for gender these were computed separately for men and for women. The results of this analysis showed that, independent of age, materialism among men is related to eating meat ($r = 0.21$, $p < 0.05$) and playing computer games ($r = 0.20$, $p < 0.10$). Women who express stronger materialism spent more time fun shopping ($r = 0.34$, $p < 0.001$) and going out for meals ($r = 0.29$, $p < 0.01$) and less time going to a farmers' market ($r = -0.25$, $p < 0.05$) than women with weaker materialism. These findings suggest that to some extent people are more likely to engage in activities that support their values, but only for materialism, only for a limited number of activities, and these activities vary between men and women.

Possessions owned and their importance

Figure 1 shows the percentage of respondents who reported owning each of the possessions presented in the questionnaire and the percentage of respondents who perceived each good as important or as very important. All participants reported owning family photographs and more than 95% of people owned electrical goods such as a mobile phone (97%) and a TV (96%). Around 90% of participants owned a car (91%) and energy saving light bulbs (91%). Fewer participants reported owning items such as a bike (60%), a compost bin (51%), a games console (38%) and a National Trust membership (29%). Only two respondents each reported owning a solar panel and a wind turbine. Figure 1 shows that, for most, possession ownership and perceived importance are related, that is, those goods that are owned by most people are also perceived to be important by most people. There are, however, a few exceptions. For some goods, the percentage of respondents who perceive them to be important is much lower than the percentage of respondents who own the goods. This is the case for the DVD player, mobile phone, TV, music collection, camera, microwave oven, portable music player, bike, arts and crafts materials and the games console. Musical instruments, wind turbines and solar panels are the only goods that are not owned by many respondents, but which are perceived to be important by a large percentage of respondents.

Correlations were computed between value orientations and importance attached to consumer goods. Table 3 shows that all values are to some extent related to the perceived importance of consumer goods. Those with stronger environmental concern and those with stronger self-transcendent values (altruism and biospherism) are particularly likely to attach importance to environmental products (e.g. solar panels, compost bins). People with stronger materialistic (and to some extent egoistic) value orientation attach more importance to a range of modern goods (TVs, microwaves, CD players, games consoles) and less to environmental goods. As materialism is related to age and gender, we again computed partial correlations to control for these effects and found that for men materialism is still positively related to importance of the TV ($r = 0.34$, $p < 0.01$), computer ($r = 0.22$, $p < 0.05$), mobile phone ($r = 0.27$, $p < 0.02$), car ($r = 0.34$, $p < 0.01$) and DVD player ($r = 0.28$, $p < 0.01$) and negatively related to the importance of a compost bin ($r = -0.31$, $p < 0.01$), solar panels ($r = -0.25$, $p < 0.05$) and a wind turbine ($r = -0.25$, $p < 0.05$). For women materialism is related to the importance of the microwave ($r = 0.34$, $p < 0.01$), the mobile phone ($r = 0.41$, $p < .001$), sports goods ($r = 0.26$, $p < 0.05$) and a CD player ($r = 0.27$, $p < 0.05$) and negatively to the importance of artwork ($r = -0.27$, $p < 0.05$), a compost bin ($r = -0.25$, $p < 0.05$), solar panels ($r = -0.34$, $p < .01$) and a wind turbine ($r = -0.28$, $p < 0.01$). Generally, these findings suggest that those who are more materialistic attach more importance to possessions

Table 4 | Relationship between values and importance of types of consumer products (results of regression analyses)

	Low-energy possessions	High-energy possessions
% explained variance	11%	19%
	($F = 17.76$ (2187), $p < 0.001$)	($F = 19.28$ (2187), $p < 0.001$)
Materialism	−0.20**	0.39***
Environmental concern	0.31**	−0.08
% explained variance	13%	6%
	($F = 13.00$ (2190), $p < 0.001$)	($F = 6.65$ (2191), $p < 0.01$)
Altruism/biospherism	0.37***	−0.03
Egoism	−0.01	0.25**

Note: Regression weights presented in the table indicate the unique correlation between the two relevant variables, controlled for the correlation between the dependent variable (importance) and the other independent variables. Beta weights can range from 0 (no relationship) to 1 (perfect relationship). *$p < 0.05$ (relationship is significant at the 95% confidence level), **$p < 0.01$ (99% confidence level), ***$p < 0.001$ (99.9% confidence level).

that are associated with higher direct and indirect energy use (e.g. TV, mobile phone, car, with the exception of sports goods) and less importance to possessions that are associated with lower energy use or with energy conservation (e.g. arts and crafts materials, a compost bin, solar panels). The reverse is true for the relationship between environmental concern and perceived importance of possessions.

Table 4 shows that value orientations account for a significant (but not large) percentage of the variance in perceived importance of consumer goods. The relative importance of possessions that are associated with low energy use or energy conservation is negatively related to materialism and positively to environmental concern and self-transcendent values (biospherism and altruism). The importance attached to possessions that are associated with higher energy use is only (positively) related to materialism.

Intentions and perceived ease of change

Tables 5 and 6 show the relationship between values on the one hand and intentions to adopt pro-environmental behaviours and perceptions of how difficult it is to adopt these behaviours on the other. Overall, these two concepts were related ($r = 0.51$, $p < 0.01$), indicating that the more likely people are to say they will adopt the behaviour, the more likely they are to say they think it is easy to do so. These correlations were the same for almost all behaviours, but they were a bit stronger for cycling more ($r = 0.72$) and flying less ($r = 0.66$) and weaker for unplugging electrical goods when on stand-by ($r = 0.30$), switching off lights when not in the room ($r = 0.41$) and installing insulation ($r = 0.40$).

Table 5 shows the relationship between values and intentions to adopt a range of pro-environmental behaviours. The relationship between behaviour intentions and environmental

Table 5 | Relationship between values and intentions to adopt pro-environmental behaviours

	Environmental concern	Materialism	Altruism/biospherism	Egoism
Energy				
Use less gas and electricity	0.12	−0.18*	0.12	0.00
Replace equipment	0.17*	−0.10	0.26**	0.09
Replace light bulbs	0.16*	−0.19**	0.14	0.13
Technology for green energy	0.18*	−0.01	0.10	0.02
Sign up to green tariff	0.29**	−0.21**	0.22**	−0.07
Turn down heating	0.22**	−0.06	0.17*	0.02
Install insulation	0.05	−0.03	0.09	0.05
Turn off lights	0.14	0.04	0.14	0.01
Unplug equipment not in use	0.21**	−0.19**	0.15*	−0.12
Transport				
Drive less	0.15*	−0.20**	0.13	0.02
Cycle more	0.10	−0.06	0.02	−0.03
Use more public transport	0.06	−0.19*	0.18*	−0.09
Avoid travelling by plane	0.19*	−0.22**	0.22**	−0.11
Weekend trips closer to home	0.16*	−0.23**	0.17*	−0.12
Change to a more efficient car	0.15*	−0.05	0.16*	0.05
Food				
Eat less meat	0.20**	−0.16*	0.14	−0.19**
Eat more organic produce	0.18*	−0.13	0.18*	−0.04
Eat more locally produced food	0.13	−0.14	0.23**	−0.03
Eat more seasonal produce	0.13	−0.21**	0.26**	−0.05
Eat more free range fish/meat	0.14	−0.16*	0.20**	−0.04
Eat or drink more Fair Trade	0.22**	−0.28**	0.32**	−0.20**

*Correlation is significant at the 0.05 level (two-tailed).
**Correlation is significant at the 0.01 level (two-tailed).

Table 6 | Relationship between values and perceived ease of adopting a range of pro-environmental behaviours

	Environmental concern	Materialism	Altruism/biospherism	Egoism
Energy				
Use less gas and electricity	0.23**	0.05	0.16*	0.04
Replace equipment	0.14	−0.08	0.16*	0.09
Replace light bulbs	0.26**	−0.04	0.08	−0.01
Technology for green energy	0.07	0.04	0.11	0.09
Sign up to green tariff	0.22**	−0.17*	0.08	−0.08
Turn down heating	0.22**	0.01	0.18*	0.05
Install insulation	0.07	−0.03	0.08	0.16*
Turn off lights	0.21**	0.02	0.06	0.06
Unplug equipment not in use	0.16*	−0.07	0.11	0.05
Transport				
Drive less	0.09	−0.04	0.14	0.02
Cycle more	0.13	0.09	0.09	0.13
Use more public transport	0.13	−0.03	0.25**	0.09
Avoid travelling by plane	0.11	−0.09	0.21**	0.05
Weekend trips closer to home	0.15*	−0.08	0.21**	−0.08
Change to a more efficient car	0.18*	−0.05	0.09	−0.02
Food				
Eat less meat	0.18*	−0.10	0.09	−0.03
Eat more organic produce	0.21**	0.03	0.11	0.03
Eat more locally produced food	0.22**	−0.02	0.18*	0.06
Eat more seasonal produce	0.22**	−0.03	0.22**	0.02
Eat more free range fish or meat	0.17*	0.03	0.15*	0.07
Eat/drink more Fair Trade	0.27**	−0.05	0.21**	−0.04

*Correlation is significant at the 0.05 level (two-tailed).
**Correlation is significant at the 0.01 level (two-tailed).

concern and materialism is stronger than the relationship with general values. Generally, it appears that the more likely people are to have strong environmental concern, the more likely they are to say they intend to adopt a range of pro-environmental behaviours, particularly some home energy and food-related behaviours. Moreover, the more materialistic respondents are, the less likely they are to say they intend to adopt these behaviours and in particular transport and some food-related behaviours.

Table 6 shows that the relationship between environmental concern and perceptions of how easy or difficult it is to adopt pro-environmental behaviours is largely similar as for intentions. People who express strong environmental concern believe it is easier to adopt most behaviours than people who do not (except for adopting green energy, installing insulation and driving less). Virtually no relationship has been found between materialism and these behaviours. This implies that people with high levels of materialism may be less inclined to behave pro-environmentally but they do not necessarily think it is more difficult to do so.

Table 7 reiterates the findings presented in Tables 5 and 6. It shows that the intentions to adopt pro-environmental behaviours are positively related to environmental concern and altruistic values and negatively to materialism and egoistic values. These relationships, however, are not strong; no more than 16% of the variance in intentions can be explained by the values. The percentage of explained variance for perceived difficulty is even smaller, suggesting that the relationship between values and perceived difficulty to adopt pro-environmental behaviours is small, although significant. The table also shows that environmental concern is positively related to intentions and perceived difficulty, and

Table 7 | Relationship between values and intentions to adopt pro-environmental behaviours (results of regression analyses)

	Intention	Difficulty
% explained variance	16%	11%
	$F = 18.29\ (2187),\ p < 0.001$	$F = 12.93\ (2185),\ p < 0.01$
Materialism	−0.26**	0.01
Environmental concern	0.26**	0.35**
	13%	7%
	$F = 15.24\ (2190),\ p < 0.001)$	$F = 8.22\ (2188,\ p < 0.001)$
Egoism	−0.11	0.06
Altruism/biospherism	0.36	0.28

Note: Regression weights presented in the table indicate the unique correlation between the two relevant variables, controlled for the correlation between the dependent variable (importance) and the other independent variables. Beta weights can range from 0 (no relationship) to 1 (perfect relationship). *$p < 0.05$ (relationship is significant at the 95% confidence level), **$p < 0.01$ (99% confidence level).

materialism is negatively related to intentions but not to perceived difficulty. However, as the tables above reveal, this relationship did vary depending on the specific behaviours.

Well-being

The extent to which respondents felt satisfied with their life is related to materialism. Respondents with stronger materialism are more likely to report a lower level of well-being ($r = -0.29$, $p < 0.001$). Reported well-being is not related to any of the other variables in this study such as perceived importance of possessions, intentions to adopt pro-environmental behaviours or activities. However, two small significant correlations are found, which suggest that those who spent more time playing sports report slightly higher well-being ($r = 0.15$, $p < 0.05$) and those who spent more time with friends report slightly higher well-being ($r = 0.16$, $p < 0.05$). However, as these are only two significant correlations out of a large number of possible tests (one for each behaviour), these findings should be interpreted with care.

CONCLUSION

We are living in an increasingly materialistic society where the acquisition of wealth and material possessions are perceived and presented as important life goals. At the same time there is increasing concern about the environmental damage current levels of consumerism cause. This article explored the extent to which people are concerned about both materialistic pursuits and environmental protection and how these values relate to consumer behaviour, pro-environmental behaviour and well-being. The respondents in the study expressed strong concern for environmental issues and much less concern for acquiring wealth and possessions (materialism). However, we did not find that people who expressed high environmental concern were necessarily less materialistic or vice versa. At least in

this study these two potentially conflicting values (one promoting consumerism, the other promoting conservation) do not appear to reflect one underlying dimension such as self-enhancement versus self-transcendence (e.g. Schwartz, 1992) or materialism–postmaterialism (e.g. Inglehart, 1990). The extent to which respondents express materialistic and environmental concerns are related, but only weakly. Materialism and environmental concern appeared to be related in different ways to different consumer variables. The more importance respondents attached to materialistic aspects in life, the more importance they tended to attach to possessions that are associated with higher direct and indirect energy use (such as TVs, mobile phones and cars), the less importance they attached to possessions associated with relatively low energy or energy conservation, and the less likely they were to say they intended to adopt a range of pro-environmental behaviours, particularly behaviours related to transport and (to some extent) food. The more value respondents placed on environmental issues, the more importance they attached to low-energy possessions and the more likely they were to say they intended to adopt a range of pro-environmental behaviours (particularly home energy use). However, environmental concern was not related to the importance attached to possessions associated with relatively high energy use.

This suggests that, at least for these variables, materialism and environmental concern may have conflicting and different influences. This is potentially problematic as it was shown that many people hold both values simultaneously. In this study, people therefore appear to be motivated by consumption as well as conservation. This has important implications for the promotion of sustainable lifestyles. Sustainable lifestyles imply household behaviour patterns with a relatively low use of energy and materials. Such lifestyles cannot be created if individuals are trying hard on the one hand to adopt pro-environmental behaviours but at the same time adopt behaviours that outdo any beneficial environmental consequences of such behaviour. This potential conflict between environmental and materialistic values should form an important focus point for interventions that aim to promote energy conservation in households.

The relationship between general values and behaviours was generally weaker than the relationship between materialism and environmental concern and behaviour. This is in line with the suggestion of Stern and Dietz (1994) that general values relate to more specific values, which in turn relate to general attitudes, specific attitudes, intentions and behaviours. The conceptual distance between values and behavioural intentions is therefore larger and one would not expect to find very strong correlations. The strength of the relationships found in this study is similar to that found in previous research (e.g. Stern, 2000; De Groot and Steg, 2008).

An interesting finding in this research was that although egoistic and biospheric values were not related and materialistic and environmental concerns were weakly related, a strong relationship was found between altruism and biospherism. In fact, this relationship was so strong that it was decided to combine these values into one value domain. A relationship between altruism and biospherism has been found elsewhere (e.g. De Groot and Steg, 2007, 2008). This relationship again raises interesting questions for the promotion of sustainable lifestyles for which it may be valuable to focus not only on environmental or biospheric aspects but also on social and altruistic aspects (see also Pepper et al., 2009).

In support of previous research, materialism was negatively related to well-being (e.g. Burroughs and Rindfleish, 2002; Kasser, 2002). At least in this study there was no indication as to the nature of this relationship. Kasser et al. (2004) proposed two paths to materialistic value internalization: experience of insecurity and exposure to social models that promote materialism. In support of this, some research has found that materialism is related to more TV viewing (Chaplin and John, 2007; Saunders, 2007). However, causal conclusions cannot, of course, be drawn on the basis of such correlational data. This study did not find a relationship between materialism and TV viewing, but we did find a number of other relationships between materialism and time spent on activities such as shopping and playing computer games. Particularly the relationship with computer use may deserve further attention in order to better understand the nature of this relationship and its potential causes and consequences.

The sample of respondents in this study is not representative of the UK household population. Although care was taken to include people from different socio-demographic groups, the context of the study has created a sample biased towards the purchase of consumer products in DIY stores. Moreover, participants were aware that they are participating in a one-year intensive study that aims to promote energy conservation in the home. When respondents were asked what kinds of behaviours they were planning to adopt or what changes they were planning to make in their households in response to participation in the project, most respondents referred to buying products for their households that would allow them to save energy. Very few respondents indicated that they would attempt to consume less or buy less. We do not know whether this is a generalizable finding, whether it is specific to the respondent group in this study or whether it is related to the context of the study. For future research it would be useful to examine whether this sample has been biased towards buying themselves out of the ecological crisis or whether this is a more general perception among UK households. This is particularly interesting in the context of materialism and environmental concern. If people are motivated by materialism and environmental concern, would it be possible to promote conservation behaviour by addressing conservation and reduction of consumption as well as by addressing materialism and promoting the purchase of more energy-efficient and environmentally friendly products? Research on materialism suggests that in order for people to use and desire material objects to cope with potential issues of insecurity (Kasser, 2002), it is essential that the symbolic value of these possessions is recognized. Existing research has shown that the reasons for valuing possessions are related to expressing, maintaining and signalling self-concept to others (e.g. Csikszentmihalyi and Rochberg-Halton, 1981; Belk, 1985; Dittmar, 1992; Jackson, 2005). In the current study correlations between materialism and the importance attached to environmental products, however, were mainly negative, suggesting that this route would only be an option if the symbolic 'status' value of environmentally friendly products was improved.

This research has shown that different values and concerns are related to consumer attitudes and behavioural intentions in different ways. The findings suggest that whereas people are motivated by environmental concern to reduce their consumption of energy and materials, they also have material concerns that motivate them to purchase new products and increase their environmental impact. In order to promote more sustainable lifestyles, it is important, therefore, not only to promote environmental awareness and concern but also, as Jackson (2009) suggests, to address material concerns, which requires looking at the larger value context in which actions are situated (Räthzel and Uzzell, 2009).

ACKNOWLEDGEMENT

The data presented in this report were collected as part of the 21st Century Living Project, a research project led by the EDEN project and funded by Homebase. We thank EDEN project and in particular Mike Harris, ACONA and Homebase for making it possible to conduct this research.

References

Abramson, P. and Inglehart, R., 1995, *Value Change in Global Perspective*, Ann Arbor, University of Michigan Press.

Arndt, J., Solomon, S., Kasser, T. and Sheldon, K., 2004, 'The urge to splurge: a terror management account of materialism and consumer behavior', *Journal of Consumer Psychology* 14, 198–212.

Axelrod, L.J. and Lehman, D.B., 1993, 'Responding to environmental concern: what factors guide individual action?' *Journal of Environmental Psychology* 13, 149–159.

Belk, R.W., 1985, 'Materialism: train aspects of living in the material world', *Journal of Consumer Research* 12, 265–280.

Brechin, S.R. and Kempton, W., 1994, 'Global environmentalism: a challenge to the post-materialism thesis', *Social Science Quarterly* 75, 245–269.

Burroughs, J.E. and Rindfleish, A., 2002, 'Materialism and well-being: a conflicting values perspective', *The Journal of Consumer Research* 29, 348–370.

Chaplin, L. and John, D., 2007, 'Growing up in a material world: age differences in materialism in children and adolescents', *Journal of Consumer Research* 34, 184.

Clump, M.A., Brandel, J.M. and Sharpe, P.J., 2002, 'Differences in environmental responsibility between materialistic groups', *Psychologia* 45, 155–161.

Cohen, P. and Cohen, J., 1996, *Life Values and Adolescent Mental Health*, Mahwah, NJ, Lawrence Erlbaum.

Csikszentmihalyi, M. and Rochberg-Halton, E., 1981, *The Meaning of Things: Domestic Symbols and the Self*, Cambridge, Cambridge University Press.

De Boer, J., Hoogland, C. and Boersema, J., 2007, 'Towards more sustainable food choices, value priorities and motivational orientations', *Food Quality and Preference* 18, 985–996.

De Groot, J.I.M. and Steg, L., 2007, 'Value orientations and environmental beliefs in five countries: validity of an instrument to measure egoistic, altruistic and biospheric value orientations', *Journal of Cross-Cultural Psychology* 38, 318–332.

De Groot, J.I.M. and Steg, L., 2008, 'Value orientations to explain beliefs related to environmental significant behaviour: How to measure egoistic, altruistic, and biospheric orientations', *Environment and Behavior* 40(3), 330–354.

DEFRA (Department for Environment, Food, and Rural Affairs), 2008, *Future Water: The Government's Water Strategy for England*, Norwich, UK, TSO.

Dietz, T., Fitgerald, A. and Shwom, R., 2005, 'Environmental values', *Annual Review of Environmental Resources* 30, 335–372.

Dittmar, H., 1992, 'Perceived material wealth and first impressions', *British Journal of Social Psychology* 31, 379–391.

Druckman, A., Bradley, P., Papathanasopoulou, E. and Jackson, T., 2008, 'Measuring progress towards carbon reduction in the UK', *Ecological Economics* 66, 594–604.

Druckman, A. and Jackson, T., 2009, 'The carbon footprint of UK households 1990–2004: A socio-economically disaggregated, quasi-multi-regional input-output model', *Ecological Ecomomics* 68(7), 2066–2077.

Dunlap, R., Van Liere, K., Mertig, A. and Jones, R.E., 2000, 'Measuring endorsement of the New Ecological Paradigm: A revised NEP scale', *Journal of Social Issues* 56(3), 425–442.

Dunlap, R.E. and Van Liere, K.D., 1978, 'The "new environmental paradigm": a proposed measuring instrument and preliminary results', *Journal of Environmental Education* 9, 10–19.

Gatersleben, B., Steg, L. and Vlek, C., 2002, 'Measurement and determinants of environmental relevant consumer behaviour', *Environment and Behavior* 34, 335–362.

Ger, G. and Belk, R.W., 1996, 'I'd like to buy the world a coke: consumption scapes of the "less affluent world"', *Journal of Consumer Policy* 19, 271–304.

Heijs, W., Carton, M., Smeets, J. and van Gemert, A., 2005, *Labyrint van leefstijlen*. Cahier Architectuur Stedebouw Eindhoven, nr. 7. Internal Report. Eindhoven University [In Dutch].

Inglehart, R., 1990, *Culture Shift in Advanced Industrial Society*, Princeton, New Jersey University Press.

Inglehart, R., 1995, 'Public support for environmental protection: objective problems and subjective values in 43 societies', *Political Science and Politics* March, 57–72.

Jackson, T., 2005, 'Live better by consuming less? Is there a 'double dividend' in sustainable consumption?', *Journal of Industrial Ecology* 9(1–2), 19–36.

Jackson, T., 2008, 'The Challenge of Sustainable Lifestyles', Chapter 4 in G. Gardner and T. Prugh (eds) *State of the World 2008: Innovations for a Sustainable Economy*, London, Earthscan.

Jackson, T., 2009, *Prosperity without Growth – Economics for a Finite Planet*, London, Earthscan.

Kasser, T., 2002, *The High Price of Materialism: A Psychological Inquiry*, MA, USA, MIT Press.

Kasser, T., 2005, 'Frugality, generosity, and materialism in children and adolescents', in K.A. Moore and L.H. Lipman (eds), *What do Children need to Flourish?: Conceptualizing and Measuring Indicators of Positive Development* (chapter 22), New York, Springer.

Kasser, T., Ryan, R.M., Couchman, C.E. and Sheldon, K.M., 2004, 'Materialistic values: their causes and consequences', in T. Kasser and A.D. Kanner (eds) *Psychology and Consumer Culture: The Struggle for a Good Life in a Materialistic World*, Washington, DC, American Psychological Association, 11–28.

Kempton, W., Boster, J.S. and Hartley, J.A., 1996, *Environmental Values in American Culture*, MA, USA, MIT Press.

Kilbourne, W., Grünhagen, M. and Foley, J., 2005, 'A cross-cultural examination of relationship between materialism and individual values', *Journal of Economic Psychology* 26, 624–41.

Maslow, A.H., 1954, *Motivation and Personality*, New York, Harper.

Maslow, A.H., 1968, *Towards a Psychology of Being*, New York, van Nostrand Reinhold.

McKenzie-Mohr, D., Nemiroff, L.S., Beers, L. and Desmarais, S., 1995, 'Determinants of responsible environmental behavior', *Journal of Social Issues* 51, 139–156.

Office of Climate Change, 2007, *OCC household emissions project: analysis pack*. Available at: www.occ.gov.uk/activities/household.htm [accessed 15 September 2008].

Pepper, M., Jackson, T. and Uzzell, D., 2009, 'An examination of the values that motivate socially conscious and frugal consumer behaviours', *International Journal of Consumer Studies* 33, 126–136.

Räthzel, N. and Uzzell, D., 2009, 'Changing relations in global environmental change', *Global Environmental Change* 19, 326–335.

Richins, M.L., 2004, 'The material values scale: measurement properties and development of a short form', *Journal of Consumer Research* 31, 209–218.

Richins, M.L. and Dawson, S., 1992, 'A consumer values orientation for materialism and its measurement: scale development and validation',

Journal of Consumer Research 19, 303–316.

Rokeach, M., 1973, *The Nature of Human Values*, New York, The Free Press.

Saunders, S.A., 2007, 'A snapshot of five materialism studies in Australia', *Journal of Pacific Rim Psychology* 1(1), 14–19.

Schultz, P.W., 2001, 'The structure of environmental concern: concern for self, other people, and the biosphere', *Journal of Environmental Psychology* 21, 1–13.

Schultz, P.W. and Zelezny, L., 1999, 'Values as predictors of environmental attitudes: Evidence for consistency across 14 countries', *Journal of Environmental Psychology* 19, 255–265.

Schwartz, S.H., 1992, 'Universals in the content and structure of values: theory and empirical tests in 20 countries', in M. Zanna (ed) *Advances in Experimental Social Psychology*, New York, Academic Press, 25, 1–65.

Schwartz, S.H., 2006, 'Value orientations: measurement, antecedents and consequences across nations', in R. Jowell, C. Roberts, R. Fitzgerald and G. Eva (eds), *Measuring Attitudes Cross-nationally – Lessons from the European Social Survey*, London, Sage.

Schwartz, S.H. and Bilsky, W., 1990, 'Toward a theory of the universal content and structure of values: Extensions and cross cultural replications', *Journal of Personality and Social Psychology* 58, 878–891.

Schwartz, S.H. and Boehnke, K., 2004, 'Evaluating the structure of human values with confirmatory factor analysis', *Journal of Research in Personality* 38, 230–255.

Sheldon, K.M. and McGregor, H., 2000, 'Extrinsic value orientation and the "tragedy of the commons"', *Journal of Personality* 68, 383–411.

Solberg, E.G., Diener, E. and Robinson, M.D., 2004, 'Why are materialists less satisfied?', in T. Kasser and A. Kanner (eds), *Psychology and Consumer Culture: The Struggle for a Good Life in a Materialistic World*, Washington, DC, American Psychological Association, 29–48.

Steger, M.E., Pierce, J.C., Steel, B.S. and Lovrich, V.P., 2005, 'Political culture, postmaterial values, and the new environmental paradigm: A comparative analysis of Canada and the United States', *Political Behaviour* 11(3), 233–254.

Stern, N.H., 2007, *The Economics of Climate Change. The Stern Review*, Cabinet Office, HM Treasury.

Stern, P., 2000, 'Toward a coherent theory of environmentally significant behavior', *Journal of Social Issues* 56, 407–424.

Stern, P., Dietz, T., Abel, T., Guagnano, G.A. and Kalof, L., 1999, 'A value-belief-norm theory of support for social movements: The case of environmentalism', *Human Ecology Review* 6, 81–97.

Stern, P.C., Dietz, T., Kalof, L. and Guagnano, G.A., 1995, 'Values, beliefs and pro-environmental action: Attitude formation toward emergent attitude objects' *Journal of Applied Social Psychology* 25, 1611–1636.

Stern, P.C. and Oskamp, S., 1987, 'Managing scarce environmental resources', in D. Stokols and I. Altman (eds), *Handbook of Environmental Psychology*, New York, Wiley, 2, 1043–1088.

Stern, P.C., 1992, 'What psychology knows about energy conservation', *American Psychologist* 47, 1224–1232.

Stern, P.C. and Dietz, T., 1994, 'The value basis of environmental concern', *Journal of Social Issues* 50, 65–84.

Tatzel, M., 2002, '"Money worlds" and well-being: an integration of money dispositions, materialism and price-related behaviour', *Journal of Economic Psychology* 23, 103–126.

Vansteenekiste, M., Duriez, B., Simons, J. and Soenens, B., 2006, 'Materialistic values and well-being among business students: Further evidence of their detrimental effect', *Journal of Applied Social Psychology* 36, 2892–2908.

ARCHITECTURAL
SCIENCE
REVIEW

Understanding barriers to social adaptation: are we targeting the right concerns?

Silva Larson*

School of Business, James Cook University, Townsville, Australia
CSIRO Sustainable Ecosystems, Davies Laboratory, PMB Aitkenvale, Queensland 4814, Australia

This article proposes that improved 'translation' of policy goals and actions into issues relevant to local stakeholders on the ground, may play an important role in stakeholders' understanding and consequent acceptance of the principles of sustainability and adaptation. In turn, the relevance of national or other higher level goals to on-the-ground stakeholders could be improved through communication of the concerns of stakeholders to policymakers. The subjective well-being concept is proposed as having the potential to improve such a communication. The article first provides an overview of key concepts in vulnerability and adaptation literature. Human well-being concept is then introduced and the results of an empirical study conducted in the Great Barrier Reef region of Australia are presented, providing evidence of factors perceived by respondents as most important to their well-being.

Keywords: Adaptation; Great Barrier Reef; subjective well-being; vulnerability

INTRODUCTION

The international body of literature increasingly acknowledges that the question of what stimuli ecosystems and communities will need to adapt to as a result of a climate change is a function not so much of the climate system itself, but rather of the nature of the system of interest (Preston and Stafford-Smith, 2009). Different regions, sectors, communities and enterprises will likely need to adapt to highly diverse aspects of climate change, depending upon those manifestations of climate that are relevant to them.

The core questions for adaptation research have been identified as (Smit et al., 2000) What are we adapting to? Who adapts? and How do we adapt?, and a significant body of literature examines these questions. However, a fourth question, 'What do we want to achieve by adaptation?', is of interest in this article, and is potentially one that has not received sufficient attention to date. What is it that we ultimately want to protect by adapting? Literature refers to the reduction of vulnerability of subjects or the minimization of impacts on social and economic systems, but what do we aim to achieve by reducing such vulnerabilities or minimizing such impacts is often not clearly stated. It can be assumed that the ultimate objective of such exercises is the long-term sustainability of the system, ensuring the maintenance of current qualities of lifestyle and levels of well-being. However, only some of the discourses and definitions of adaptation specifically refer to the improvement of

social well-being (Kane and Yohe, 2000) or health and well-being (Burton, 1992). Others attach more importance to the maintenance or enhancement of economic activity (Smith, 1993; Smith et al., 1996). Empirical research, however, also indicates that maintenance of quality of life is the main desirable outcome reported by participants, for themselves, their families and the societies they live in (Eckersley, 1999, 2000; GIAB, 2004).

On-the-ground stakeholders may find such goals of adaptation or sustainability difficult to operationalize (Larson, 2009). The understanding and acceptance of the principles and goals of adaptation by local stakeholders on the ground could be improved if goals were 'translated' into issues relevant to them. Improved information and knowledge are acknowledged as important for improved adaptation; however, the bulk of relevant literature deals with issues of top-down communication, such as the creation of policies and institutions that would enable or enhance adaptive capacity or facilitate learning about the science of climate change (Scheffer et al., 2000; Smit et al., 2000; Berkes et al., 2002; Yohe and Tol, 2002; Lemos et al., 2007). Little research appears to have been carried out on the bottom-up direction, that is, trying to convey factors that are of importance to ordinary people to policy and decision makers. Nonetheless, the relevance of national or other higher level goals to on-the-ground stakeholders could be improved through communication of the concerns of stakeholders to the policymakers (Larson, 2009).

*Email: silva.larson@csiro.au

doi:10.3763/asre.2009.0103 ©2010 Earthscan ISSN: 0003-8628 (print), 1758-9622 (online) www.earthscan.co.uk/journals/asre
earthscan

This article first provides an overview of key concepts in vulnerability and adaptation literature. The human well-being concept is then introduced and the results of an empirical study conducted in the Great Barrier Reef region of Australia are presented, providing evidence of factors perceived by respondents as most important to their well-being. The discussion section further explores what it is that we want to achieve by adaptation. The article concludes that a better understanding of what is most important to people and societies is needed if we are to adapt in a way that protects what we care about most. Also, better communication of such priorities between policy and decision makers on the one hand and communities and individuals on the other hand may result in better adaptation choices and outcomes. The article also proposes that this two-way improved communication has an important role in the facilitation of changes in behaviours of individuals and other agents, as changes in behaviours are more likely to occur when agents are able to translate the potential impact to their own situations, to understand how their own well-being would be negatively impacted if no change occurs and thus actively acquiesce to changes in behaviour.

VULNERABILITY, ADAPTATION AND RESILIENCE: OVERVIEW OF KEY CONCEPTS FROM THE LITERATURE

Adaptation can be defined as a procedural response to a real or perceived potential for harm, in order to manage the impacts of and responses to a hazard (Preston and Stafford-Smith, 2009). Several concepts are discussed in the context of 'potential for harm', such as 'risk', 'hazard', 'impact', 'vulnerability' or 'consequence'; however, the concept of 'vulnerability' is of particular interest to this discussion as it relates to the ability of individuals or social groups to cope with the hazards (Adger and Vincent, 2005; Adger et al., 2005).

The Intergovernmental Panel on Climate Change (IPCC) defines vulnerability specific to climate change as a degree to which a system is susceptible to, or unable to cope with, adverse effects of climate change, including climate variability and extremes (Carter et al., 2007). The concept of vulnerability is often presented as consisting of three key components: exposure, sensitivity and adaptive capacity (Smit and Wandel, 2006; Preston et al., 2008). In the context of climate change, exposure and sensitivity to climate hazards create potential impacts, with 'adaptive capacity' being a capacity to adapt to the results of such impacts. Exposure to climate hazards lies more in the domain of biophysical science, whereas sensitivity depends on the inherent characteristics of the system being exposed. Adaptive capacity on the other hand is the ability of the system to change in a way that makes it better equipped to manage its exposure and sensitivity to climatic

influences (Preston and Stafford-Smith, 2009). Thus, one is considered to be more vulnerable if one's adaptive capacity is low (Adger and Vincent, 2005). From the point of view of social systems in the context of climate change, therefore, adaptive capacity is a key concept of interest.

Another related concept is that of resilience. Resilience in ecological and social systems is the ability to undergo change and still retain the same controls on function and structure, the capability to self-organise, and the ability to build and increase the capacity for learning and adaptation (Resilience Alliance, 2009). Views differ regarding the relationship between adaptive capacity and resilience (Gallopin, 2006). Folke et al. (2002) maintain that resilience is key to enhancing adaptive capacity, although Walker et al., (2002) remark that 'adaptive capacity is an aspect of resilience', which together suggest a mutually reinforcing relationship between these concepts. One view is that resilience is about negotiating vulnerability and adaptation under different conditions; 'true resilience will lie in knowing when to change course and when to forge ahead' (Redman and Kinzig, 2003).

IPCC (2001) defines adaptive capacity as 'the general ability of institutions, systems, and individuals to adjust to climate change (including climate variability and extremes) to moderate potential damage, to take advantage of opportunities, or to cope with the consequences'. This definition has been adopted widely by other scholars and scientific assessments such as the Millennium Ecosystem Assessment (2005).

Adaptive capacity is viewed as dependent on five capitals, that is, financial, built, natural, human and social (Nelson et al., 2007). In addition, Lemos et al. (2007) propose that adaptive capacity can be enhanced by investing in information and knowledge, both in their production and in the means of distributing and communicating them, and by encouraging appropriate institutions that permit evolutionary change and learning to be incorporated.

Adaptive capacity is perceived to be enhanced by a rich social memory of alternative situations and responses, and by the accumulation of social capital in the form of networks of trust, shared knowledge and actual materials needed to facilitate those responses (Bohensky et al., in press).

Preston and Stafford-Smith (2009) suggest that one of the most neglected aspects of adaptive research and assessment is the evaluation of constraints on adaptation and changes in behaviours. Hulme et al. (2007) distinguish between two different types of constraints – limits and barriers. A limit to adaptation implies an absolute barrier, that is, one that is unsurpassable, and often arising from biophysical constraints. A barrier to adaptation on the other hand exists because of the way a society is organized or because of the values it propagates. Such barriers are often perceived as tied to measures of wealth – such as access to financial capital and credit, access to technology and education, and access to knowledge. As a result of such conceptualizations of adaptation barriers, developing nations are generally regarded as having low adaptive capacity (Preston and Stafford-Smith, 2009). However, barriers can run much deeper within the community and individuals, including social, cultural and even cognitive barriers (see e.g. Adger *et al.*, 2007; Koch *et al.*, 2007; Lorenzoni *et al.*, 2007; Marx *et al.*, 2007; Urwin and Jordan, 2008). These may arise from differences in world views of the environment and economy, different perceptions of vulnerability, adaptive capacity and risk, and competition among issues for public attention and a space on political agendas (e.g. climate change or environmental issues in general vs the economy or national security).

Vulnerability assessments often combine climate, landscape, economic and social factors indicate areas of greater or lesser vulnerability. For example, Nelson *et al.* (2007) evaluated Australian national datasets and, in consultation with specialists, evaluated the human, social, natural, physical and financial capital of regional Australia to create maps of areas of greater and lesser adaptive capacity. Such analyses however do not necessarily provide one with an indication of what specific adaptation measures should be implemented or their relative costs and benefits, thus impeding their utility in decision support (Preston and Stafford-Smith, 2009). An alternative approach to lists of indicators based on secondary data sources is elicitation of perceptions of individuals, communities or societies of their own capacity to adapt (Bryant *et al.*, 2000; Hertin *et al.*, 2003; Grothmann and Patt, 2005; Lorenzoni *et al.*, 2007; Bohensky *et al.*, in press). There are trade-offs associated with each approach. Inductive (elicitation of perceptions) approaches run the risk of missing factors that are critically important to understanding adaptive capacity but not readily recognized by actors in the system, whereas deductive approaches, based on theoretical grounds, frameworks and pre-set lists of indicators, may fail to capture factors that are relevant on the ground. Using both together, however, enables a more complete picture of the factors, including perceptions, that are likely to enhance or erode adaptive capacity. Bohensky *et al.* (in press) therefore propose that it may be beneficial to use measures of adaptive capacity drawn from theory or conceptual frameworks of researchers, alongside inductive measures that are defined by the affected actors.

Roles of participation and social learning in enabling behavioural change in relation to climate-related issues have been discussed in the literature (e.g. Pelling and High, 2005). But how to ensure participation in issues that are not perceived as important? For example, work by Bohensky *et al.* (in press) in the Great Barrier Reef region suggests that climate change and adaptation are not seen as important by individuals and organizations interviewed. Thus, although the region has been assessed as having high adaptive capacity based on secondary data indicators (Nelson *et al.*, 2007), Bohensky and colleagues suggest that this adaptive capacity may not be turned into active adaptation until a crisis occurs, and acknowledge the significant danger that this may come too late. Indeed, the prevailing belief

among the region's resource users, managers and leaders is that a catastrophe is the most likely pathway to change, and this is rather unsettling, argue Bohensky and colleagues (in press). Theoretical definitions suggest that adaptive capacity is latent and harnessed in response to stimuli, but at which point the stimuli will be sufficient to provoke a response, these authors wonder.

Adaptive capacity can be enhanced by appropriate understanding of a problem and possible responses and can be constrained when deep-rooted attitudes and behaviours of an individual or society undermine the ability to adapt to new situations. Thus, the understanding of social, cultural and cognitive barriers to adaptation and behavioural change warrants further research. One concept that has a potential to aid in the exploration of social barriers, by capturing perceptions, attitudes and values held by individuals, is that of subjective human well-being. It will therefore be introduced in the next section.

SUBJECTIVE PERCEPTIONS OF WELL-BEING

The well-being concept is an integrative concept with a scope that can investigate social, ecological, economic, institutional, cultural and other domains of relevance to humans. Historically, the concept has been linked to research in the areas of human health and psychology (Diener *et al.*, 1999) and social policy and economics (Nussbaum and Sen, 1993). However, in recent years, the well-being concept has expanded beyond social and economic concerns to incorporate ecological, institutional, cultural and other domains.

Human well-being is becoming an increasingly important aspect of investigations in planning and management (Hagerty *et al.*, 2001; Veenhoven, 2002; Hassan *et al.*, 2005). Evaluations of the urban quality of life are well documented (Grayson and Young, 1994; Giannias, 1998; Pacione, 2003; van Kamp *et al.*, 2003; Ge and Hokao, 2006), representing either general approaches or focusing on particular domains of the urban quality of life such as health, social cohesion, safety or leisure (e.g. Berger-Schmitt, 2002; Lloyd and Auld, 2002; Bell, 2006). Several recent frameworks are based on integration of natural environment with human well-being (Jacobs, 1991; Narayan *et al.*, 2000; Prescott-Allen, 2001; Alkire, 2002; van Kamp *et al.*, 2003; Hassan *et al.*, 2005), as improvements in human well-being are increasingly viewed as dependent on improving ecosystem management and ensuring conservation and sustainable use of resources (Hassan *et al.*, 2005).

Two types of approaches to the well-being and quality of life have developed – the objective and the subjective. The objective approach to well-being focuses on data related to material and social circumstances typically collected at the national level, such as income in dollars or housing in square metres (Nussbaum and Sen, 1993; Hagerty *et al.*, 2001; Veenhoven, 2002). However, the objective approach does not provide any insight into individual satisfaction with income or perceived adequacy of the housing (Veenhoven, 2002). This is the main focus of the subjective approach to well-being (Andrews and Withney, 1976; Campbell *et al.*, 1976; Nussbaum and Sen, 1993; Veenhoven, 2002; Cummins *et al.*, 2003). The importance of both objective and subjective indicators of well-being, as sources of different information that aids in reporting, planning, policy and decision making at various spatial levels, has been acknowledged in the literature (Veenhoven, 2002; Easterlin, 2003).

The environment we reside in is not 'given'; it is created and interpreted by humans (Irwin, 2001). Therefore, there is a need for an adequate understanding of how individuals and communities see and interpret the environment in which they reside. Approaches that take into account individual experiences help us understand and communicate the interpretations, priorities and needs of individuals (Diener and Suh, 1997). Measuring quality of life is not easy, argues Jacobs (1991), as what is important is not the amount spent on services, but the amount of well-being people derive from it. In some sense, therefore, quality of life is a subjective notion, which cannot be entirely reduced to objectively measurable indicators. Furthermore, research into subjective well-being acknowledges that cultural background or internal, individual factors such as temperament, cognition, goals and coping methods may have a larger impact on satisfaction with life than external resources and demographic factors such as educational levels, income, age or gender (Andrews and Withney, 1976; Campbell *et al.*, 1976; Diener *et al.*, 1999).

A major challenge for implementing adaptation options is the inherent dynamic nature of both the climate and the ecological and socio-economic systems (Preston and Stafford-Smith, 2009). Thus, we always run the risk that seemingly adaptive actions taken today will eventually prove to be maladaptive in a future context, due to acquisition of new knowledge or simply due to changes in societal preferences (Burton *et al.*, 2002; Næss *et al.*, 2007; Vogel *et al.*, 2007). A good understanding of what is important to people is therefore vital for moving beyond the acknowledgement of a change in a general sense into the implementation of context-specific adaptation policies and measures of relevance to local stakeholders. Data from a survey of more than 350 residents in two rural regions of the Great Barrier Reef region in Australia are presented here to provide an empirical illustration of this point, and as a potential approach to capturing and measuring key factors of importance to local residents, as perceived by those residents themselves.

The methodological approach used in the study was based on an integrated conceptual model of well-being that includes factors of well-being from ecological, social and economic domains, and allows for subjective quantification of the factors of well-being most important to the respondent (Larson, 2009). The well-being factors included in the questionnaire were selected based on a two-step process. First, a generic list of ecological, social, economic and services-related factors was compiled from the literature, influenced mainly by frameworks based on the integration of natural environment with human well-being (Veenhoven, 1996; Hassan *et al.*, 2005; Millennium Ecosystem Assessment, 2005; Prescott-Allen, 2001; Alkire, 2002; van Kamp *et al.*, 2003). Then, the list was refined as a result of discussions with peers, government agency representatives and community representatives from the proposed case study areas. Twenty-seven well-being factors included in the final questionnaire were grouped into three domains:

- Society – Family and community domain, consisting of family relations; community relations; personal/family safety; cultural identity; personal/family health; civil and political rights; personal/family education levels; council relations; and sports, travel and entertainment.
- Ecology – Natural environment domain, consisting of air quality; water quality; soil quality; access to natural areas; biodiversity; swimming, bushwalking and other activities in nature; fishing, hunting, collecting produce; beauty of the landscape and beaches; and condition of the landscape and beaches.
- Economy and services domain, consisting of work; income/financial security; housing; health services; recreational facilities; condition of the roads; public infrastructure and transport; training and education services; and support services.

The selection of participants was based on a randomly chosen first number, followed by a selected number entry in the original database until the desired sample size was achieved. A total of 824 surveys were mailed out, using Dillman's (2000) tailored survey method technique. A total of 354 valid responses were received. The sample was tested for non-response error by comparing the demographic data of respondents with demographic data from the Australian Bureau of Statistics (ABS), for the case study shires as a whole. The comparison included gender, age, marital status, cultural background, education and sector of employment. The non-response testing did not reveal any major gaps between survey sample and total population.

Participants were asked to choose five to seven of the well-being factors that they considered the most important. They were then asked to assign to those factors relative levels of importance by allocating points between 1 (least important) and 100 (most important) to each factor selected. Respondents were instructed that more than one factor could receive the same weights. The percentage of scale maximum method (Cummins, 2003) was used to process and standardize thus collected individual weights to 1. Weights that respondents assigned to well-being factors were then aggregated using the double de Borta voting method (Feldman, 1980), that is, the relative importance of the factor was determined both by the average weight assigned to each well-being factor by respondents and by the percentage of respondents identifying that particular factor as being

Table 1 | Importance assigned to the emerging top 10 contributors to regional well-being and the summary scores for each of the three domains of well-being ($n = 354$)

Contributors to Regional Well-being	Importance	Std. Deviation
Well-being factors	sum = 1	
Family relations	0.129	0.137
Personal/family health	0.111	0.106
Income/financial security	0.084	0.082
Personal/family safety	0.080	0.086
Health services	0.078	0.094
Water quality	0.068	0.077
Work	0.041	0.079
Roads condition	0.041	0.073
Air quality	0.040	0.066
Condition of the landscape/beaches	0.034	0.065
(All other well-being factors)	(0.294)	
Well-being domains	sum = 1	
Family and community domain	0.426	0.210
Economy and services domain	0.309	0.185
Natural environment domain	0.257	0.192

important to their well-being. Relevant results from the study are summarized in Table 1.

The results suggest that well-being factors from the family and community domain, in particular family relations and personal and family health and safety, were of highest importance to the largest numbers of respondents in the case study regions, with the family and community domain accounting for 42.6% of importance overall. Factors from the society domain have both been selected by the largest proportion of respondents and received highest scores as well-being contributors.

Income/financial security also rated high, as well as a number of other economic factors and services, such as work, health services and condition of the roads, bringing the economy and services domain to a total of 30.9% of importance overall. Water and air quality and condition of the landscape and beaches were factors from the natural

environment domain that have qualified into 10 most important regional contributors to well-being, with the natural environment receiving 25.7% of all weights.

Data collected in this survey provided information on residents' wants and priorities, which are not readily available in standard data sources. Central statistical agencies such as the ABS provide information on some of the contributors to well-being, such as housing or education, and are useful measures of change over time and across regions. However, such data are based on the normative objective approach and do not contain information on how those objective indicators are perceived by people. A combination of secondary data indicator-based assessments and primary subjective data-based assessment may provide additional information of high relevance to the climate change vulnerability discussion.

DISCUSSION AND CONCLUSIONS

This article proposes that improved 'translation' of policy goals and actions into issues relevant to local stakeholders on the ground may play an important role in stakeholders' understanding and consequent acceptance of the principles of sustainability and adaptation. In turn, the relevance of national or other higher level goals to on-the-ground stakeholders could be improved through communication of the concerns of stakeholders to policymakers. The subjective well-being concept has been proposed as having the potential to improve the communication of sustainability and adaptation goals between the policy level and the individual (personal) level (Larson, 2009). Ultimately, better communication and better understanding of what people value, and consequent targeting of such issues, may help change peoples' behaviours towards behaviours that, in the long term, preserve the things perceived as of importance. For this to occur, however, a good understanding of factors of importance to people, and a better understanding of what they want to achieve by adapting, is needed. Is current policy sufficiently informed by views of the people? And are current views held by people sufficiently informed and aware of big policy issues?

Effective engagement and social learning have been identified as crucial for the long-term improvement of adaptive capacity and outcomes (Bellamy, 2007). In turn, capacity building and social learning that develop during engagement processes play a role in legitimizing new institutions (Lemos and Oliveira, 2004; Larson, 2006; Ostrom, 2007). However, a recent review of the understanding of institutional arrangements in the Great Barrier Reef region identified significant gaps between community concerns and the perceptions of government agencies responsible for managing those concerns, and the actual institutional arrangements and responsibilities (Larson and Stone-Jovicich, 2008). This finding highlighted a need for better communication between various scales and social groups. However, it might be unlikely for the community engagement to occur unless issues proposed to be discussed are perceived as important and relevant by those who policy-makers want to engage. Without initial engagement, the opportunity to learn is lost, and consequent engagement might be even less likely.

Subjective perspectives of well-being are gaining increasing recognition as being important in policymaking (Veenhoven, 2002; New Zealand Ministry of Social Development, 2004; McAllister, 2005), in particular in assessing the impact of political and economic decisions on individuals' lives (McAllister, 2005). This article argues that the subjective well-being approach may also contribute research in the area of vulnerability, adaptive capacity and resilience, and that further research in this direction is warranted.

Barriers to adaptation, argue Hulme and colleagues (2007), are essentially created by the way a society is organized or by values it propagates. Such barriers are also perceived as tied to measures of wealth (Preston and Stafford-Smith, 2009). However, the findings presented in this article indicate that factors related to the natural environment, family, community and the economy and services are all of importance to people. The majority (70%) of respondents in the study included factors from each domain as contributing to their personal and family well-being. The survey has highlighted the importance of social factors to the individual well-being of respondents, and has also demonstrated the significant role that natural environment plays in the well-being of individuals. Thus, concepts and assessments that go beyond potential negative impacts on incomes and assets, and deal with issues broader than material wealth, also warrant further research.

This article has briefly presented one methodological approach that can prioritize components as perceived by respondents as important to their individual and family well-being. The article argues that at least some of the cultural and social barriers to adaptation can be removed with improved communication, and that research that provides further insight in this area would be valuable. The improved understanding of factors of importance to people can support decision makers in devising desirable and therefore acceptable options for adaptation at the appropriate scale. The required behavioural changes and resulting 'trade-offs' would likely not only promote goals of long-term sustainability, but would also appeal to local residents.

ACKNOWLEDGMENTS

Useful comments on the earlier drafts of this article were provided by Drs Natalie Stoeckl, Nadine Marshall and John Gardener. Funding was provided by CSIRO Water for a Healthy Country Flagship and Climate Adaptation Flagship. Sincere thanks to Mr Peter Wiegand for his assistance with mail-out and data entry. This research project was approved by the James Cook University Human Ethics Subcommittee in March 2006 (Approval number H2314).

References

Adger, W.N., Agrawala, S., Mirza, M.M.Q., Conde, C., O'Brien, K., Pulhin, J., Pulwarty, R., Smit, B. and Takahashi, K., 2007, 'Assessment of adaptation practices, options, constraints and capacity', in M.L. Parry, O.F. Canziani, J.P. Palutikof, P.J. van der Linden and C.E. Hanson (eds), *Climate Change 2007: Impacts, Adaptation and Vulnerability; Contribution of Working Group II to the Fourth Assessment Report of the Intergovernmental Panel on Climate Change*, Cambridge, UK, Cambridge University Press, 717–743.

Adger, W.N., Arnell, N.W. and Tompkins, E., 2005, 'Successful adaptation to climate change across scales', *Global Environmental Change* 15, 77–86.

Adger, W.N. and Vincent, K., 2005, 'Uncertainty in adaptive capacity. C.R.', *Geoscience* 337, 399–410.

Alkire, S., 2002, 'Dimensions of human development', *World Development* 30(2), 191–205.

Andrews, F. and Withney, S., 1976, *Social Indicators of Wellbeing: American Perceptions of Quality of Life*, New York, Plenum Press.

Bell, D., 2006, *Review of Research into Subjective Well-being and its Relation to Sport and Culture*, Edinburgh, UK, Scottish Executive Education Department.

Bellamy, J., 2007, 'Adaptive governance: the challenge for regional natural resource management', in A.J. Brown and J.A. Bellamy (eds), *Federalism and Regionalism in Australia: New Approaches, New Institutions?*, Canberra, Australian National University E Press, 95–118.

Berger-Schmitt, R., 2002, 'Considering social cohesion in quality of life assessments: concept and measurement', *Social Indicators Research* 58, 403–428.

Berkes, F., Colding, J. and Folke, C., 2002, *Navigating Social-Ecological Systems: Building Resilience for Complexity and Change*, Cambridge, Cambridge University Press.

Bohensky, E., Stone-Jovicich, S., Larson, S. and Marshall, N. (in press), 'Adaptive capacity in theory and reality: implications for governance in the Great Barrier Reef region', in D. Armitage and R. Plummer (eds) *Adaptive Capacity: Building Environmental Governance in an Age of Uncertainty*, Heidelberg, Springer.

Bryant, C.R., Smit, B., Brklacich, M., Johnston, T.R., Smithers, J., Chiotti, Q. and Singh, B., 2000, 'Adaptation in Canadian agriculture to climatic variability and change', *Climatic Change* 45(1), 181–201.

Burton, I., 1992, *Adapt and Thrive, Canadian Climate Change Centre*, unpublished manuscript, Ontario, Canada, Downsview.

Burton, I., Huq, S., Lim, B., Pilifosova, O. and Schipper, E.L., 2002, 'From impacts assessment to adaptation priorities: the shaping of adaptation policy', *Climate Policy* 2, 145–159.

Campbell, A., Converse, P. and Rodgers, W., 1976, *The Quality of American Life: Perceptions, Evaluations and Satisfaction*, New York, Russell Sage Foundation.

Carter, T.R., Jones, R.N., Lu, X., Bhadwal, S., Conde, C., Mearns, L.O., O'Neill, B.C., Rounsevell, M.D.A. and Zurek, M.B., 2007, 'New assessment methods and the characterisation of future conditions', in M.L. Parry, O.F. Canziani, J.P. Palutikof, P.J. van der Linden and

C.E. Hanson (eds), *Climate Change 2007: Impacts, Adaptation and Vulnerability; Contribution of Working Group II to the Fourth Assessment Report of the Intergovernmental Panel on Climate Change*, Cambridge, UK, Cambridge University Press, 133–171.

Cummins, R.A., 2003, 'Normative life satisfaction: measurement issues and a homeostatic model', *Social Indicators Research* 64, 225–256.

Cummins, R.A., Eckersley, R., Pallant, J., Van Vugt, J. and Misajon, R., 2003, 'Developing a national index of subjective well-being: the Australian Unity Wellbeing Index', *Social Indicators Research* 64, 159–190.

Diener, E. and Suh, E., 1997, 'Measuring quality of life: economic, social, and subjective indicators', *Social Indicators Research* 40, 189–216.

Diener, E., Suh, E.M., Lucas, R.E. and Smith, H.L., 1999, 'Subjective well-being: three decades of progress', *Psychological Bulletin* 125(2), 276–302.

Dillman, D.A. 2000, *Mail and Internet Survey: The Tailored Design Method*, 2nd edition, New York, John Wiley and Sons.

Easterlin, R.A., 2003, 'Explaining happiness', *Proceedings of the National Academy of Science* 100, 11176–11183.

Eckersley, R., 1999, 'Dreams and expectations: young people's expected and preferred futures and their significance for education', *Futures* 31, 73–90.

Eckersley, R., 2000, 'The state and fate of nations: implications subjective measures of personal and social quality of life', *Social Indicators Research* 52, 3–27.

Feldman, A., 1980, *Welfare Economics and Social Choice Theory*, Boston, MA, Martinus Nijhoff Publishing.

Folke, C., Carpenter, S., Elmqvist, T., Gunderson, L., Holling, C.S. and Walker, B., 2002, 'Resilience and sustainable development: building adaptive capacity in a world of transformations', *Ambio* 31, 437–440.

Gallopin, G.C., 2006, 'Linkages between vulnerability, resilience, and adaptive capacity', *Global Environmental Change* 16, 293–303.

Ge, J. and Hokao, K., 2006, 'Research on residential lifestyles in Japanese cities from the viewpoints of residential preference, residential choice and residential satisfaction', *Landscape and Urban Planning* 78, 165–178.

Giannias, D., 1998, 'A quality of life based ranking of Canadian cities', *Urban Studies* 35(12), 2241–2251.

GIAB (Growth Innovation Advisory Board), 2004, *Research on Growth and Innovation*, Wellington, New Zealand, Prepared by the Growth & Innovation

Advisory, Board Ministry of Research Science and Technology.

Grayson, L. and Young, K., 1994, *Quality of Life in Cities. An Overview and Guide to the Literature*, London, UK, The British Library/London Research Centre.

Grothmann, T. and Patt, A., 2005, 'Adaptive capacity and human cognition: the process of individual adaptation to climate change', *Global Environmental Change* 15, 199–213.

Hagerty, M.R., Cummins, R.A., Ferriss, A.L., Land, K., Michalos, A.C., Peterson, M., Sharpe, A., Sirgy, J. and Vogel, J., 2001, 'Quality of life indexes for national policy: review and agenda for research', *Social Indicators Research* 55, 1–96.

Hassan, R., Scholes, R. and Ash, N. (eds), 2005, *Ecosystems and Human Wellbeing: Current State and Trends, Millennium Ecosystem Assessment*, Volume 1, Washington, DC, Island Press.

Hertin, J., Berkhout, F., Gann, D. and Barlow, J., 2003, 'Climate change and the UK house building sector: perceptions, impacts and adaptive capacity', *Build Research and Information* 31(3), 278–290.

Hulme, M., Adger, W.N., Dessai, S., Goulden, M., Lorenzoni, I., Nelson, D., Naess, L.-O., Wolf, J. and Wreford, A., 2007, 'Limits and barriers to adaptation: four propositions', Tyndall Briefing Note No. 20, Tyndall Centre for Climate Change Research, University of East Anglia, Norwich, UK.

IPCC (Intergovernmental Panel on Climate Change), 2001, *Climate Change 2001: Impacts, Adaptation and Vulnerability. Summary for Policy Makers*, Geneva, World Meteorological Organisation.

Irwin, A., 2001, *Sociology and the Environment. A Critical Introduction to Society, Nature and Knowledge*, Cambridge, UK, Polity Press.

Jacobs, M., 1991, *The Green Economy: Environment, Sustainable Development and the Politics of the Future*, London, UK, Pluto Press.

Kane, S. and Yohe, G., 2000, 'Societal adaptation to climatic variability and change: an introduction', *Climatic Change* 45, 1–4.

Koch, I.C., Vogel, C. and Patel, Z., 2007, 'Institutional dynamics and climate change adaptation in South Africa', *Mitigation and Adaptation Strategies for Global Climate Change* 12, 1323–1339.

Larson, S., 2006, 'Wellbeing function as a support tool for communication of the stakeholder priorities and goals on catchments scale', in A. Tanik, I. Ozturk, M. Gurel, M.S. Yazgan and E. Pehlivanoglu-Mantas (eds), *Proceedings of the 10th International*

Conference on Diffuse Pollution and Sustainable Basin Management*. Istanbul, Turkey, 18–22 September 2006, p. 122 and CD proceedings.

Larson, S., 2009, 'Communicating stakeholder priorities in the Great Barrier Reef region', *Society and Natural Resources* 22(7), 650–664.

Larson, S. and Stone-Jovicich, S., 2008, 'Community perceptions of water quality and current institutional arrangements in the Great Barrier Reef region of Australia', in P. Cherallier, B. Pouyard and E. Servat (eds), *Proceedings of the 13th International Water Resources Association World Water Congress*. Montpelier, France, 1–4 September 2008.

Lemos, M.C., Boyd, E., Tompkins, E.L., Osbahr, H. and Liverman, D., 2007, 'Developing adaptation and adapting development', *Ecology and Society* 12(2), 26.

Lemos, M.C. and Oliveira, J.L., 2004, 'Can water reform survive politics? Institutional change and river basin management in Ceará, northeast Brazil', *World Development* 32(12), 2121.

Lloyd, K. and Auld, C., 2002, 'The role of leisure in determining quality of life: Issues of content and measurement', *Social Indicators Research* 57, 43–71.

Lorenzoni, I., Nicholson-Cole, S. and Whitmarsh, L., 2007, 'Barriers perceived to engaging with climate change among the UK public and their policy implications', *Global Environmental Change* 17, 445–459.

Marx, S.M., Weber, E.U., Orlove, B.S., Leiserowitz, A., Krantz, D.H., Roncoli, C. and Phillips, J., 2007, 'Communication and mental processes: experimental and analytic processing of uncertain climate information', *Global Environmental Change* 17, 47–58.

McAllister, F., 2005, *Wellbeing: Concepts and Challenges*. Discussion Paper prepared for the Sustainable Development Research Network. Available at www.sd-research.org.uk/wellbeing/wellbeing/documents/SDRNwellbeingpaper-Final_000.pdf [accessed 8 August 2007].

Millennium Ecosystem Assessment, 2005, *Millennium Ecosystem Assessment, Ecosystems and Human Well-being*, Washington, DC, Island Press.

Næss, L.O., Norland, I.T., Lafferty, W.M. and Aall, C., 2007, 'Data and processes linking vulnerability assessment to adaptation decision-making on climate change in Norway', *Global Environmental Change* 16, 221–233.

Narayan, D., Chambers, R., Shah, M.K. and Petesch, P., 2000, *Voices of the*

Poor: Crying out for Change, New York, Oxford University Press for the World Bank.

Nelson, R., Brown, P.R., Darbas, T., Kokic, P. and Cody, K., 2007, *The Potential to Map the Adaptive Capacity of Australian Land Managers for NRM Policy using ABS Data*. CSIRO, Australian Bureau of Agricultural and Resource Economics, Canberra, National Land and Water Resources Audit.

New Zealand Ministry of Social Development, 2004, *The Social Report*, Wellington, NZ, Ministry of Social Development.

Nussbaum, M. and Sen, A. (eds), 1993, *The Quality of Life*, Oxford, UK, Clarendon Press.

Ostrom, E., 2007, 'Multiple institutions for multiple outcomes', in A. Smajgl and S. Larson (eds), *Sustainable Resource Use: Institutional Dynamics and Economics*, London, Earthscan, 23–49.

Pacione, M., 2003, 'Urban environmental quality and human well-being – a social geographical perspective', *Landscape and Urban Planning* 65, 19–30.

Pelling, M. and High, C. 2005, 'Understanding adaptation: what can social capital offer assessments of adaptive capacity?', *Global Environmental Change* 15, 308–319.

Prescott-Allen, R., 2001, *The Wellbeing of Nations: a Country by Country Index of Quality of Life and the Environment*, Washington DC, Island Press.

Preston, B.L. and Stafford-Smith, M., 2009, *Framing Vulnerability and Adaptive Capacity Assessment*, Discussion paper, CSIRO Climate Adaptation Flagship Working paper No. 2. Available at: www.csiro.au/files/files/ppgt.pdf.

Preston, B.L., Smith, T., Brooke, C., Gorddard, R., Measham, T., Withycombe, G., McInnes, K., Abbs, D., Beveridge, B. and Morrison, C., 2008, *Mapping Climate Change Vulnerability in the Sydney Coastal Councils Group*. Prepared for the Sydney Coastal Councils Group and the Commonwealth Department of Climate Change. CSIRO Climate Adaptation Flagship, Melbourne, Australia.

Redman, C.L. and Kinzig, A.P., 2003, 'Resilience of past landscapes: resilience theory, society, and the *longue durée*', *Conservation Ecology* 7(1), 14.

Resilience Alliance, 2009, *Adaptive Capacity*. Available at: www.resalliance.org/565.php

Scheffer, M., Brock, W. and Westley, F., 2000, 'Mechanisms preventing optimum use of ecosystem services: an interdisciplinary theoretical analysis', *Ecosystems* 3, 451–471.

Smit, B., Burton, I., Kelin, R.J.T. and Wandel, J., 2000, 'An anatomy of adaptation to climate change and variability', *Climatic Change* 45, 223–251.

Smit, B. and Wandel, J., 2006, 'Adaptation, adaptive capacity and vulnerability', *Global Environmental Change* 16, 282–292.

Smith, B. (ed), 1993, *Adaptation to Climatic Variability and Change*, Canada, Environment Canada, Guelph.

Smith, B., McNabb, D. and Smithers, J., 1996, 'Agricultural adaptation to climate change', *Climatic Change* 33, 7–29.

Urwin, K. and Jordan, A., 2008, 'Does public policy support or undermine climate change adaptation? Exploring policy interplay across different scales of governance', *Global Environmental Change* 18, 180–191.

van Kamp, I., Leidelmeijer, K., Marsman, G. and de Hollander, A., 2003, 'Urban environmental quality and human well-being: Towards a conceptual framework and demarcation of concepts', *Landscape and Urban Planning Journal* 65, 5–18.

Veenhoven, R., 1996, 'Happy life-expectancy: a comprehensive measure of quality-of-life in nations', *Social Indicators Research* 39, 1–58.

Veenhoven, R., 2002, 'Why social policy needs subjective indicators', *Social Indicators Research* 58, 33–45.

Vogel, C., Moser, S.C., Kasperson, R.E. and Dabelko, G.D., 2007, 'Linking vulnerability, adaptation, and resilience science to practice: Pathways, players, and partnerships', *Global Environmental Change* 17, 349–364.

Walker, B., Carpenter, S., Anderies, J., Abel, N., Cumming, G.S., Janssen, M., Lebel, L., Norberg, J., Peterson, G.D. and Pritchard, R., 2002, 'Resilience management in social-ecological systems: a working hypothesis for a participatory approach', *Conservation Ecology* 6(1), 14.

Yohe, G. and Tol, R.S.J., 2002, 'Indicators for social and economic coping capacity: moving toward a working definition of adaptive capacity', *Global Environmental Change* 12, 25–40.

ARCHITECTURAL
SCIENCE
REVIEW

Cooling exposure in hot humid climates: are occupants 'addicted'?

Christhina Cândido[1,3]*, Richard de Dear[2], Roberto Lamberts[3] and Leonardo Bittencourt[4]

[1]Department of Environment and Geography, Faculty of Science, Macquarie University, Sydney, NSW 2109, Australia
[2]The University of Sydney, Sydney NSW, Australia
[3]Federal University of Santa Catarina, Florianópolis/SC, Brazil
[4]Federal University of Alagoas, Maceio/AL, Brazil

According to the Fourth Assessment Report of the Intergovernmental Panel on Climate Change (IPCC), it is clear that the buildings sector presents the biggest potential for deep and fast CO_2 emission reductions on a cost-effective basis. Interestingly, this assessment was premised exclusively on technical (engineering) measures, but ignored completely the behavioural and lifestyle dimensions of energy consumption in the buildings sector. Behavioural change in buildings, however, can deliver even faster and zero-cost improvements in energy efficiency and greenhouse gas (ghg) emission reductions. With this in mind, designers are beginning to shift their attention to how they can widen the range of opportunities available in a building to provide comfort for the occupants, both in new-build and retrofit contexts. This in turn has re-awakened an interest in the role of natural ventilation in the provision of comfort. This discussion about adaptive comfort raises several questions, including the following: How can we shift occupants' comfort expectations away from the static indoor climates of the past towards the more variable thermal regimes found in naturally ventilated buildings? Are building occupants 'addicted' to static environments, i.e. air-conditioning (AC)? If so, how tolerant or compliant will they be when the thermally constant conditions provided by AC are replaced by the thermally variable conditions that characterize naturally ventilated spaces? Does the frequency of prior exposure to AC bias building occupants' thermal expectations and, if so, what are the implications of this bias for their acceptance of naturally ventilated indoor climates? Does prior exposure to AC lead building occupants to actually prefer AC over natural ventilation? This article addresses these questions in the context of a large field study of building occupants in a hot and humid climate zone in Brazil (Maceio). The temperature preferences registered on 975 questionnaires in naturally ventilated buildings are statistically analysed in relation to occupants' prior exposure to AC in their workplaces.

Keywords: Air conditioning; energy conservation; hot-humid climate; natural ventilation; thermal comfort; thermal history

INTRODUCTION

The Fourth Assessment Report of the Intergovernmental Panel on Climate Change (IPCC, 2007) highlighted the potential of the buildings sector to achieve greenhouse gas (ghg) emission reductions, above other sectors such as transport and industry. This assessment was premised on a technical approach related to architectural and engineering solutions that can be grouped into four themes: (1) reducing heating, cooling and lighting loads; (2) improving and using the thermal mass of the building; (3) increasing the efficiency of appliances and heating, ventilation and air-conditioning (HVAC) systems; and (4) increasing the efficiency of lighting systems.

Interestingly, this assessment was premised exclusively on technical (engineering) measures but completely ignored the behavioural and lifestyle dimensions of energy consumption in the buildings sector. Behavioural change in buildings, however, can deliver even faster gains in energy efficiency, and ghg reductions, at zero cost. Bearing this concept in mind, designers would benefit from shifting their attention to opportunities available in all buildings to adapt to a wider range of indoor thermal conditions. Building designers should explore ways of maximizing adaptive opportunities within indoor environments as much as possible, thus reinforcing passive cooling strategies as an essential energy conservation strategy. The maintenance of narrow temperature ranges requires significant energy inputs, but these static environments do not necessarily result in appreciably higher levels of occupant satisfaction (Arens et al., 2010). This focus is re-awakening an interest in natural ventilation (Tanabe and Kimura, 1989; de Dear and Brager, 2002; Toftum, 2004; Zhang et al., 2007).

*Corresponding author: *Email:* ccandido@els.mq.edu.au

ARCHITECTURAL SCIENCE REVIEW 53 | 2010 | 59–64
doi:10.3763/asre.2009.0100 ©2010 Earthscan ISSN: 0003-8628 (print), 1758-9622 (online) www.earthscan.co.uk/journals/asre

Particularly in hot and humid regions, buildings should avoid external heat gains while dissipating internal ones. Shading is crucial and thermal mass is designed to maximize the storage potential for free heating and cooling while avoiding discomfort from over-heating or cooling, especially during the night-time. Natural ventilation is the main bioclimatic strategy to improve thermal comfort conditions inside buildings without resorting to air-conditioning (AC). In addition, naturally ventilated buildings provide more dynamic environments that have been shown to be associated with more stimulating and pleasurable indoor environments (Cabanac, 1971; de Dear, 2009). Despite these positive characteristics, naturally ventilated environments have been increasingly replaced by air-conditioned ones as a result of a myriad of complex reasons that vary from early design stage decisions to occupants' expectations (Brown, 2009).

The discussion about widening the acceptable indoor temperature comfort bands raises the question of the extent to which occupants' comfort expectations can vary from the narrow temperature bands promoted by the predicted mean vote and predicted percentage dissatisfied methodologies used internationally by HVAC engineers, allowing natural ventilation with limited acceptance penalties. Previous results suggested that occupants of air-conditioned buildings tended to prefer such buildings whereas occupants of non-air-conditioned buildings preferred not to have AC (de Dear and Auliciems, 1988), and also that occupants' thermal history influences their thermal perception (Chun et al., 2008). These observations suggest that building occupants become 'addicted' to static environments, i.e. AC, but does it mean that they will present differences in terms of thermal preference when the thermal constancy of AC is replaced by the thermal variability that characterizes natural ventilation? Does prior exposure to AC lead building occupants to actually prefer AC over natural ventilation? This article addresses these questions in naturally ventilated indoor environments located for the hot and humid climatic zone of Brazil (Maceio city).

METHOD

Researchers combined nearby indoor climate measurements with simultaneous questionnaires filled in by occupants of naturally ventilated spaces. A survey including 975 questionnaires was used for this study.

Air temperature, humidity, globe temperature and air velocity were measured with laboratory precision as well as individualized air velocity values for each occupant. The instruments used to perform the field experiments were:

- microclimatic station, including globe thermometer, psychrometer for dry- and wet-bulb temperatures and a hot wire anemometer
- portable hot wire anemometer (Airflow Developments, model TA35 sensor)
- smoke sticks.

The microclimatic station was able to take measurements and store the data collected into a data logger during the experiment period; it was located in the centre of the room. The portable hot wire anemometer was used in order to register air velocity values for each occupant. Complementarily, smoke sticks were used to verify the main airflow direction during measurements of individualized air velocity. The method for obtaining instantaneous thermal comfort and sensation responses as well as the indoor microclimatic measurement procedures have been detailed in an earlier article (Cândido et al., 2010).

Maceio's climatic environment and outdoor meteorological conditions during the survey

Maceio city is located on the northeast coast of Brazil (latitude 9°40' south). The climate is classified as hot and humid, with small daily and seasonal temperature fluctuations combined with a high vapour pressure. Seasons are divided into two: winter and summer. Summer is classified as a hot season and winter as a cool one.

The mean annual temperature is around 26°C and the annual thermal amplitude is 3.4°C (the highest monthly average occurs in February–26.7°C and the lowest monthly average is in July–23.7°C). Typically, the hottest days are from November to February and the coolest days are from June to August. Despite Maceio's equable climate, the surveys were performed during the cool and hot seasons for comparative purposes. Table 1 shows statistical summaries of these outdoor conditions.

Measurement rooms and occupants' profile

The buildings were occupied by university students performing sedentary activities. Monitored rooms were used for drawing activities (studios) and were normally occupied by 20 students. All rooms offered large open spaces and natural ventilation was intentionally the main cooling strategy. The windows were easily controlled collectively by the occupants and ceiling fans provided supplemental air movement inside the rooms. The study was carried out

Table 1 | Outdoor meteorological conditions during the surveys

Measurement	Seasons					
	Hot			Cool		
	Ave	Max	Min	Ave	Max	Min
Outdoor temperature (°C)	25.2	28.6	22.4	24.0	26.8	21.4
Outdoor relative humidity (%)	73.8	88.9	56.1	75.0	91.0	57.0
Mean monthly outdoor temperature (°C)	25.3	30.2	23.7	23.5	27.1	20.2

Table 2 | Biographical characteristics of the samples

Characteristic	Cooling exposition at their workplace	
	Exposed to AC systems	Without exposure to AC systems
Number of occupants	445	530
Percentage females	75.3%	69.8%
Percentage males	24.7%	30.2%
Age – average (years)	22.4	21.2

considering concepts of personal control and the adaptive model (de Dear and Brager, 2002).

For this analysis, occupants were classified into two groups according to their responses for cooling exposure at their workplace: occupants exposed to AC systems at their work environment and those not exposed. Table 2 summarizes biographical characteristics of the sample.

Questionnaire

The questionnaire was presented in three parts. The first one corresponded to subjects' demographic and anthropometric characteristics such as age, height, weight and gender.

The second part included questions related to thermal comfort, air movement acceptability and also the pattern of AC usage. In the thermal comfort part, subjects were asked about their own thermal comfort condition, their personal preferences and also about the room itself, at the time of the questionnaire. This article focuses on cooling exposition and preference questions.

The third and last part of the questionnaire related to subjects' activities (metabolism) during the measurement process. It also recorded information about the occupants' clothing by way of a garment checklist (insulation).

RESULTS

The research questions posed resulted in a set of responses, identifying how occupants inside naturally ventilated buildings classify their indoor environment depending on their previous exposure to workplaces with and without AC systems. Results were analysed for thermal sensation votes, thermal preferences and cooling preferences.

The occupants' thermal sensation rated on the seven-point scale was similar for both groups, as depicted in Figure 1. No significant differences were observed when comparing thermal sensation votes for occupants with AC systems at their workplace and occupants without exposure to AC systems at their workplace. For both groups the majority of thermal sensation votes were concentrated into 'neutral',

'slightly warm' and 'warm' categories. Only occupants without AC systems at their workplace voted for 'slightly cool' (5%) and only occupants with AC systems at their workplace voted for 'hot' (4%).

Despite the similarity of their thermal sensations votes, preferences varied depending on AC exposure. Figures 2a and b show the distribution of occupants' thermal preference votes within operative temperature bands. The percentages of occupants preferring 'no change' were significantly higher for those without AC systems at their workplace. This fact is noticeable within all operative temperature bands. Thermal preferences for 'cooler' were significantly higher for occupants who had been exposed to AC systems at their workplace compared with occupants without AC exposure.

Occupants were also asked about their cooling preference at that moment as a complement to their thermal sensation and preference votes. The question was: 'If you could choose, which one of these cooling strategies would you like to have in this room?' Their options were natural ventilation, natural ventilation and fans, and AC. The overall cooling preference results were subsequently cross-tabulated with those of occupants' cooling exposure at their workplace (see Figures 3a and b).

Two thirds of occupants exposed to AC systems at their workplace preferred AC systems (65.7%), while the remaining one third (34.3%) indicated preference for natural ventilation or natural ventilation plus fans.

In contrast, the results were completely the opposite for occupants without exposure to AC systems at their workplace. In this sample, two thirds of cooling preference responses preferred natural ventilation and natural ventilation and fans whereas only one third preferred AC systems.

Figure 4 shows occupants' cooling preference votes across operative temperature bins. Once more it is clear that occupants with AC systems at their workplace indicated a preference for AC systems, and these percentages increased when the operative temperature also increased (from 50% for an operative temperature of 24.5°C increasing to 88% at 29.5°C). In contrast, the percentage of occupants preferring natural ventilation and natural ventilation and fans decreased with increasing operative temperature values from 50% at 24.5°C down to only 12% at 29.5°C.

For occupants without AC systems at their workplace, the preference for natural ventilation and natural ventilation and fans was significantly higher than for those preferring AC systems. The percentages of occupants preferring natural ventilation decreased from 98% at 24.5°C operative temperature to 60% at 29.5°C.

Table 3 shows the cross-tabulated percentages for cooling and thermal preferences for both AC and no AC exposed samples. These results showed variations in terms of thermal preferences between occupants with the same cooling exposure at their workplace but preferring different cooling strategies. For occupants without AC exposure at their workplace, thermal preferences were broadly similar

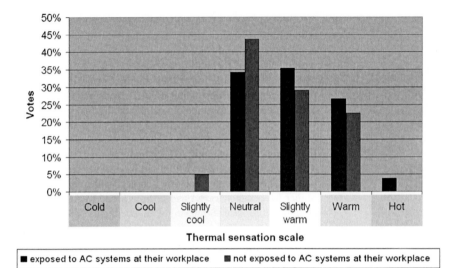

Figure 1 | Occupants' thermal sensation votes exposed to AC systems at their workplace

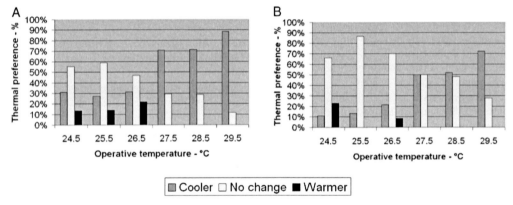

Figure 2 | Occupants' thermal preference votes within operative temperature values: (a) occupants exposed to AC systems at their workplace and (b) occupants without exposure to AC systems at their workplace

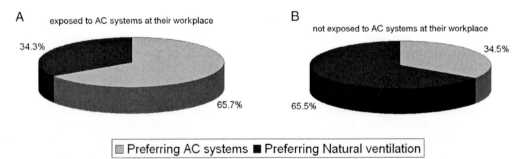

Figure 3 | Overall cooling preference votes: (a) occupants exposed to AC systems at their workplace and (b) occupants without exposure to AC systems at their workplace

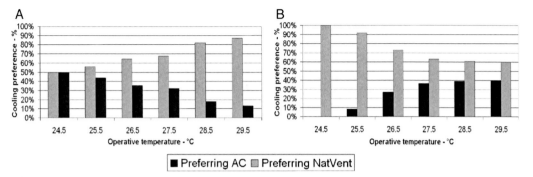

Figure 4 | Occupants' cooling preference votes within operative temperature values: (a) occupants exposed to AC systems at their workplace and (b) occupants without exposure to AC systems at their workplace

Table 3 | Cross-tabulated percentages for cooling and thermal preferences

Cooling exposure	Cooling preference	Thermal preference		
		Cooler	No change	Warmer
Occupants not exposed to AC systems at their workplace	Preferring AC systems	70.0%	30.0%	0.0%
	Preferring natural ventilation	68.4%	31.6%	0.0%
Occupants exposed to AC systems at their workplace	Preferring AC systems	78.3%	21.7%	0.0%
	Preferring natural ventilation	52.0%	48.0%	0.0%

regardless of AC and natural ventilation preference. For occupants with AC systems at their workplace, the results presented significant differences in their cooling preference. In this sample, occupants who preferred AC systems also indicated a preference for being 'cooler' in a majority (78.3%). However, 52% of occupants who preferred natural ventilation indicated 'want cooler' as their thermal preference.

DISCUSSION

This article investigated differences in terms of thermal sensation, heating preferences and cooling preferences into naturally ventilated buildings based on occupants' prior cooling exposure in their workplace (air-conditioned or naturally ventilated indoor environments).

Thermal sensation votes were broadly similar for both samples, for those with and without AC at their work environments. However, expectations of their indoor environments were significantly different in terms of thermal preferences and also cooling preferences. Occupants with AC systems at their workplace were less tolerant of operative temperature variations when exposed to naturally ventilated indoor environments than those without prior AC exposure. The majority of AC occupants also voted 'want cooler' for their thermal preference even though they happened to be experiencing broadly similar indoor temperatures at the time of the questionnaire as occupants who did not have prior AC exposure. The AC-exposed sample seemed to be less tolerant and less adaptable when the thermal constancy of the AC environment was replaced with the thermal variable.

Occupants who were constantly exposed to air-conditioned buildings tended to prefer such buildings, while occupants of non-air-conditioned buildings preferred not to have AC. These results suggest an 'addiction' to static thermal environments. They also indicate that occupants' thermal history directly influences their thermal perception and preferences (Chun *et al.*, 2008). Past experience and behaviour influence occupants' thermal perception of the indoor environment, and hence they should be taken into account in the design of bioclimatic architecture. It is indeed a hard mission to control what sort of environment occupants will be exposed to outside their workplace. However, when inside these indoor environments, they will bring their expectations with them.

CONCLUSIONS

This article has demonstrated the importance of occupants' thermal history as an influence on their perception of indoor thermal environment. The percentages of occupants preferring natural ventilation or natural ventilation combined with fans provide unequivocal indication that passive strategies are welcomed by these occupants, and should be exploited as much as possible. For warm and humid regions such as Maceio, it is important to consider whether prior AC exposure also influences the preference and acceptability of indoor air movement levels and humidity values. Complementary field experiments are necessary in order to understand these important subjective aspects of indoor air quality.

Conversely, these findings raise important questions about the role that rising comfort expectations resulting from increased AC usage might play in hindering the implementation of adaptive comfort principles in bioclimatic buildings and the return to more naturally ventilated buildings. Can this upward trend in comfort expectations that has accompanied rising AC penetration rates in recent decades be reversed as designers attempt to scale back society's reliance on energy-intensive compressor-based cooling over the coming decades? To what extent are comfort expectations amenable to modification with information and 'ethical persuasion'?

These questions are currently being addressed by the Japanese Ministry of Environment's 'Cool Biz' campaign in which summertime AC set points have been raised to 28°C in conjunction with a vigorous education campaign regarding that country's Kyoto Protocol commitments being aired across the media.

In Brazil, educational campaigns were effective during the energy crisis of 2001, when the population had to consider energy conservation strategies on a daily basis.

References

Arens, E., Humphreys, M.A., de Dear, R. and Zhang, H., 2010, 'Are 'class A' temperature requirements realistic or desirable?', *Building and Environment* 45, 4–10.

Brown, G.Z., 2009, 'Pleasure and performance', *26th International Conference on Passive and Low Energy Architecture*. Quebec City, Les Presses de l'Université Laval.

Cabanac, M., 1971, 'Physiological role of pleasure', *Science* 17, 1103–1007.

Cândido, C., de Dear, R., Lamberts, R. and Bittencourt, L., 2010, 'Air movement acceptability limits and thermal comfort in Brazil's hot humid climate zone', *Building and Environment* 45, 222–229.

Chun, C., Kwok, A., Mitamura, T., Miwa, N. and Tamura, A., 2008, 'Thermal diary: connecting temperature history to indoor comfort', *Building and Environment* 43, 877–885.

de Dear, R. and Auliciems, A., 1988, 'Air-conditioning in Australia - II - User attitudes', *Architectural Science Review* 31, 19–27.

de Dear, R.J., 2009, 'The theory of thermal comfort in naturally ventilated indoor environments: "the pleasure principle"', *Third Symposium of Natural Ventilation*. Tokyo.

de Dear, R.J. and Brager, G.S., 2002, 'Thermal comfort in naturally ventilated buildings: revisions to ASHRAE Standard 55', *Energy and Buildings* 34(6), 549–561.

IPCC, 2007, 'Fourth Assessment Report - Working Group III - Mitigation of Climate Change', *Intergovernmental Panel on Climate Change*.

Tanabe, S. and Kimura, K., 1989, 'Thermal comfort requirements under hot and humid conditions', *Proceedings of the First ASHRAE Far East Conference on Air Conditioning in Hot Climates*. Singapore, ASHRAE, 3–21.

Toftum, J., 2004, 'Air movement – good or bad?', *Indoor Air* 14, 40–45.

Zhang, H., Arens, E., Fard, S.A., Huizenga, C., Paliaga, G., Brager, G. and Zagreus, L., 2007, 'Air movement preferences observed in office buildings', *International Journal of Biometeorology* 51, 349–360.

Twentieth century standards for thermal comfort: promoting high energy buildings

Sue Roaf*, Fergus Nicol, Michael Humphreys, Paul Tuohy and Atze Boerstra

School of the Built Environment, Heriot Watt University, Edinburgh, EH14 4AS, UK

The urgent need to reduce anthropogenic greenhouse gas (GHG) emissions in a bid to meet increasingly stringent GHG targets has focused the attention of scientists on the built environment. The reason is that nearly 50% of all the energy in the developed world is consumed in buildings and it is here that the easiest savings can be made. Although the theoretical trend in building regulations is to favour lower carbon buildings, in reality new buildings have typically become more energy profligate year after year. Much of this results from increased mechanization, poorer building fabric and design, and the resource consumption patterns. Modern thermal comfort standards are partly responsible for increased levels of energy consumption in buildings as well as for encouraging unhealthier, less comfortable buildings because they drive the designers towards higher use of air-conditioning. A first step towards the radical overhauling of our approach to the artificial conditioning of buildings is to revise these standards. This article describes the evolution of the current standards and the problems inherent in the buildings they shape and serve and then proceeds to propose new methods of regulating thermal comfort in a warming world in which the cost of energy is rising.

Keywords: Adaptive; buildings; carbon emissions; climate change; energy; regulations; thermal comfort

BACKGROUND

Two dominant factors are driving the global imperative to reduce energy consumption and related greenhouse gas (GHG) emissions: climate change legislations and rising energy costs resulting from fossil fuel depletion. The built environment is responsible for up to half of all the GHGs produced by countries and, consequently, vast amounts of money are currently being spent on related research. However, many of the current legislative trends are resulting in increased, not decreased, emissions from buildings (Roaf *et al.*, 2009). In the UK, current building regulations are driving designers towards the use of air-conditioning and away from the less energy-intensive natural ventilation of buildings (Tuohy, 2008). In America, the widely used Leadership in Energy and Environmental Design (LEED) rating system discourages the use of natural ventilation in buildings if owners want to achieve a platinum or gold rating (Shaviv, 2008).

Spurred on by such incentives, the trend towards the mechanization of buildings is rapidly rising despite the long-held understanding of the negative environmental impacts of the very high energy demands of air-conditioning (Roaf, 1992; Kolokotroni *et al.*, 1996). The trend is less justifiable in countries where there has been a limited need for its use. For instance, in the temperate climates of the UK, air-conditioning is simply not needed for the control of indoor temperatures, either in current or future climates, in well-designed passive and low energy architecture buildings (Haves *et al.*, 1998; Hacker, 2005; Tuohy *et al.*, 2010).

The easiest reasonable way to save energy in a building that is heated or cooled is to alter the setting of the thermostat. A well-rehearsed rule of thumb in the UK Department of Education design office used to be that a 1K difference in the right direction on the thermostat would result in a heating energy saving of 10%. In the plethora of studies published so far on the subject of achieving emission reductions from buildings, much is said about mechanical and constructional strategies for energy efficiency as well as integrated renewable energy systems, but thermal comfort standards and related behavioural strategies are very seldom mentioned despite their being some of the lowest hanging, and lowest cost, 'fruits on the tree' (see Energy Savings Trust (www.energysavingstrust.org.uk) and the Carbon Trust (www.carbontrust.co.uk)). The widely held assumption that the health, well-being and comfort of building occupants depend on the close control of indoor climates will be shown, in this article, to be erroneous. We will demonstrate that the regulations that posit this view promote the values of certain professional and cultural groups and ignore local cultural, economic, climatic and environmental factors.

The basic premise of this article is that a radical new approach to thermal comfort standards is urgently needed

*Corresponding author: *Email:* s.roaf@sbe.hw.ac.uk

because of the very high energy and environmental penalties that result from the strategy of the close temperature control of indoor climates. Optimal indoor environments are, in reality, a function of the physical design of the building itself and its social and economic constraints, not just of its services. What matters most for the provision of reasonably priced comfort is the building's form in relation to function and macro- and micro-climatic design as well as the thermal responses, habits, culture, resources availability and wealth of its occupants. This being the case, it must be possible to produce thermal comfort standards for buildings which do not resort to specifications of supposedly 'universally appropriate' indoor temperatures. Rather, standards must be directly related to the occupants' own perception of whether a space in a building is providing adequate comfort, or not, in the local context, and the ability of the occupants to manage their own personal thermal comfort experience through interaction with the building. The characteristics of a building, in terms of its design, construction, adaptable elements, controls (blinds, shutters, curtains, shades and windows) and management in relation to the local climate, culture and economy, should be sufficient to provide that opportunity to individuals to establish a comfortable indoor temperature. This, of course, was the case in good traditional buildings. Standards that put thermal control into the hands of building users would be more meaningful to, and usable by, building designers (particularly architects) and occupants alike; consequently, they are more likely to be well understood and therefore will be useful to reduce energy use in, and GHG emission from, buildings (Nicol and Humphreys, 2002).

Two steps are needed to underpin the new standards:

- Responsibility for the long-term performance and impacts of the building must revert to the building designer, and not just be the responsibility of the subsequently hired services engineer who has little power to influence the form and functioning of the building itself.
- Day-to-day energy use in buildings must be clearly the responsibility of its occupants and must be controlled, monitored and paid for by them.

A range of new regulations will be necessary to achieve this. New thermal comfort standards that not only enable local control to occur but also allow occupants to choose their own preferred temperature will be needed. Such new national and international standards (Nicol and Humphreys, 2009a) and building design strategies will need to anticipate and accommodate the new responsibilities allocated to building designers, managers and occupants alike (Nicol and Roaf, 2007).

This article outlines the history of thermal comfort standards, with particular reference to the adaptive nature of thermal comfort. It describes the strengths and weaknesses of current standards and outlines possible scenarios for future standards. Tuohy et al. (2010) take the theoretical scenarios and, using simulation, study them for a typical office block in the London climate of 2005 and the

London climate predicted for 2080 to provide an idea of the respective energy use and GHG emissions of each regulation strategy. They conclude with a discussion of what this tells us about how comfort regulations should be most effectively and responsibly directed in the 21st century, away from the close control of indoor temperatures.

THE CHANGING NEED FOR REGULATING INDOOR ENVIRONMENTS

The needs addressed by thermal guidelines have changed in the course of time. Studies on the physiology of the body in relation to its environment were begun in the 18th century (Arbuthnot, 1733) and continued into the 19th century (Davey, 1814). During the 19th century, research began to concentrate more on comfort in relation to building heating systems (Reid, 1844; Tomlinson, 1850) and health in buildings (Galton, 1880). Research interests included the health of workers in mills and factories, particularly through the work of bodies such as the Industrial Research Boards on Fatigue and Health in London (Hambly and Bedford, 1921; Vernon, 1926; Farmer and Chambers, 1929); this was because of the high sickness and mortality rates among workers. Later, detailed studies of specialist buildings such as theatres (Badham et al., 1928) and factories (Bedford, 1936) were undertaken. Studies also concentrated on vulnerable populations such as school children (Vernon et al., 1930) and hospital patients. The resulting codes and guidelines were developed in a very different age, during which the cost and environmental impacts of high energy use were not an issue. Rather, they were driven by the need to secure the health and productivity of the work force (Braverman, 1974). Increasingly, in the 20th century, the emphasis changed to the need to stimulate new markets for spending by the emerging middle classes (Cooper, 1998; Ackermann, 2002), and ultimately to promote sales of the systems that would provide the vital 'product' of comfort.

Early studies in the area also addressed other questions. The high death rates among the armed forces travelling to the very different climates of the Empire led to significant studies in the course of time and to the adaptation of military uniforms, habitations and behavioural regimes for different climates (Benedict, 1929). Important early studies on comfort and of hyperthermia centred on the working conditions in the hot, deep mines of South Africa, where deaths among workers were the motivation for some excellent but ethically questionable science that continued right through to the 1970s (Jones, 1924; Wyndham et al., 1966; Wyndham and Heyns, 1973).

Considerable work was done on the acclimatization of populations and related health issues as white populations from North West Europe colonized an increasingly wide range of new territories and climates. One early 19th century Australian pioneer was Sir Raphael Cilento, originally based at the School of Tropical Medicine in

Townsville, Queensland, who performed very influential studies on climatic adaptation of populations in relation to health and prosperity (Yarwood, 1991; Fisher, 1994).

Such studies laid the foundations of medical and behavioural science from which the ideas of physiological limits for 'civilized' living developed, providing fodder for the once popular School of Climate Determinists, epitomized by the very influential book by Ellsworth Huntington on climate and civilization (Huntington, 2001). One of his followers, who was still being quoted by research scientists in the early 1960s, was S.F. Markham, who published his book titled *Climate and the Energy of Nations* in 1944 (Markham, 1944). In this book, he pointed out, to a Britain unfamiliar with air-conditioning, the miracle of this new technology that would enable non-adapted colonizing peoples to live in comfort anywhere in the world. Markham, in a heroic conjoining of the aspirations of Empire and Capitalism (Hulme, 2009), pointed out that air-conditioning liberated Westerners to live all the year round in cool buildings, regardless of the climate outside (see Figure 1).

Auliciems (2009), commenting on the influence of the climate determinists, points outs that 'oversimplified

interpretations of climate impacts, by Ellsworth Huntington and his contemporaries, led to academic alienation and at times misguided social policy'. He makes the important point that 'Man–atmosphere interrelationships and adaptations are embedded within complex homeostatic and dynamic systems, which operate at several levels of human organization' and goes on to affirm that 'given the uncertainty of both climate change and human responses, it is emphasized that adaptability of society and individuals is preferable to attaining adaptation to particular environmental conditions'.

COMFORT STANDARDS FOR BUILDINGS

Air-conditioning requires indoor temperature set-points

If one owns a machine that can produce air at any temperature in an otherwise uncomfortable climate, then one can simply adjust the machine until the environment is comfortable. Of course, it then becomes important to decide what the right temperature is to be. If there is a group of people in a space,

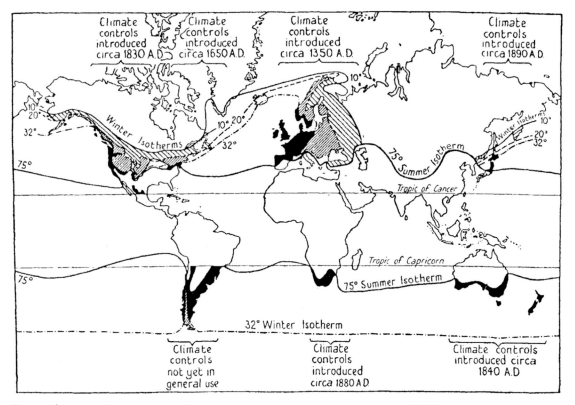

Figure 1 | Areas of the world where the warmest months do not exceed a mean of 75°F and for the coldest month do not fall below a mean of 32, 20 or 10°F. Tropical areas within these limits have been excluded because of the greater intensity of solar radiation. These were areas that Markham considered to be of optimal climate that require minimal heating and cooling to maintain indoor comfort
Source: Markham (1944, p98)

then an agreed temperature must be settled on; this results in a lack of persistent discomfort for most of the population. Hence, by the 1920s, engineers had devised temperature standards that would fulfil this requirement for the setting of temperatures to suit the many rather than the individual (Houghton and Yagloglou, 1923a, b). They were exploring how best to measure comfort (Vernon, 1926) and the contributing factors to summer and winter comfort, particularly in the workplace (Yagloglou and Drinker, 1928; Bedford, 1936).

This early climate-laboratory work by Houghton and Yagloglou (1923a, b) in the USA provided the framework for standards that would be developed to give the building engineer two set temperatures, one for winter and one for summer, for the mechanical controls. This climate chamber work was later developed by others including Ole Fanger, who developed the internationally recognized predicted mean vote (PMV) method on which the international standard ISO 7730 and some other standards are based. From the PMV of the space, the predicted percentage of occupants dissatisfied (PPD) is calculated (Fanger, 1970). The PMV and PPD methods provide the air-conditioning industry with a serviceable standard for calculating the required indoor temperatures for buildings in use. The PMV/PPD standard has encouraged the wholesale commodification of the building design process, taking power away from the building designers and putting it squarely in the hands of the building services engineers who now controlled the standards. So, for example, Fanger writes, 'Creating thermal comfort for man is a primary purpose of the heating and air conditioning industry, and this has had a radical influence...on the whole building industry ...thermal comfort is the 'product' which is produced and sold to the customer...' (Fanger, 1970).

If comfort is a 'product' of the heating and air-conditioning industry, then it needed to be defined in order to provide a means of testing compliance with the standards. However, a very different approach to the role and specification of comfort in buildings is taken by those who, in parallel, developed the adaptive model of thermal comfort.

The origins and principles of the adaptive model of thermal comfort

The adaptive model of thermal comfort rests on field-study research. This research takes place in real buildings in everyday conditions, with the participants continuing their normal activities. The classic pattern for the thermal comfort field study was set by Thomas Bedford in his study of the wintertime comfort of workers in light industry in the UK (Bedford, 1936). He made comprehensive measurements of the thermal environment, enquired of some 3000 participants how warm or cool they were feeling, and used multiple regression analysis to predict the subjective thermal sensation from the environmental data and thence obtain an optimum temperature for comfort.

Charles Webb could be regarded as the originator of the adaptive approach to thermal comfort along with his collaborators Michael Humphreys and Fergus Nicol. They brought together extensive field data from Singapore, Baghdad (Iraq), Roorkee

(North India) and Watford (UK). They noticed that the respondents were comfortable with the mean conditions they experienced, whether in Singapore, North India, Iraq or UK. This suggested that they had somehow *adapted* to the mean conditions they had experienced. The mean warmth sensation (the mean 'comfort vote') depended very little on the mean room temperature, depending rather on the departure from the mean.

Nicol and Humphreys developed a flow diagram showing thermal comfort as a self-regulating adaptive system that included both physiological and behavioural adaptations (Nicol and Humphreys, 1973). Figure 2 shows the heat flow from the body to the environment (the subject of the PMV model) to be but part of a larger whole that included voluntary and involuntary feedbacks tending to secure comfort.

Other studies were collected and an analysis performed by Humphreys (1976). From most of these studies, it was possible to find the optimum temperature for comfort and the sensitivity of the respondents to temperature changes. If people had adapted to their normal indoor environment, the optimum temperatures for comfort should correlate with the mean temperatures they experienced. Figure 3 shows this was so (correlation $(r) = 0.95$, $p < 0.001$). The range of neutral temperatures was far too wide to be explained by the newly available PMV equation (Fanger, 1970).

Also, the mean subjective warmth changed little over a wide range of mean indoor temperatures. Figure 4 shows this to be so. The results of Humphreys' analysis therefore both confirmed the adaptive hypothesis and drew attention to a limitation of the PMV equation.

Next, the data were analysed in relation to the outdoor temperatures obtained from published world meteorological tables. The neutral temperatures were related to the corresponding mean outdoor temperatures (Humphreys, 1978). The strongest relation was for the 'free-running' mode of operation (no heating or cooling in use at the time of survey). The result is shown in Figure 5.

After publication of these meta-analyses, other researchers began to explore adaptive comfort. Ian Griffiths conducted

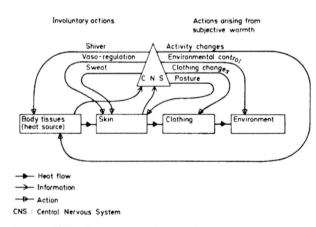

Figure 2 | The thermal regulatory system
Source: Nicol and Humphreys (1973)

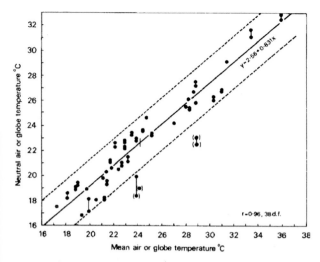

Figure 3 | Scatter diagram of mean temperatures and neutral temperature
Source: Humphreys (1976)

surveys in the UK and Europe (Griffiths, 1990); John Busch in Bangkok, Thailand (Busch, 1990, 1995); Auliciems and de Dear in Australia (Auliciems and de Dear, 1986); Gail Schiller Brager and de Dear in the USA (Brager and de Dear, 1998). These surveys all included estimates of the clothing insulation, and so it was possible to calculate the comfort temperatures predicted by the PMV model. These researchers found adaptation to be taking place, sometimes to an extent inexplicable on the PMV model. The discrepancies were most noticeable at higher indoor temperatures.

Auliciems extended the adaptive model to include psychological and social effects, as well as climate and building technology. He suggested that energy could be saved by using a 'thermobile' rather than a 'thermostat'. The thermobile would adjust the indoor temperature set-point according to the prevailing outdoor temperature (Auliciems and de Dear, 1986). There were other conceptual developments too. Baker and Standeven linked comfort to the available means of thermal adaptation – the 'adaptive opportunity' (Baker and Standeven, 1996). If just a little adaptive opportunity were

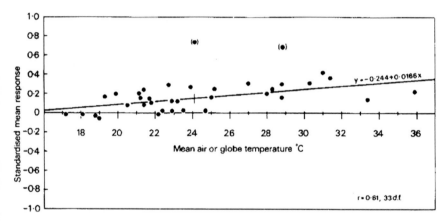

Figure 4 | Scatter diagram of standardized mean response and mean temperature
Source: Humphreys (1976)

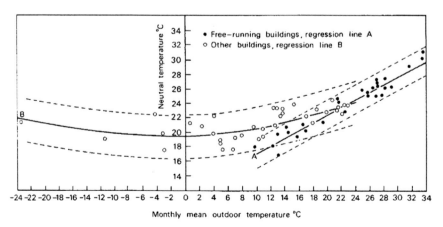

Figure 5 | Scatter diagram of neutral temperature
Source: Humphreys (1978)

available to building occupants, discomfort was more likely to occur. Bordass *et al.* (2002) and Bordass and Leaman (2005) developed protocols for the post-occupancy evaluation of buildings. Their results showed that people who had control over their environment were more tolerant of it (Bordass and Leaman, 2007) and they called this the 'forgiveness factor'. If the occupants could not control their environment, discomfort was more likely to occur. Shove, accepting the adaptive hypothesis, argued that comfort was a 'social construction' – different societies, historically and geographically, have had different comfort temperatures (Shove, 2003). This suggests that societies could be encouraged to adopt solutions that are both environmentally responsible and thermally comfortable.

The American Society of Heating Refrigeration and Air-conditioning Engineers (ASHRAE) commissioned new field studies of thermal comfort from different climate zones. A characteristic of these studies was the comprehensive and accurate measurement of the thermal environment, together with the assessment of clothing insulation and metabolic rate. de Dear and Brager (1998) did a meta-analysis of these and other good quality field studies. Their database comprised some 20,000 sets of observations, each with a subjective vote (7 point scale). The data came from nine countries, included 160 buildings, and had a wide coverage of climate. The 2004 revision of Standard 55 used their result to provide a graphical relation between comfort indoors and the outdoor mean temperature. de Dear and Brager's results broadly confirmed the findings of Humphreys' meta-analyses of 1978–1981, as shown in Figures 6 and 7 (Humphreys and Nicol, 2000).

In 2003 a new Dutch guideline, the *Adaptieve Temperatuur Grenswaarde* (ATG), introduced the concept of adaptive opportunity into the range of indoor conditions that are accepted in buildings. This was based on a concept that a building with adaptive opportunity was necessary for occupants to be able to make themselves comfortable at temperatures

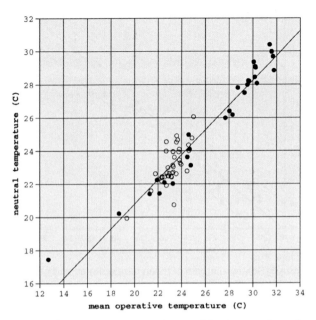

Figure 6 | Mean room temperature and the temperatures for comfort (neutrality) correlate with each other ($r > 0.9$). Solid points are for the free-running mode and open points for the heated/cooled mode. Data come from the de Dear database of 100+ observations
Source: Michael Humphreys

beyond the narrow envelope of temperatures acceptable in existing international standards: the International Organization for Standardization (ISO), the American ASHRAE and the European Comité Européen de Normalisation (CEN) standards based on PMV (van der Linden *et al.*, 2006).

Based on the ATG and on recent work sponsored by Chartered Institution of Building Services Engineers

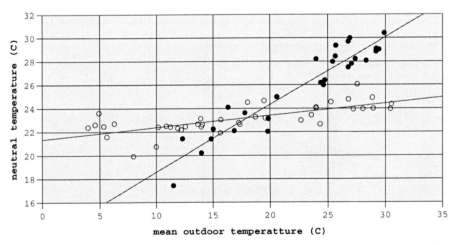

Figure 7 | Indoor neutral temperatures and daily mean outdoor temperatures for the de Dear database. Solid points are for the free-running mode, open points for the heated/cooled mode
Source: Michael Humphreys

(CIBSE), and using data from the meta-analysis of the European project SCATs (McCartney and Nicol, 2002), CEN has developed a new adaptive standard for free-running buildings as part of EN15251 (2007). The standard uses the running mean of the outdoor temperature to predict comfort temperatures in free-running European buildings and predicts comfort according to the category descriptions shown in Table 1 for free-running buildings, allowing $\pm2°$ as the comfort band for category I, $\pm3°$ for category II and $\pm4°$ for category III. The derivation of the comfort temperature is explained in Nicol and Humphreys (2009a).

Differences between the heat-balance and the adaptive approaches

There are basic differences between the heat-balance model used in indices such as PMV and the model that underlies the adaptive approach. These differences arise from the philosophy and procedures embodied in the two approaches. The heat-balance approach, which underpins PMV, tries to generalize from the limited experiments that are possible in climate laboratories, where the experimental conditions are under the control of the experimenter and where detailed and precise measurement of physiological responses can more easily be made. The adaptive approach takes the responses of the subjects to real life, where the conditions are not controlled by the experimenter but are, to some extent, decided by the control that the subjects may have over their own environment. Because the heat-balance approach uses generalized relationships in a controlled environment, it is unable to shed light on the precise way in which subjects will respond to any particular environment, so it frequently has to make assumptions about what will actually happen, such as assumed clothing insulation levels. In the field experiment, on the other hand, while many of the real responses to the environment can be measured (use of windows or actual clothing insulation) there is the problem of generalizing from these responses what may be special to the circumstances of the particular survey. Field studies can be used to investigate a range of aspects of the thermal environment:

- As discussed above, meta-analyses can be performed on the results from a number of surveys (Humphreys, 1976; de Dear and Brager, 1998). This procedure has led to the development of statistical relationships between indoor comfort and outdoor temperature in naturally ventilated buildings.
- The use of controls such as windows, shades and fans to control indoor conditions are well tried and understood by building users, but the simulation of their use is complicated by the fact that there is a stochastic element in the way the controls are used. People do not all open a window at a particular temperature but as the temperature rises there is an increasing likelihood that they will do so. A number of researchers have been addressing this problem including Rijal et al. (2007a, b), Haldi and Robinson (2009) and Yun and Steemers (2008). In each case the aim is to provide algorithms to allow computer simulations to include the effect of window opening or other user behaviour in thermal simulations of naturally ventilated buildings under user control.

Table 1 | Applicability of the classes in ISO 7730 (2006) and categories (Cat) in EN15251 (CEN, 2007) and their associated acceptable ranges of PMV and operative temperature (mechanically cooled offices)

ISO Class	CEN Cat.	Category Description (CEN)	Limit PMV	Temperature Range
A	I	High level of expectation recommended for spaces occupied by very sensitive and fragile persons with special requirements, such as the handicapped, sick, very young children and elderly persons	±0.2	Summer: 23.5–25.5°C Winter: 21–23°C
B	II	Normal level of expectation should be used for new buildings and renovations	±0.5	Summer: 23.0–26.0°C Winter: 20.0–24.0°C
C	III	An acceptable moderate level of expectation that may be used for existing buildings	±0.7	Summer: 22.0–27.0°C Winter: 19.0–25.0°C
	IV	Values outside the criteria for the above categories (only acceptable for a limited period)		

Assumed clothing insulation of 0.5Clo for summer and 1.0Clo for winter, metabolic rate of 1.2Met.

- Changing one's clothing is the most obvious behavioural adaptation to temperature. So studying clothing change will reveal how quickly and to what extent people adapt to their thermal environment. Humphreys undertook a number of field studies to explore this adaptation by quantifying the clothing changes of secondary and primary school children, of people outdoors while shopping or visiting a zoo park (Humphreys, 1973, 1977), and bed clothing during sleep (Humphreys, 1979). These studies found that there was surprisingly little adaptive change during the day, that there was more adaptive change from day to day and more still from week to week. Clothing changes lagged behind the temperature changes, and people sometimes 'traded' thermal comfort for fashion (social comfort). Similar results were found by Morgan *et al.* (2002), who also showed that the change of clothing can be an important guide to the change in temperature preference.

The adaptive approach sees change as natural and stasis as only one possible way of achieving comfort in buildings. The heat-balance model, while formally allowing change in clothing and activity as an option, cannot in fact give advice on the ways in which people actually adapt, since the experimental work that underlies it was done under climate chamber conditions that cast no light on such behaviour. This means that assumptions must be made about clothing and activity, tending to limit the applicability of the results to static environments such as what are found in air-conditioned buildings.

It is unfortunate that the adaptive approach has become almost totally identified with the relationship between indoor comfort temperatures and the outdoor temperature, much to the neglect of the model seen as a totality, a misunderstanding that largely arises from an incomplete understanding of the basic principles of the adaptive model, of which we now give a brief overview.

Overview of the adaptive model

Fundamental is the adaptive principle: 'If a change occurs that produces discomfort, people will tend to act to restore their comfort' (Humphreys and Nicol, 1998). The return towards comfort is pleasurable, as has been amply demonstrated by the experimental work of Cabanac (1969). People are not passive receptors of their thermal environment, but continually interact with it. It follows that adaptive thermal comfort is an example of a 'complex adaptive system'. These systems are mathematically intractable, may have multiple equilibria and, if disturbed, may settle at a new equilibrium position. Thus, many different comfort temperatures are possible at different times and in different circumstances. Other examples of complex adaptive systems are the world climate system and the world economic system. As a consequence of the adaptive principle, except in extreme climates, people become adjusted to the conditions they normally experience. People must therefore be studied in their everyday habitats if the system is to be understood and quantified.

It is useful to classify the different kinds of adaptation that may occur:

Physiological adaptations to coldness include vasoconstriction, shivering and eating more food. It is uncertain whether people acclimatize long term to cold, in the sense of the body resetting its metabolic processes. Physiological adaptations to warmth include vasodilatation, sweating and eating less food. Heat acclimatization is well documented, and includes the lowering of the body core temperature, associated with the onset of sweating. Acclimatization to heat takes a week or so to complete.

Behavioural adaptations to coldness may include increased activity, increased clothing, closing the posture, cuddling up, heating the room, finding a warmer place, closing windows, avoiding draughts, modifying the building or emigrating. Adaptations to warmth may include reduced activity, reduced clothing, adopting an open posture, separating from other people, cooling the room, finding a cooler place, opening a window, using a fan, modifying the building or emigrating.

Psychological adaptations are not yet well defined or well documented, but they may include expecting a range of conditions, accepting a range of sensations, enjoying a variety of sensations, accepting behavioural adaptations and accepting responsibility for control.

In some circumstances there may be insufficient opportunities for adaptive actions to be fully effective. They may be constrained by, for example, the climate, culture and fashion, work requirements, the features of the building, the environment in which the building is placed and the personality profile of the occupant. Insufficient adaptive opportunity leads to discomfort, but if the combined effect of the various actions is sufficient, comfort will be achieved.

Summary points:
- The adaptive model shows that comfort temperatures are variable (we have seen populations comfortable in rooms as low as 17°C and as high as 35°C).
- Comfort temperatures in the buildings in free-running mode depend strongly on the prevailing mean outdoor temperature.
- The comfort temperature is the current equilibrium position of a complex adaptive system.
- Modifying the pattern of constraints acting on the system will modify the position of the equilibrium.
- Gradual changes in the constraints are unlikely to produce discomfort.
- Inadequate adaptive opportunity, or too much constraint, will produce discomfort.
- Thermal physiology and heat-exchange models of thermal comfort are components of the adaptive model.

METHODOLOGICAL PROBLEMS WITH CURRENT STANDARDS

Quantifiable comfort standards are inevitably required by engineers and designers to indicate a temperature that they can use to size a heating or cooling system or to decide whether the building they have designed will remain comfortable. The existing standards for indoor comfort are administered by various bodies. The most influential standards are those of the ISO, which apply in ISO member countries throughout the world, the CEN, whose standards are recognized in Europe, and the American National Standards Institution, whose comfort standard for indoor environments is administered by ASHRAE and is generally referred to as the ASHRAE Standard (ASHRAE, 2004). These three comfort standards have moved closer together in recent years and, for mechanically heated and cooled buildings, are now virtually identical, being based on Fanger's PMV method.

International comfort standards give 'classes' or 'categories' for indoor environments according to the closeness with which the indoor conditions are controlled. In ISO 7730, classes A–C imply that close control denotes a superior building (ISO, 2006). The new CEN Standard 15251 (CEN, 2007) uses a slightly different categorization (Table 1) in terms of the type of building rather than the assumed quality, but the limits of these categories are identical to those of ISO 7730 and it is probable that they will be used to indicate 'quality', especially as 'high expectation' is associated with category I. ASHRAE standards may soon follow suit, despite considerable reservations already aired about the veracity of such assumptions (Arens et al., 2010).

In heated or air-conditioned buildings, closer control almost always implies higher energy use. Thus, the categorization in these standards means that buildings with high energy use are characterized as superior to those with lower energy use. The categorization is therefore working against the aim of reducing the energy impact of buildings. Nicol and Humphreys (2009b) have suggested an alternative approach where buildings are categorized according to their energy use rather than their indoor climate such as what is suggested in Table 2.

The measurement of the environment required to test compliance with Standard ISO 7730 is set out in ISO 7726 (ISO, 1998), which defines the measurements required for evaluation of Fanger's (1970) PMV. In order to evaluate PMV sufficiently accurately to be sure that it can be kept with ±0.2PMV (Table 1), accurate measurement of the six variables on which it depends is required. There are four physical variables

(namely air and radiant temperatures, humidity, and air movement) that can, but not without some difficulty, be measured with sufficient accuracy (Humphreys and Nicol, 2002). But there are also two 'personal' variables, namely clothing insulation and the rate of metabolic heat production, the accurate measurement of which is notoriously difficult. Because of this difficulty, assumed values are often assigned to the personal variables (Nicol and Humphreys, 2009b), and it is therefore impossible to know whether, in an occupied building in daily life, the standard has been met.

Although both the ASHRAE (2004) and the CEN standards include separate 'adaptive' rules for buildings that are not air-conditioned, these also favour narrower ranges of internal temperatures promoting close control as desirable, and much of the wording of the standards suggests that mechanical cooling is superior.

The use of 'rational', 'precise', 'close control' indices such as PMV has had a number of drawbacks:

- In an attempt to meet unrealistic indoor air temperature limits, heating and cooling systems and their controls have become too complex – often resulting in different parts of the system 'fighting' one another (Bordass et al., 2002).
- Inherent flaws in the PMV model lead to needless and sometimes uncomfortable cooling in summer (Humphreys and Nicol, 2001; Mendell and Mirer, 2009).
- Thermal comfort predicted by PMV correlates poorly with thermal delight (Hershong, 1979) and modern buildings seldom offer opportunities to sensually delight in warmth, or coolth, or the breath of a cool breeze over the skin on a warm day.

By favouring narrow limits of PMV, current standards promote the use of air-conditioning. This itself has a number of interconnected and adverse results, some of which are not commonly admitted, for the well-being of occupants, for running costs and for the quality of building design.

Well-being:

- Ventilation is poor in many closely controlled buildings, not least where employers try to minimize energy use by recycling air, resulting in higher incidence of sick building syndrome (SBS). 'Most studies completed to date indicate that relative to natural ventilation air conditioning, with or without humidification, was consistently associated with a statistically significant increase in the prevalence of one or more SBS symptoms by approximately 30–200%' (Seppanen and Fisk, 2002). Not least because poor maintenance practices lead to unhealthy systems.
- SBS symptoms in office workers worldwide are more common in mechanically heated and cooled buildings. They are of uncertain origin. One cause is thought to be contaminants related to the characteristics of heating, ventilating and air-conditioning (HVAC) systems. In one study, data from 97 representative air-conditioned US office buildings

Table 2 | Suggested categories for building energy use in line with the need for low carbon buildings

Category	Explanation
I	Building requiring no energy to remain comfortable
II	Buildings requiring energy only at limited times of year to remain comfortable
III	Buildings requiring all the year round energy input to remain comfortable

Source: Nicol and Humphreys (2009a, b)

in the Building Assessment and Survey Evaluation study found clear evidence for associations between building-related symptom outcomes and HVAC characteristics. Outdoor air intakes less than 60m above ground level were associated with significant increases in most symptoms. Humidification systems with poor condition/maintenance were associated with significantly increased upper respiratory symptoms, eye symptoms, fatigue/difficulty in concentrating and skin symptoms (Mendell *et al.*, 2008; Seppanen and Fisk, 2002).

- Studies have shown that there are significant health impacts for building occupants. 'Simply put, avoiding overcooled buildings in the summer, and keeping buildings at the cooler end of the recommended temperature range in the winter, may result in a substantial decrease in building-related symptoms. This should still maintain thermal comfort in the buildings in winter and should actually improve comfort in the summer' (Mendell and Mirer, 2009).

Costs:

- The use of air to circulate heat and coolth moved the industry away from the potentially more efficient use of water as the heat transfer medium in heating and cooling systems.
- Soaring energy costs are gaining significance on boardroom balance sheets.
- As the machinery required to 'safeguard' comfort begins to dominate building costs, the actual fabric of the building becomes cheaper and buildings themselves are eventually reduced to thin, tight, low-cost envelopes (Ackermann, 2002; Cooper, 1998).

Building design:

- Designers, both engineers and architects, have largely lost the skills to design passive low energy buildings (Nicol and Roaf, 2007).
- Engineers routinely insist that the opening of windows interferes with the proper functioning of the mechanical systems so windows are increasingly designed not to open. Consequently, the poorer quality buildings in temperate and cold regions that were originally only heated in winter now require cooling in summer too. In warmer regions, buildings that would require cooling for only a few weeks or months a year now had to be mechanically heated, cooled and ventilated all the year round, all at phenomenal costs in terms of energy, GHG emissions and money. Seventy per cent of electricity generated in the USA is now used to condition buildings.

DISCUSSION: IS TIGHT CONTROL OF TEMPERATURE REALLY NEEDED?

Clothing and comfort: 'Cool Biz': a radical example from Japan

An important experiment, indicating that summertime temperatures in buildings need not adhere to current tight standards, was instigated by the Japanese Ministry of the Environment in 2005 when occupants of central government ministry buildings were ordered to adjust air-conditioning start-up temperatures to 28°C until the beginning of September. The 'Cool Biz' dress code was introduced and workers were advised to wear trousers made from materials that are air-permeable and absorb moisture, and short-sleeved shirts, without jackets or ties. Even some of those who liked the idea of dressing more casually occasionally became self-conscious when commuting and surrounded by non-government employees who were wearing standard business suits. Many government workers said they felt it was impolite not to wear a tie when meeting counterparts from the private sector. However, Prime Minister Koizumi was frequently interviewed without a tie or jacket, so calming such fears effectively.

On 28 October 2005, the Japanese Ministry of the Environment announced the results of a web-based questionnaire survey on the Cool Biz campaign covering some 1200 men and women randomly extracted from an internet panel recruited by a research company. The survey results indicated that almost all respondents knew about Cool Biz, and around a third reported that their offices set the air-conditioner thermostat higher than in previous years. Based on these figures, the ministry estimated that the campaign resulted in a 460,000-ton reduction in CO_2 emissions, equivalent to the CO_2 emitted by about 1 million households for 1 month (http://www.env.go.jp/en/press/2005/1028a.html). The results for 2006 were even better, resulting in an estimated CO_2 emission savings equivalent to 2.5 million households for 1 month. The campaign is ongoing and is considered a significant success, and this indicates that step changes in temperature control can indeed be extremely effective if handled appropriately.

Productivity and comfort

One argument used to persuade designers and clients of the need for tight control of indoor air temperatures rests on productivity. Recent work on the relationship between temperature and task performance published by REHVA (REHVA, 2007) rests chiefly on a meta-analysis by Seppanen and Fisk (2002) that combines numerous studies of performance of different kinds of work, but chiefly that of telephone call centres, where the performance criterion was the time taken to answer an enquiry. They found an optimum for performance at around 22°C, but with quite a wide band of uncertainty.

The meta-analysis awaits a thorough critique, and its relevance to office work in general is uncertain, chiefly because variation in the performance of single attributes of single tasks bears only a loose relationship to the wider concept of productivity in industry.

There is also a danger that the relation between room temperature and performance found in the study will be interpreted simplistically. The relation is indirect: performance, in its thermal aspect, depends on the thermal state of the body rather than on that of the room. It follows that, as people adapt to their room temperatures by for example seasonal changes of clothing, the room temperature for optimum performance of a particular task will show a corresponding change. Further, different kinds of task show optima at different body thermal states. Thus, it is probable that there is no single optimum temperature for task performance. Performance is therefore likely to be best at the temperatures the workers find comfortable. And we have shown that these temperatures can be as low as 17°C and as high as 35°C, and all points between these extreme values.

When Le Corbusier coined his famous phrase 'a house is a machine for living in' (Le Corbusier, 1986) he did not imply, as do some approaches to the study of productivity, that people are machines for living and working in buildings. Productivity is notoriously hard to define in a way that can be measured simply. Its assessment must include related indicators such as staff turnover, absence rates for sickness, as studies have shown that the push for higher productivity has often resulted in very poor working environments, high staff turnover levels and ill-heath (Bergqvist *et al.*, 1995), with high energy cost too.

The key element in the evolution of machinery and its use, as noted by Braverman (1974), 'is not its size, complexity, or speed, but the manner in which its operations are controlled'. The issue of who dictates the conditions in which workers operate is also key, and the ability to control one's own working conditions has been shown to improve perceived levels of comfort and, in turn, how productive people feel they are (Bordass and Leaman, 2007). This is borne out by the findings of a study of typical office workers across a wide range of European locations from Sweden to Portugal and Greece. Inspection of self-assessed productivity found that, over a wide range of room temperatures, people

rated themselves most productive when they were most comfortable – and the temperature for comfort varied widely between the different countries and climates of Europe (Humphreys and Nicol, 2007).

CLOSING COMMENT

We stand at the end of the age of cheap fossil energy, and at the threshold of a future of increasingly extreme weather. The cost of running buildings is increasingly a commercial concern as energy costs are being made visible, for instance in Europe through the mechanism of energy rating assessments and energy performance certificates for homes and larger public buildings required under the European Performance of Buildings Directive (EPBD). This visibility is already influencing market values of buildings, with low energy buildings being increasingly favoured as 'green' and more affordable, leaving some buildings owners with 'energy hog' buildings that are, in the long term, little more than 'investment nightmares' (Gensler, 2005). It is inevitable that in future, buildings will be increasingly classified according to their actual energy consumption and carbon footprint rather than by how they perform against the PMV-based standards. It may well be that in a resource-constricted future, there will come a time when such standards are ignored altogether if building occupants are comfortable enough without them. This happened overnight with the Cool Biz project in Japan. The need to transform the 'comfort in buildings markets' with new far-sighted standards is clearly outlined above. How this may be achieved is discussed in Tuohy *et al.* in their 2010 article on '21st century standards for thermal comfort: fostering low carbon building design and operation' in this volume.

References

Ackermann, M., 2002, *Cool Comfort: America's Romance with Air-Conditioning*, Washington, DC, Smithsonian Institution Press.

Arbuthnot, J. 1733, *An Essay Concerning the Effects of Air on Human Bodies*, London, Tonson and Draper.

Arens, E., Humphreys, M.A., de Dear, R. and Zhang, H., 2010, 'Are "class A" temperature requirements realistic or desirable?' *Building and Environment* 45(1), 4–10.

ASHRAE/ANSI Standard 55, 2004, *Thermal Environment Conditions for Human Occupancy*, Atlanta, GA, American Society of Heating Refrigeration and Air-conditioning Engineers.

Auliciems, A., 2009, 'Human adaptation within a paradigm of climate determinism and change', in K. Ebi, I. Burton and G. McGregor (eds) *Biometeorology*

for Adaptation to Climate Variability and Change, Chapter 11, Netherlands, Springer.

Auliciems, A. and de Dear, R., 1986, 'Air conditioning in Australia I: human thermal factors', *Architectural Science Review* 29, 67–75.

Badham, C., Assheton, C.F. and Rayner, H.E., 1928, On the index of comfort in the ventilation of theatres in Sydney, N.S. Wales, *Studies in Industrial Hygiene*, No. 10, Report to the Director of Public Health of NSW.

Baker, N. and Standeven, M., 1996, 'Thermal comfort for free-running buildings', *Energy and Buildings* 23(3), 175–182.

Bedford, T., 1936, *The Warmth Factor in Comfort at Work; A Physiological Study of Heating and Ventilation*, London, HMO Stationery Office.

Benedict, F.G., 1929, 'Human skin temperature as affected by muscular activity, exposure to cold and wind

movement', *American Journal of Physiology* 87, 633.

Bergqvist, U., Wolgast, E., Nilsson, B. and Voss, M., 1995, 'Musculoskeletal disorders among visual display terminal workers: individual, ergonomic, and work organizational factors', *Ergonomics* 38(4), 763–776.

Bordass, B. and Leaman, A., 2005, 'Making feedback and post-occupancy evaluation routine 1: a portfolio of feedback techniques', *Building Research and Information* 33(4), 347–352.

Bordass, B. and Leaman, A., 2007, 'Are users more tolerant of "green" buildings?' *Building Research and Information* 35(6), 662–673.

Bordass, B., Leaman, A. and Cohen, R., 2002, 'Walking the tightrope: the probe team's response to BRI commentaries', *Building Research and Information* 30(1), 62–72.

Brager, G. and de Dear, R., 1998, 'Thermal adaptation in the built environment: a literature review', *Energy and Buildings* 27(1), 83–96.

Braverman, H., 1974, *Labor and Monopoly Capital: The Degradation of Work in the Twentieth Century*, from chapter 9 on Machinery, New York, NY, Monthly Review Press.

Busch, J.F., 1990, 'Thermal response to the Thai office environment', *ASHRAE Transactions* 96(1), 859–872.

Busch, J.F., 1995, 'Thermal comfort in Thai air-conditioned and naturally ventilated offices', in J. Nicol, M. Humphreys, O. Sykes and S. Roaf (eds) *Standards for Thermal Comfort: Indoor Air Temperature Standards for the 21st Century*, London, E and F N Spon, 114–131.

Cabanac, M., 1969, 'Pleasantness or unpleasantness of a thermal sensation and homeoregulation', *Physiology and Behavior* 4, 359–364.

CEN, 2007, *Standard EN15251 Indoor Environmental Input Parameters for Design and Assessment of Energy Performance of Buildings – Addressing Indoor Air Quality, Thermal Environment, Lighting and Acoustics*, Brussels, Belgium, Comité Européen de Normalisation.

Cooper, G., 1998, *Air-Conditioning America: Engineers and the Controlled Environment, 1900–1960*, Johns Hopkins Studies in the History of Technology, Baltimore, MD, Johns Hopkins University Press.

Davey, J., 1814, 'An account of some experiments on arterial heat', *Transactions of the Philosophical Society* 104, 590, London.

de Dear, R.J. and Brager, G.S., 1998, 'Developing an adaptive model of thermal comfort and preference', *ASHRAE Technical Data Bulletin* 14(1), 27–49.

EPBD. For information on the European Performance of Buildings Directive, see: www.epbd-ca.org/.

Fanger, P.O., 1970, *Thermal Comfort*, Copenhagen, Denmark, Danish Technical Press.

Farmer, E. and Chambers, E.G., 1929, 'A study of personal qualities in accident proneness and proficiency', Report to the Industrial Health Research Board, No. 55, London.

Fisher, F.G., 1994, *Raphael Cilento, a Biography*, Brisbane, University of Queensland Press.

Galton, D. 1880, *Healthy Dwellings*, Oxford, Clarendon Press.

Gensler, 2005, *Faulty Towers: Is the British Office Block Sustainable?* www.gensler.com.

Griffiths, I.D., 1990, 'Thermal comfort in buildings with passive solar features',

Report ENS-090-UK, Department of Psychology, University of Surrey.

Hacker, J., 2005, *Beating the Heat*. Available at: www.arup.com/_assets/_download/download396.pdf. See also CIBSE TM 33.

Haldi, F. and Robinson, D., 2009, 'A comprehensive stochastic model of window usage: theory and validation', *Proceedings of Building Simulation 2009, 11th International IBPSA Conference, Glasgow*.

Hambly, J.D. and Bedford, T., 1921, 'Preliminary notes on atmospheric conditions in boot and shoe factories', Report to the Industrial Fatigue Research Board, No. 11, London.

Haves, P., Roaf, S. and Orr, J., 1998, 'Climate change and passive cooling in Europe', *Proceedings of PLEA Conference. Lisbon*, James & James Science.

Hershong, L., 1979, *Thermal Delight in Architecture*, Cambridge, MA, MIT Press.

Houghton, F.C. and Yaglohglou, C.P., 1923a, 'Determining lines of equal comfort', *Journal of American Heating and Ventilating Engineers* 29, 165–176.

Houghton, F.C. and Yaglohglou, C.P., 1923b, 'Determination of the comfort zone', *Journal of American Heating and Ventilating Engineers* 29, 515–536.

Hulme, M., 2009, *Why We Disagree About Climate Change*, Cambridge, Cambridge University Press, 22–25.

Humphreys, M.A., 1973, 'Classroom temperature, clothing and thermal comfort – a study of secondary school children in summertime', *Journal of the Institute of Heating and Ventilating Engineers* 41, 191–202

Humphreys, M.A., 1976, 'Field studies of thermal comfort compared and applied', *Journal of the Institute of Heating and Ventilating Engineers* 44, 5–27.

Humphreys, M.A., 1977, 'Clothing and the outdoor microclimate in summer', *Building & Environment* 12, 137–142.

Humphreys, M.A., 1978, 'Outdoor temperatures and comfort indoors', *Building Research and Practice* 6(2), 92–105.

Humphreys, M.A., 1979, 'The influence of season and ambient temperature on human clothing behaviour', in P.O. Fanger and O. Valbjorn (eds) *Indoor Climate*, Copenhagen, Denmark, Danish Building Research, 699–713.

Humphreys, M.A. and Nicol, J.F., 1998, 'Understanding the adaptive approach to thermal comfort', *ASHRAE Technical Data Bulletin: Field Studies of Thermal Comfort and Adaptation* 14, 1–14.

Humphreys, M.A. and Nicol, J.F., 2000, 'Outdoor temperature and indoor

thermal comfort: raising the precision of the relationship for the 1998 ASHRAE database of field studies', *ASHRAE Transactions* 106(2), 485–492.

Humphreys, M.A. and Nicol, J.F., 2001, 'The validity of ISO-PMV for predicting comfort votes in every-day thermal environments', *Proceedings of the Windsor Conference on Moving Thermal Comfort Standards into the 21st Century*, Oxford Brookes University.

Humphreys, M.A. and Nicol, J.F., 2002, 'The validity of ISO-PMV for predicting comfort votes in every-day life', *Energy and Buildings* 34, 667–684

Humphreys, M.A. and Nicol, F., 2007, 'Self-assessed productivity and the office environment: monthly surveys in five European countries', *ASHRAE Transactions* 113(1), 606–616.

Huntington, E., 2001, *Civilization and Climate*, reprinted from the 1915 edition, Honolulu, HI, University Press of the Pacific.

ISO, 1998, Standard ISO7726, *Ergonomics of the Thermal Environment – Instruments for Measuring Physical Quantities*, Geneva, Switzerland, International Organization for Standardization.

ISO, 2006, Standard ISO7730, *Ergonomics of the Thermal Environment – Analytical Determination and Interpretation of Thermal Comfort using Calculation of the PMV and PPD Indices and Local Thermal Comfort Criteria*, Geneva, Switzerland, International Organization for Standardization.

Jones, J.S., 1924, 'Hygrometry for deep mines', *Bulletin of the Institute of Mining and Metallurgy* 240, London.

Kolokotroni, M., Kukadia, V. and Parera, M., 1996, 'NATVENT – European project on overcoming technical barriers to low-energy natural ventilation', *Proceedings of the CIBSE/ASHRAE Joint Conference: Part 1*, London, Chartered Institute of Building Service Engineers, 36–41.

Le Corbusier, [1928] 1986, *Towards a New Architecture*, London and Mineola, NY, Dover Publications. This is a translated reprint of Corbusier's original book *Vers une Architecture*, first published in 1928 in Paris.

Markham, S.F., 1944, *Climate and the Energy of Nations*, Oxford, Oxford University Press.

McCartney, K.J. and Nicol, J.F., 2002, 'Developing an adaptive control algorithm for Europe: results of the SCATs Project', *Energy and Buildings* 34(6), 623–635.

Mendell, M. and Mirer, G., 2009, 'Indoor thermal factors and symptoms in office workers: findings from the US EPA Base Study', *Indoor Air* 19(4), 291–302.

Mendell, M., Lei-Gomez, Q., Mirer, A., Seppanen, O. and Brunner, G., 2008, 'Risk factors in heating, ventilating, and air-conditioning systems for occupant symptoms in US office buildings: The US EPA BASE', *Proceedings of Indoor Air* 18(4), 301–316.

Morgan, C.A., de Dear, R.J. and Brager, G., 2002, 'Climate clothing and adaptation in the built environment', *Proceedings of the 9th International Conference on Indoor Air Quality and Climate*, 5, 98–103.

Nicol, J.F. and Humphreys, M.A., 1973, 'Thermal comfort as part of a self-regulating system', *Building Research and Practice* 6(3), 191–197.

Nicol, J.F. and Humphreys, M.A., 2002, 'Adaptive thermal comfort and sustainable thermal standards for buildings', *Energy and Buildings* 34, 563–572.

Nicol, J.F. and Humphreys, M.A., 2009a, 'Derivation of the equations for comfort in free-running buildings in CEN Standard EN15251, Special Issue Section: International Symposium on the Interaction Human and Building Environment', *Buildings and Environment* 45(1), 11–17.

Nicol, J.F. and Humphreys, M.A., 2009b, 'New standards for comfort and energy use in buildings', *Building Research and Information* 37(1), 68–73.

Nicol, J. and Roaf, S., 2007, 'Adaptive thermal comfort and passive buildings', in M. Santamouris (ed) *Passive Cooling*, London, James & James Science Publishers.

REHVA, 2007, 'How to integrate productivity in life-cycle cost analysis of building services' in P. Wargorcki and O. Seppänen (eds), Report 6 of the Federation of European Heating, Ventilating and Air-Conditioning Associations (REHVA), Brussels.

Reid, D.B., 1844, *Illustrations of the Theory and Practice of Ventilation*, London,

Longmans, Brown, Green and Longmans.

Rijal, H.B., Tuohy, P., Nicol, F., Humphreys, M., Samuel, A. and Clarke, J., 2007a, 'Using results from field surveys to predict the effect of open windows on thermal comfort and energy use in buildings', *Energy and Buildings* 39, 823–836.

Rijal, H.B., Tuohy, P., Nicol, F., Humphreys, M., Samuel, A. and Clarke, J., 2007b, 'Development of an adaptive window opening algorithm to predict the thermal comfort, energy use and over heating in buildings', *Journal of Building Performance Simulation* 1(1), 17–30.

Roaf, S., 1992, 'Ozone loopholes – A case study of air-conditioning in Britain', *Proceedings of the World Renewable Energy Congress. Reading*.

Roaf, S., Crichton, D. and Nicol, F., 2009, *Adapting Buildings and Cities for Climate Change*, 2nd edition, Oxford, Architectural Press.

Seppanen, O. and Fisk, W.J., 2002, 'Association of ventilation system type with SBS symptoms in office workers', *Indoor Air* 12, 98–112.

Shaviv, E., 2008, 'Passive and low energy architecture (PLEA) v. green architecture (LEED)', in O. Lewis (ed), *Proceedings of the PLEA Conference. Dublin*.

Shove, E., 2003, *Comfort, Cleanliness and Convenience: The Social Organisation of Normality*, Oxford, Berg.

Tomlinson, C., 1850, *A Rudimentary Treatise on Warming and Ventilation*, London, J. Weale.

Tuohy, P., 2008, 'Air-conditioning: the impact of UK regulations, the risks of un-necessary air-conditioning and a capability index for non-air conditioned naturally ventilated buildings', *Proceedings of the 2008 Windsor Conference on Air Conditioning and the Low Carbon Cooling Challenge*. Available at: www.nceub.org.uk/index.php?pagename=Research. WindsorConference2008.

Tuohy, P., Roaf, S., Nicol, F., Humphreys, M. and Boerstra, A., 2010, '21st

century standards for thermal comfort: fostering low carbon building design and operation', *Architectural Science Review* 53(1), 78–86.

van der Linden, A.C., Boerstra, A.C., Raue, A.K., Kurvers, S.R. and De Dear, R.J., 2006, 'Adaptive temperature limits: a new guideline for the Netherlands', *Energy and Buildings* 38(11), 8–17.

Vernon, H.M., 1926, 'Is effective temperature or cooling power the better index of comfort?' *Journal of Industrial Hygiene* 8, 392.

Vernon, H.M., Bedford, T. and Warner, C.G., 1926, 'A physiological study of the ventilation and heating of certain factories', Report to the Industrial Fatigue Research Board, No. 35, London.

Vernon, H.M., Bedford, T. and Warner, C.G., 1930, 'A study of heating and ventilation in schools', Report to the Industrial Health Research Board, No. 58, London.

Wyndham, C.H. and Heyns, A., 1973, 'The probability of heat stroke developing at different levels of heat stress', *Archives de Sciences Physiologique* 27(4), 545–562.

Wyndham, C.H., Stryndom, N., Willaims, C., Morrison, J. and Bredell, G., 1966, 'The heat reactions of bantu males in various states of acclimatization – II. The limits of heat stress for a moderate rate of work', *Internationale Zeitschrift für Angewandte Physiologie Einschliesslich Arbeitsphysiologie* 23(1), 79–92.

Yagloglou, C.P. and Drinker, P., 1928, 'The summer comfort zone: climate and clothing', *Journal of Industrial Hygiene* 8, 5.

Yarwood, A.T., 1991, 'Sir Raphael Cilento and the White Man in the tropics', *Health and Healing in Tropical Australia*, 47–63.

Yun, G.Y. and Steemers, K., 2008, 'Time dependent occupant behaviour models of window control in summer', *Building and Environment* 43(9), 1471–1482.

ARCHITECTURAL
SCIENCE
REVIEW

Twenty first century standards for thermal comfort: fostering low carbon building design and operation

Paul Tuohy*, Sue Roaf, Fergus Nicol, Mike Humphreys and Atze Boerstra

Energy Systems Research Unit, University of Strathclyde, Glasgow, G1 1XJ, UK

Nearly 50% of energy consumed in the developed world is consumed in buildings. Despite regulation intent, many new buildings are energy profligate. Thermal comfort standards are partly responsible for this increase in consumption. In this volume, Roaf *et al.* have described the evolution of current comfort standards and problems inherent in buildings they shape, and have discussed two new methods of regulating thermal comfort in buildings which recognize human adaptation and have potential for reduced energy demand. These new methods incorporate adaptation through a fixed heating and cooling threshold approach (similar to Japanese Cool-Biz) or through heating and cooling setpoints calculated based on outdoor conditions (using CEN standard equations). The impact on comfort and energy demand of these new approaches is investigated for a London office building. Variables such as future climate, future building upgrades, setback temperatures, internal gains and ventilation are also explored. Adoption of the new approaches gave a 50% reduction in heating and cooling energy for the simulated office. The new approach together with optimized setback temperatures, ventilation strategies and higher efficiency equipment gives predicted heating and cooling energy demand close to zero. Recommendations for future regulation, design and operation of buildings are proposed.

INTRODUCTION

The recent trend particularly evident in non-domestic buildings has been for increasing adoption of heating, ventilation and air-conditioning (HVAC) systems, the trend being in part driven by the wide acceptance of the predicted mean vote (PMV) criterion for indoor comfort. However, the extent of adaptation predicted using the PMV criterion is around half that found in practice in field studies (Humphreys, 1976), particularly in buildings where occupants have some opportunity to adapt themselves and their environment to maintain comfort. In the present article, we investigate the potential of two new alternative approaches to PMV, which are based on the adaptive comfort criteria currently included in the UK Chartered Institution of Building Services Engineers' guide (CIBSE, 2006), in the American Society of Heating, Refrigerating and Air-conditioning Engineers' standards (ASHRAE, 2004) and in the European Comité Européen de Normalisation standards (CEN, 2007). The historical background and rationale for these two new approaches are described in Roaf *et al.* (2010).

The application of adaptive criteria has so far been restricted by these standards to free-running buildings where occupants can adapt their dress, behaviour and local environment to maintain thermal comfort, and the criteria have primarily been used for naturally ventilated buildings in summer. There is, however, some justification for using adaptive criteria more widely. The survey data used in the formulation of the CEN adaptive standard included several buildings where the occupants had the use of local heating and cooling appliances (Roaf *et al.*, 2010). Surveys of German buildings with centrally controlled thermally active building systems (TABS) have suggested that adaptive criteria best represent occupant comfort in these circumstances (Kalz *et al.*, 2009) and the recent 'Cool Biz' initiative in Japan successfully applied fixed threshold temperatures for the cooling of government offices and occupant adaptation by changing to less formal dress was encouraged (Wikipedia, 2009).

In this article, we illustrate the potential reduction in energy use that could be realized if buildings were designed and operated so that the adaptive criteria are applied. The impacts of other measures such as reduced setback temperatures during unoccupied hours, reduced energy use by equipment and lighting and the use of free cooling through enhanced ventilation are also analysed. The analysis includes likely future building standards for new or retrofit designs

*Corresponding author: *Email:* paul.tuohy@strath.ac.uk

doi:10.3763/asre.2009.0112 ©2010 Earthscan ISSN: 0003-8628 (print), 1758-9622 (online) www.earthscan.co.uk/journals/asre

earthscan

and the analysis is repeated for both a current climate and a predicted future climate.

The aim of the analysis is to inform the development of future regulations and design operational guidance that will assist in realizing robust, comfortable, low energy buildings in practice.

COMFORT TEMPERATURES AND CLIMATE

Adaptive comfort criteria for buildings have been incorporated in the CEN and ASHRAE standards and CIBSE guidelines. In this study, we will use the adaptive comfort criteria of the CEN standard and CIBSE guidelines, which define comfort temperature (Tcomf) and running mean outdoor temperature (Trm) and relate them as shown in equation 1.

$$Tcomf = 0.33\,Trm + 18.8 \qquad (1)$$

In our study, we investigate the impact of using the proposed alternative approaches for an example London office using dynamic simulation. The analysis tool used in this study is ESP-r (Clarke, 2001). It should be noted that all temperatures in this article are given in centigrade.

There are various sources of current and future climate information for London. CIBSE recently published current and future UK climate datasets for use in building simulation based on the UKCIP02 projections (CIBSE, 2009). There is also the recently revised, probabilistic UKCIP09 set of projections. Dru Crawley of the US Department of Energy recently defined algorithms for incorporating both climate change and urban heat island effects into climate files for building simulation (Crawley, 2007). For this article, we have chosen to use the 2005 and 2080 London climate files from this dataset as the basis of our analysis.

The running mean outdoor temperatures (Trm) and the indoor comfort temperatures (Tcomf) calculated using equation 1 are shown in Figure 1. The shift between 2005 and 2080 in the annual average running mean temperature is +3.3°C, whereas in the summer period the average shift is larger at +5.5°C. The corresponding shifts in indoor adaptive comfort temperatures are +1.1°C for the annual average and +1.7°C for the summer average.

APPROACHES TO THERMAL COMFORT IN BUILDINGS

Roaf *et al.* (2010) describe in more detail the rationale behind the proposed two new approaches based on adaptive comfort criteria. The first approach is to impose a heating set-point of 18°C and a cooling set-point of 28°C (label: h18c28). This approach is somewhat similar to that taken in the Japanese Cool Biz programme where a fixed cooling threshold was applied. The second approach (label: Adapt) is based directly on the CEN adaptive comfort criteria. In this case, heating and cooling set-points are calculated based on the running

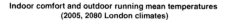

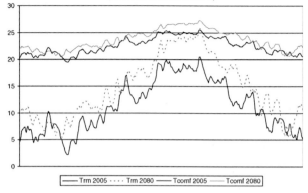

Figure 1 | Outdoor running mean temperature for the 2005 (Trm 2005) and projected 2080 climates (Trm 2080). Indoor adaptive comfort temperatures for the 2005 (Tcomf 2005) and projected 2080 (Tcomf 2080) climates

mean temperature using equations 2 and 3.

$$Tcool = Tcomf + 3 \qquad (2)$$
$$Theat = Tcomf - 3 \qquad (3)$$

A base case scenario representing existing typical practice was used to impose a fixed heating set-point of 21°C and a fixed cooling set-point of 23°C (label: h21c23). This h21c23 scenario was chosen to represent operation in accordance with the Federation of European HVAC Associations (REHVA) guideline, which suggests a constant 22°C as the optimum temperature (Plocker and Wijsman, 2009). All three control methods are illustrated in Figure 2. The adaptive control (Adapt) is derived from the running mean temperature and, hence, will be different for the 2080 and 2005 climate cases, while the h18c28 and h21c23 approaches are climate independent. One observation is that in 2005 the Adapt and h18c28 cooling thresholds are both around 28°C in July and August, but that in 2080 the Adapt cooling threshold is around 29.5°C; it would of course be feasible to adjust the h18c28 set-points through time in order to synergize with a change in climate. A second observation is that the h18c28 thresholds are much wider than the Adapt thresholds although the differences between heating set-points during times of peak heating and the differences between cooling set-points during times of peak cooling are not so pronounced.

EXAMPLE OFFICE

To illustrate the impact of the different control strategies, a simulation model of a London office was used. The model represents a 180m² mid-floor section of a larger office building with windows facing north and south. The section analysed includes both cellular and open plan office areas. Two versions of the office building were used: one representing a typical 1990s construction and the other representing a more advanced

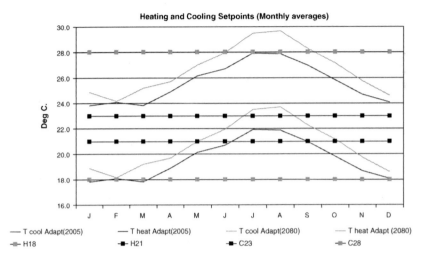

Figure 2 | Illustration of the three approaches to control indoor comfort for the London 2005 and projected 2080 climates

construction with insulation and infiltration close to EU Passive House standards (as promoted by the EU since 1998) and incorporating some simple over-window shading and some exposed thermal mass (exposed lightweight concrete ceiling, etc.). Figure 3 gives some sketch images of the office and Tables 1 and 2 give construction and operation details. The analysis output includes the indoor and outdoor environmental conditions on a sub-hourly time step and the heating or cooling energy required to be supplied into the space. The analysis presented here does not take account of heating or cooling system efficiencies or auxiliary energy for any pumps and fans associated with heating, cooling and ventilation.

Details of internal gains, setback temperatures and ventilation rates are given in Tables 3–6 and are discussed in more detail later in this section. The ventilation during occupied hours (as explained in Table 6) for the office is assumed to be sufficient to maintain fresh air but could be supplied by mechanical systems or through window opening or by other passive means. The infiltration outside of occupied hours is set to be appropriate for the construction standards applied.

The construction and operation of the building assumed for this example office are set deterministically and do not represent the variations and uncertainties in construction, building use or occupant behaviours that would be experienced over the life of a real building. We have taken this simplified approach here in order to clearly illustrate the potential impacts of the new approaches to comfort. To fully explore the robustness and capability of a building design, these variations and uncertainties should be incorporated in a probabilistic analysis.

IMPACT ON HEATING AND COOLING ENERGY DEMANDS

The performance of the typical 1990s version and the advanced version of the office was analysed with each

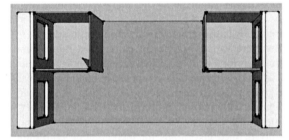

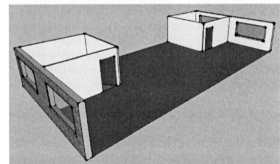

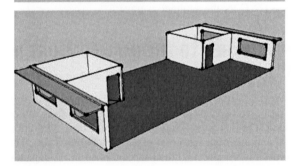

Figure 3 | Three sketches illustrating the simulated office: a plan view (top image), a view of the typical 1990s version (middle image) and a view of the advanced version (lower image)

Table 1 | Construction details for the typical 1990s and the advanced versions of the office (construction layers are listed from outside to inside)

	1990s	**Advanced**
Walls	Masonry; internal insulation; plasterboard; $U = 0.6$	External insulation; conc block; plaster; $U = 0.13$
Floor	Insulation; wood board; carpet	Light concrete; carpet
Ceiling	Insulation; plasterboard	Light concrete
Glazing	Double; $U = 3.3$	Triple; $U = 0.8$
Partition	Plasterboard; insulation; plasterboard	Plasterboard; insulation; plasterboard
External shade	No	Shaded

Table 3 | Three setback conditions for the h21c23 control: the baseline has no setback, setback 1 includes heating and cooling setpoints of 18°C and 26°C, respectively, in the setback period, and setback 2 has setpoints of 15°C and 32°C

	Baseline	**Setback 1**	**Setback 2**
H-C setpoints (occ)	21–23	21–23	21–23
H_C setpoints (setback)	21–23	18–26	15–32

Table 4 | Two setback conditions for the h18c28 and Adapt controls: the baseline includes heating and cooling setpoints of 18°C and 30°C, respectively, in the setback period and setback 2 has setpoints of 15°C and 32°C

	Baseline	**Setback 2**
H-C setpoints (occ)	18–28/Adapt	18–28/Adapt
H_C setpoints (setback)	18–30	15–32

Table 2 | Operational details for the office model

Occupancy	8.30–18.30 (Mon–Fri)
Heat/cool period	6.00–19.00 (Mon–Fri)
Setback period	All except the heat/cool period
Control point	Resultant temperature (0.5MRT, 0.5AT)
Systems	Ideal

Note: The resultant temperature is made up of 0.5× the mean radiant temperature (MRT) and 0.5× the mean air temperature (AT).

Table 5 | Internal gains scenarios

	Baseline	**Low Gains**	**High Gains**
Gains (occupied)	15	12	20
Gains (not occupied)	4	1	4

Gains are given in W per m^2 floor area.

of the three control strategies applied (h21c23, h18c28 and Adapt) for the 2005 and 2080 climates. Figure 4 shows the calculated total heating and cooling energy demand for each of the combinations of building, climate and controls.

The advanced office performs significantly better than the typical 1990s office for all the combinations of climate and controls in terms of overall energy demand for heating and cooling. However, both the typical and advanced versions perform significantly worse in the 2080 climate. The new control approaches (h18c28 and Adapt) both perform significantly better from an energy perspective than the baseline h21c23 control, with the h18c28 performing the best.

Table 6 | Ventilation scenarios

	Typical Building	**Advanced Building**	**Advanced with X-vent**	**Advanced with X-vent + NC**
Air change (occupied)	1.6	1.6	5	5
Air change (not occupied)	0.25	0.1	0.1	5

The ventilation rate of the baseline office during occupied hours is 1.6ac/h, which corresponds to 10L/s/person; outside of occupied hours, the air change rate is due to infiltration. A scenario is created for the advanced office case where cross-flow ventilation (X-vent or XV) can be achieved with a ventilation rate of 5ac/h during occupied hours; a second scenario is where this can also be achieved during unoccupied hours (X-vent + NC). (NC = night cooling.)

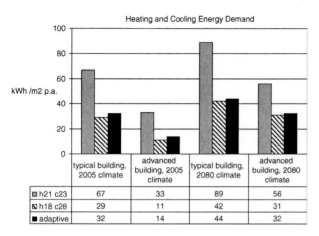

Figure 4 | Calculated total heating and cooling energy demand for each of the combinations of building, climate and controls

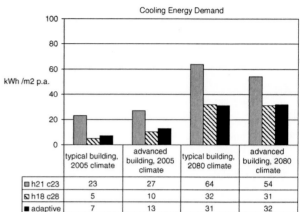

Figure 6 | Calculated total cooling energy demand for each of the combinations of building, climate and controls

Figures 5 and 6 show the heating and cooling energy demand separated. Heating demand is close to zero for the advanced building, while there is a general trend towards reduced heating in 2080. Cooling is increasingly dominant in the advanced building type or 2080 climate.

The scenarios analysed so far have included the baseline setback conditions, that is, no setback with the h21c23 control and heating and cooling setpoints of 18°C and 30°C with the proposed h18c28 and Adapt controls. The effect of setback was investigated by running the model with the range of setback temperatures described in Tables 3 and 4 and with the results shown in Figure 7. Results obtained show that reduced setback temperatures cause significant benefits in the typical 1990s version but much less benefits in the advanced case. The reduced effect in the advanced case is caused by the higher stability of the indoor environment due to the improved insulation

and air tightness and the higher thermal mass in this version of the building.

Another parameter with high uncertainty that can have a high impact on the overall energy use in buildings is the energy consumed by lights, equipment and appliances. There are various current projections for future equipment and lighting energy use and associated internal gains in offices; initiatives such as the US Energy Star and the EU Lighting and Equipment Directives, etc. promise reduced energy demand. However, increased density of electronic equipment in offices may act to offset these improvements. In order to evaluate the impact of internal gains, three scenarios were analysed as outlined in Table 5 (Figure 8). The effect of higher gains from energy consumption on the 1990s building did not show a large change; this was due to increased gains, causing reduced heating and increased

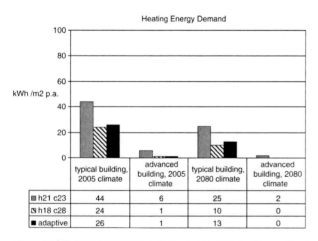

Figure 5 | Calculated total heating energy demand for each of the combinations of building, climate and controls

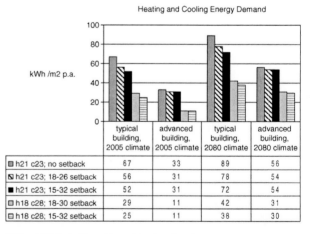

Figure 7 | Calculated impact of setback temperature on heating and cooling energy demand for the combinations of building, climate and controls

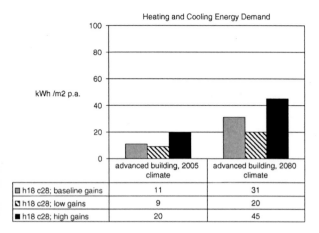

Figure 8 | Example of the impact of internal gains on the calculated heating and cooling energy demand for the advanced office with the h18c28 controls

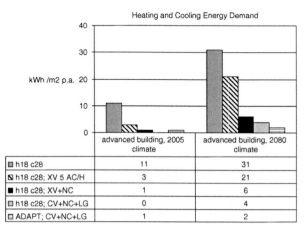

Figure 9 | Calculated impact of various ventilation (cross ventilation: XV; cross ventilation plus night cooling: XV + NC) and gain (low gains: LG) combinations on heating and cooling energy demand for the advanced building, climate and controls (h18c28 and Adapt) scenarios

cooling in similar amounts or vice versa, whereas for the reduced gains case, the net effects on total energy demand for heating and cooling are approximately neutral. The situation in the advanced building is not the same as the energy demand for heating is close to zero. For the advanced office the impact of increased internal gains from equipment would be to significantly increase the cooling energy demand and the total for heating and cooling. Similarly, reduced internal gains caused a reduction in the total energy demanded for heating and cooling. Internal gains have a very large impact in this case.

The cooling load is increased and dominates the energy performance of the advanced building. This effect is caused by the reduction in free cooling available through conduction and infiltration because of the improved insulation and infiltration characteristics of the advanced envelope. This effect can possibly be offset if opportunities that exist for free cooling with outdoor air can be realized. Several ventilation scenarios were investigated (Table 6) for the proposed new controls (h18c30 and Adapt) and the results are shown in Figure 9. The first enhanced free cooling ventilation scenario that was investigated was the opening of windows during occupied hours to establish cross-flow ventilation, achieving an assumed five air changes per hour; the second enhanced ventilation scenario investigated is the use of secure night ventilation in summer in combination with daytime cross-flow ventilation, the assumption being that these night-time ventilation paths allow the five air changes per hour to be maintained throughout unoccupied hours. It should be stated that while these deterministic assumptions for air flows used here are well-established assumptions given in guidelines (CIBSE, 2005; BRE, 2008), in practice more detailed consideration of ventilation openings, occupant behaviour and other uncertainties is recommended to achieve a robust building design (Tuohy, 2009). When these cross ventilation and night cooling air

change rates can be achieved in practice, cooling demand will be greatly reduced to around zero for the 2005 climate and an 80% reduction is predicted for the 2080 climate case. In combination with low internal gains, the enhanced ventilation can almost eliminate the calculated requirement for cooling even for the 2080 climate.

For the example office, the new control strategies in combination with the advanced fabric, shading, low internal gains and effective summer ventilation are predicted to achieve close to zero energy demand for heating and cooling.

IMPACT ON INTERNAL TEMPERATURES

The impact of the different approaches to building controls on the internal temperatures experienced in the office space is significant. Figure 10 shows the monthly average, maximum and minimum indoor resultant temperatures predicted for the typical 1990s office space and the 2005 climate for the baseline office of Figure 4 with the h18c28 and Adapt controls applied. Figure 11 shows in more detail the calculated resultant temperatures during occupied hours for an example week in April 2005. This example week is one where outdoor conditions are cooler at the beginning of the week but become significantly warmer as the week progresses. The typical 1990s building has a higher daily and monthly range of indoor temperatures than the advanced building – illustrating the effect of the external shading in limiting gains and the thermal mass in moderating temperatures, although only a very simple shade and medium mass (e.g. lightweight partitions) were used in this example. The advanced building is generally warmer than the typical 1990s building, which could be expected due to

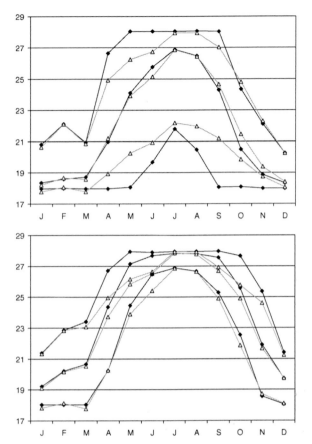

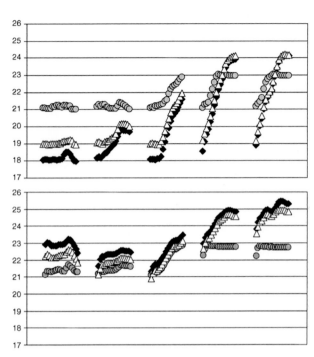

Figure 11 | Indoor resultant temperature (degrees C) during occupied hours for a week in April 2005 for the Adapt (white triangle), the h18c28 (black diamond) and the h21c23 (grey circle) control options. The top graph is for the typical 1990s construction and the bottom graph is for the advanced construction

Figure 10 | Monthly mean, maximum and minimum indoor resultant temperatures (degrees C) for the Adapt (white triangles on a grey line) and h18c28 (black diamond on a black line) control options for the 2005 climate. The top graph is for the typical 1990s construction and the bottom graph is for the advanced construction

does not provide particularly effective solar protection in this April week due to the sun angles. Optimizing shading or using solar control glazing or increasing mass could further reduce the temperature range for the advanced building if required.

DISCUSSION

The human species is inherently resilient and adaptable. However, adaptive comfort standards, although well established, are currently cautiously interpreted and viewed as only being applicable in occupant-controlled naturally ventilated buildings during periods when they are in free-running mode (no heating or cooling). Roaf *et al.* (2010) explore the history behind the current situation and propose much more widespread application of the adaptive comfort standards as a mechanism for significant reduction in unnecessary energy use. The proposal is that people can and do adapt themselves and their immediate surroundings in order to be comfortable across a range of indoor conditions. This approach is in contrast to the approach provided for guidance by commercial building service engineering organizations, which generally advocate much tighter temperature tolerances or fixed setpoints that require system-intensive solutions. The expertise

the higher insulation levels and the reduced infiltration rates of the advanced building construction.

There are significant periods of the year when the h18c28 controls result in conditions that are outside of the adaptive comfort range (Tcomf ± 3°C) and would be predicted to result in some discomfort (cool in spring, summer and autumn in the typical 1990s building and warm in the shoulder months for both buildings). These warm discomfort periods could potentially be reduced or eliminated where opportunities for free cooling through enhanced ventilation exist as described in the previous section; however, the cool periods would require occupants to adapt beyond ± 3°C of the comfort temperature (Tcomf). The daily range in temperatures is much higher for the typical 1990s building than for the advanced building. If there is a possibility to increase free cooling in the buildings through ventilation, then some of the variation could be controlled by the occupants. For the advanced building, the simple shade used of building services engineers typically covers the design and control of mechanical systems within the building, for which they are paid, but not the design of the basic form and fabric and natural lighting and ventilation systems within the building. These are under the control of the architect, who is increasingly de-skilled in such matters and who often does not bear the contractual responsibility for performance in building projects. This paradox is in reality a large pitfall in the production of low energy buildings.

Before the middle of the 20th century, many buildings were constructed with high thermal mass, deep set windows and optimized natural ventilation schemes, which resulted in a stable internal environment. The trend since then has been away from these methods, in part driven by higher internal gains from equipment but also driven by increasing reliance on automated systems. The typical 1990s building in this study gives an example of a building that does not, by itself, provide a stable internal environment, while the advanced building results in a more stable environment but is prone to overheating or a high cooling load unless it is operated to take advantage of free cooling.

The study carried out in this work is a parametric analysis aimed at clearly demonstrating the effects of each of the investigated factors. For building design, the authors advocate a more detailed probabilistic approach for realizing a building that is robust to future variations, for example, patterns of use and local climates, etc. This work focuses on the energy required to be delivered to the indoor environment to maintain the required heating and cooling setpoints. The input energy to the systems (including system efficiencies and losses, pumps and fans, etc.) used to deliver this energy to the space is not addressed here, but current and probable future system performance is discussed in another article (Tuohy, 2009). It is increasingly the case that energy for heating and cooling is delivered by the same system with similar efficiencies.

The underlying assumption here is that the building occupants find their environment acceptable and they feel that they are able to adapt to maintain their personal comfort, for example, more clothes in winter, fewer clothes in summer, etc. A key point may be that the occupants do not feel at risk in such an environment, for they are confident that the building will maintain comfortable conditions even in extremes, either through robust passive design and operation or through available systems.

Both of the proposed methods for incorporating human adaptation in building operation (h18c28 and Adapt) resulted in more than 50% reduction in calculated energy demand for heating and cooling across all combinations of construction type and climate. The h18c28 approach has the advantage of being very simple to communicate but resulted in indoor climates that were at times outside of the Tcomf $\pm$ 3°C range with an associated increased risk of discomfort. The Adapt approach is more complex to communicate and implement but gives better comfort performance. Possible

future implementation of an Adapt scheme could involve a link with weather forecasting services, such as that already in use for pre-charging electric storage heaters, etc.

Further operational factors were also found to have a significant impact on building energy performance. The setback temperatures applied outside of the occupied periods were found to have a large impact for the typical 1990s building with high heat losses but were not so important for the advanced building. Internal gains from equipment gave significantly increased cooling demand in the advanced office but this effect was offset by reduced heating demands for the typical 1990s office. In fact, the increased electricity used for appliances may still give an increase in input energy for all the cases where a high efficiency heat pump is used for heating and cooling.

The more advanced building construction has almost no heating demand but increased cooling demand due to the lower unintended free cooling (heat losses to the environment) of the advanced construction. This effect could be offset and the cooling load of the advanced office reduced to almost zero even in the 2080 climate if effective ventilation strategies could be implemented to achieve day and night free cooling.

Public awareness of the approach being taken and the reasons for doing so may be important to gain acceptance for a change to the proposed new standards. Feedback mechanisms such as public display of the current setpoint temperatures and the buildings' current and cumulative energy use would increase awareness as well as ensure that any problems were detected.

CONCLUSIONS

There is a huge opportunity for reducing energy consumption in buildings. This study suggests that for a typical office, a combination of strategies could achieve close to zero energy demand for heating and cooling for the 2005 and predicted 2080 London climates.

The combination of measures recommended as the basis of future standards is:

- Design or retrofit buildings passively to provide intrinsically robust internal environments with low heating and cooling energy demands.
- Alter building contracts to put the responsibility for building performance squarely in the hands of both the architect and the services engineer.
- Provide opportunities for adaptation by building occupants through the building design and operation regime including dress codes, etc.
- Apply adaptive standards to heating and cooling system controls.
- Minimize setback temperatures outside of occupied periods.
- Minimize internal gains.
- Maximize opportunities for free cooling.

- Maximize heating, cooling and ventilation system efficiencies or eliminate the requirement for them.

- Publicize the approach being taken to reduce operational energy use and provide performance feedback mechanisms.

References

ASHRAE/ANSI Standard 55, 2004, *Thermal Environment Conditions for Human Occupancy*, Atlanta, GA, American Society of Heating Refrigeration and Air-conditioning Engineers.

BRE, 2008, SAP: *The UK Government Standard Assessment Procedure*, Building Research Establishment Publication. Available at: http://projects.bre.co.uk/sap2005/ [accessed 27 December 2009].

CEN, 2007, *Standard EN15251: Indoor Environmental Input Parameters for Design and Assessment of Energy Performance of Buildings – Addressing Indoor Air Quality, Thermal Environment, Lighting and Acoustics*, Brussels, Comité Européen de Normalisation.

CIBSE, 2005, *AM10: Natural Ventilation in Non-domestic Buildings*, London, Chartered Institution of Building Services Engineers.

CIBSE, 2006, *Environmental Design Guide A*, 7th edition, London, Chartered Institution of Building Services Engineers.

CIBSE, 2009, *TM48: The Use of Climate Change Scenarios for Building Simulation: the CIBSE Future Weather Years*, London, Chartered Institution of Building Services Engineers.

Clarke, J., 2001, *Energy Simulation in Building Design*, 2nd edition, Oxford, Butterworth-Heinemann.

Crawley, D., 2007, 'Creating weather files for climate change and urbanisation impacts analysis', *Proceedings of the Building Simulation Conference, 2007*.

Humphreys, M., 1976, 'Field studies of thermal comfort compared and applied: Building Services Engineer', *Journal of the Institution of Heating and Ventilating Engineers* 44, 176–180.

Kalz, D.E., Pfafferott, J., Herkel, S. and Wagner, A., 2009, 'Building signatures correlating thermal comfort and low-energy cooling: in-use performance', *Building Research Information* 37, 413–432.

Plocker, W. and Wijsman, A., 2009, 'Productivity and sick leave integrated into building simulation', *Proceedings of the IBPSA Conference, Glasgow*.

Roaf, S., Nicol, F., Humphreys, M., Tuohy, P. and Boerstra, A., 2010, '20th century standards for thermal comfort: Promoting high energy buildings', *Architectural Science Review* 53, 65–77.

Tuohy, P., 2009, 'Regulations and robust low carbon buildings', *Building Research Information* 37, 433–455.

Wikipedia, 2009, Available at: http://en.wikipedia.org/wiki/Cool_Biz_campaign

Automate and motivate: behaviour-reliant building technology solutions for reducing greenhouse gas emissions

J. K. Ward, J. Wall* and S. D. White
CSIRO Energy Technology, PO Box 330, Newcastle, NSW 2300, Australia

An adequate response to climate change requires that commercial buildings achieve substantial reductions in greenhouse gas emissions. To realize maximum reductions, the adoption of bioclimatic architectural principles and incorporation of renewable energy technologies will be imperative. As these couple building conditions to the local climate, we anticipate a shift away from fixed indoor comfort conditions towards adaptive comfort control. Trials are currently being conducted in Australian commercial office buildings to demonstrate the effectiveness of advanced heating, ventilation and air conditioning (HVAC) control. These include behaviour-reliant technologies to actively manage occupant expectations, influence comfort perception and promote thermal acceptability. This article describes the approach taken and presents some early results. We suggest that deep emission reductions will require the integration of advanced HVAC control with behavioural change centric techniques – that is, to automate and motivate.

Keywords: Behavioural change; energy efficiency; intelligent HVAC control; occupant comfort

INTRODUCTION

Deep carbon emission cuts will be required from the commercial buildings sector to achieve an adequate response to climate change. Indeed, zero emission buildings are being proposed, at least as an aspirational target.

The best pathway to achieving zero emission commercial buildings is uncertain. On the one hand, a traditional engineering approach would examine all the sources of consumption and find the most energy-efficient appliances, before then using renewable energy solutions to mitigate the 'unavoidable' remaining energy consumption. This approach tries to avoid interfering with the building design and building occupants and maintains the current predominant paradigm regarding acceptable indoor conditions.

On the other hand, the second 'bioclimatic' architecture approach looks to create an occupied space that is more in tune with the local environment. Architecture reflects, incorporates and internalizes the outdoor environment. Day-lighting and natural ventilation are introduced where feasible, and indoor conditions are more responsive to adaptive comfort needs.

Optimum solutions are likely to comprise a seamless combination of both approaches. An initial scan of the breakdown of greenhouse gas emissions in the Australian commercial building sector (Figure 1) suggests that lighting and heating, ventilation and air conditioning (HVAC) services (heating, ventilation and cooling services) are the primary source of greenhouse gas emissions. Fortunately, emissions from these activities can be minimized or, in some cases, eliminated by a combination of improved engineering and bioclimatic architecture.

Office equipment and food refrigeration are responsible for significant emissions, but are less amenable to deep cuts in greenhouse gas emissions. Presumably, renewable energy solutions will be required to offset the emissions from these activities to thereby achieve a zero emission building. However, the introduction of renewable energy technologies to buildings, creates an intermittent supply of energy, which must somehow be integrated with the variable demand for energy in the building. Balancing supply and demand in these circumstances is not obvious.

Underpinning the work in this article is the expectation that the use of both (i) bioclimatic architecture and (ii) renewable energy technologies forms part of the likely pathway to future zero emission commercial buildings. It is further the contention of this article that such buildings must necessarily incorporate more sophisticated interaction with the behaviour (and perceptions) of the occupant. In particular:

*Corresponding author: *Email:* Josh.Wall@csiro.au

doi:10.3763/asre.2009.0105 ©2010 Earthscan ISSN: 0003-8628 (print), 1758-9622 (online) www.earthscan.co.uk/journals/asre

earthscan

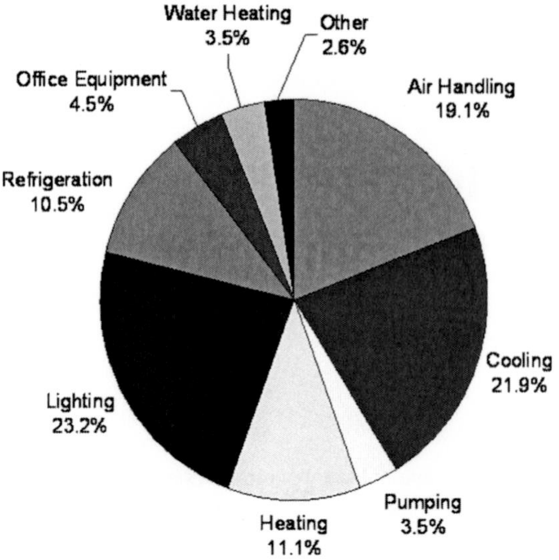

Figure 1 | End-use shares of electricity consumption in Australian commercial buildings
Source: Wilkenfeld and Associates (2002)

- Emissions saving HVAC and day-lighting opportunities, stemming from more bioclimatic architecture, will lead to greater variability in conditions in the occupied space and therefore require a greater sensitivity to individual comfort perceptions.
- Emissions saving renewable energy technologies will not always be able to supply the full needs of the building with certainty. Rather than pay for two sets of energy supply infrastructure (renewable supply and grid supply), bioclimatic variability in comfort conditions provides an opportunity to avoid the need for excessive backup building energy supply infrastructure.

The following sections introduce some novel building-integrated renewable energy and comfort management technological solutions that illustrate possible pathways to zero emission buildings. These technologies have particular focus on (i) HVAC solutions and (ii) the integration of optimal building control with some form of behavioural change to achieve significant gains in building energy efficiency and greenhouse gas savings.

THE COMFORT OPPORTUNITY

Current comfort standards, such as ISO 7730 (ISO, 2005), predict conditions of the indoor thermal environment that a majority of occupants find acceptable. In addition to an analytical method based on the predicted mean vote – predicted percentage dissatisfied (PMV-PPD) indices, the ASHRAE Standard 55 (ASHRAE, 2004) introduced an adaptive comfort model for naturally ventilated buildings.

The adaptive comfort model was derived from a global database of 21,000 measurements taken primarily in office buildings from four different continents. The research found that, when occupants have control over operable windows and are accustomed to conditions that are more connected to the natural swings of the outdoor climate, the subjective notion of comfort and preferred temperatures change as a result of availability of control, different thermal experience and resulting shifts in occupant perceptions or expectations. Moreover, environmental psychologists have long known that human reaction to sensory stimulus is modified when a person has control over that stimulus (de Dear and Brager, 1998). A related explanation is that people are more accepting of variations that come from a known source having predictable behaviour (Bordass *et al.*, 1994), which is often the case in a naturally ventilated building.

Previous research has also shown that when occupants have some form of control over their local environment, for example, operable windows (Brager *et al.*, 2004), the subjective notion of comfort and preferred temperatures change, with occupants often accepting wider operating conditions than those mandated by traditional comfort models.

An example of where traditional comfort models have been extended over wider operating conditions (in this case increased air velocity) is defined in Addendum d to ASHRAE Standard 55-2004. Addendum d allows airspeed to be used to efficiently cool people indoors in the temperature range 22.5–26°C (72.5–79°F) as a way of improving comfort (Arens *et al.*, 2009). In this temperature range, the preference for more air movement is greater than it is for less air movement. The standard currently allows modest increases in operative temperature beyond the PMV-PPD limits as a function of airspeed and turbulence intensity.

It is clear from this research that there is potential for indoor conditions to change significantly while maintaining satisfactory comfort conditions. This is good news, because it has the potential to enable bioclimatic architecture and renewable energy sources to operate successfully over large portions of the year without the necessity to override the inherent comfort fluctuations with energy-intensive HVAC systems. Examples are provided in the following sections.

Comfort opportunities applied to autonomous solar air conditioning

Solar photovoltaics (PV) is a well-known renewable energy technology that can be installed on a building with minimal building interaction/interference. The building could be viewed as merely the host surface for mounting the modules.

In contrast to PV, solar air conditioning is a prospective building-integrated renewable energy technology (Henning, 2007) that offers a number of opportunities for positive integration with building HVAC systems and is more attuned to bioclimatic architecture principles.

In this technology, heat collected from the sun is converted into useful cooling with a thermally driven cooling process such as an absorption chiller. In this way, fossil fuel-derived electricity is replaced with renewable solar energy, with resulting greenhouse gas savings.

Whereas a conventional chiller takes advantage of a reliable supply of electricity from the grid, a solar thermal absorption chiller operates on the intermittent supply of energy from the sun. Matching this variable supply of solar energy with the variable demand for cooling in the building becomes a complex integration issue. The temptation for a conservative design engineer is to provide additional conventional mechanical chiller capacity, to act as a backup in case solar heat is not available when required. Unfortunately this duplicates chiller infrastructure, increases costs and increases greenhouse gas emissions.

Alternatively, it is possible to operate an autonomous solar air conditioning system without backup mechanical cooling. This appears logical when considering the strong correlation between the demand for air conditioning and the availability of solar radiation in many commercial building applications.

However, some components of the heat load do not correlate perfectly with diurnal solar radiation intensity. As a result, greater fluctuations in thermal comfort conditions would be expected in an autonomous solar air-conditioned building.

White *et al.* (2009) modelled temperature fluctuations in a typical commercial building with an autonomous solar desiccant air conditioning system. The predicted frequency and magnitude of high-temperature events are illustrated in Figure 2.

This profile of indoor temperature conditions would appear to provide acceptable comfort levels for most of the year. It shows that the autonomous solar air conditioning system successfully moderates conditions in occupied space, during periods of high ambient temperature, without forcing a rigid temperature condition on the occupants. In this way, the predicted temperature fluctuations display some level of correlation with desirable conditions suggested by the adaptive comfort models discussed previously.

Importantly, this indoor temperature profile results from a dynamic 'floating' balance between intermittent solar heat availability and instantaneous cooling demand, without tight control of the core cold-generating equipment. Without the ability to tightly control the supply of cooling, greater emphasis is likely to be required on shifting control closer to the occupants, to satisfy more localized comfort requirements, utilizing a greater variety of comfort tools than simply controlling air temperature. This represents a shift towards bioclimatic building principles.

If comfort can be managed, the cash crop of autonomous solar air conditioning is the potential to (i) achieve large greenhouse gas savings and (ii) balance intermittent solar energy supply and energy demand without the need for dedicated storage technology. This contrasts with most other renewable energy technologies that require significant backup infrastructure.

Comfort opportunities applied to natural and hybrid ventilation systems

When ambient conditions are mild, outside air can be used directly for cooling the internal space. Outside air can be delivered to the occupied space by natural ventilation through the opening of windows. The quantity of outside air can be enhanced through the use of a range of architectural features such as solar chimneys. In some cases, cooling can be further enhanced by the evaporative cooling effect obtained from water features in the indoor space.

Backup conventional mechanical air conditioning, with its associated air-circulation requirements, can be used when ambient conditions become too extreme for natural ventilation. Clearly, there is a significant increase in HVAC energy consumption and greenhouse gas emissions during those times when it is necessary to resort to the backup conventional mechanical air conditioning system.

During periods of natural ventilation, air flow is likely to be less uniformly distributed with resulting increased variability in air temperatures through the occupied space. Furthermore, increasing the upper temperature control setpoint allows natural ventilation to operate for longer, with a concomitant increase in greenhouse gas savings. In both cases, the ability to satisfy localized comfort requirements provides the tool for maximizing savings.

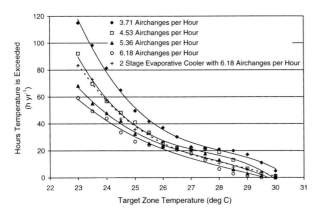

Figure 2 | Influence of (i) target zone temperature and (ii) conditioned air flow rate on the number of hours that the target temperature is exceeded, with a fixed solar panel area of $500m^2$ ($0.167m^2$ panel/m^2 floor area) in Melbourne, Australia

TECHNIQUES FOR MANAGING COMFORT (AUTOMATE AND MOTIVATE)

A wide range of techniques and technologies are available for managing comfort. These can be applied to increase the range of acceptable comfort conditions in the occupied space and thereby achieve the desired increase in greenhouse gas savings, and even increase occupant satisfaction.

Behavioural change centric techniques

Informative techniques that exploit human psychology have the potential to break through traditional comfort barriers by improving occupant satisfaction with their local environment – not only from the direct physical effect of occupant adjustments on indoor climate but also from the empowerment of the occupants. Similarly, informative means, psychology and occupant education can be used to extend the range of temperatures over which occupants find their local environment acceptable.

Considering these approaches, the authors have developed and are trialling an automated virtual comfort sensing and messaging software tool for measuring thermal comfort and inducing behaviour change among building occupants related to promoting thermal acceptability and encouraging energy saving behaviour.

This tool is a remotely triggered pop-up on staff computer screens, which is designed to perform the following functions:

- Inform occupants in real time of key performance indicators including electricity tariff information such as the current electricity cost or status of peak periods; HVAC operating modes such as air conditioning on/off and natural ventilation; and historical building performance related to energy consumption and CO_2 emissions.
- Provides a means of measuring and quantifying occupant comfort and satisfaction levels in real time.

Figure 3 is an example screen shot of the pop-up, which shows how the comfort tool can be used for informing occupants of electricity tariff information and HVAC operating modes.

To assess occupant comfort and satisfaction, the tool enables real-time feedback via a customizable electronic survey, including but not limited to thermal comfort, indoor environment quality (indoor air quality, noise, lighting) and the reporting of faults directly to building operators. This survey can be issued on-demand by a building operator

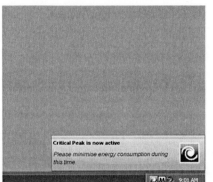

Figure 3 | An example of the comfort tool notifying building occupants about the commencement of an electricity peak period via a colour-coded icon and associated pop-up notification

to any number of occupants, or initiated by the occupants themselves. As surveys can be automatically scheduled and invasively issued in real time by a building operator, higher survey response rates are able to be achieved compared with more traditional web-based or paper surveys, thus improving the sample size and spatio-resolution over which comfort data are obtained.

The benefits of using this invasive approach to measure occupant comfort in real time include the following:

- *Improved comfort and productivity*: Conventional HVAC systems try to maintain a fixed temperature throughout the day regardless of ambient conditions or the comfort levels of individual occupants. Occupant comfort data obtained via the electronic survey can be used to quantify comfort levels for use in identifying problematic zones and to fine-tune HVAC controls accordingly, which can lead to improved occupant comfort and ultimately to an increase in productivity.
- *Support for management and operation decisions*: Analysis of the comfort data can be used to equip building and portfolio managers with quantitative thermal comfort metrics to assist in supporting building management and operation decisions relating to energy efficiency and operational costs.
- *Promoting thermal acceptability*: The potential to break through traditional comfort barriers is facilitated through improved occupant satisfaction with their indoor environment – not only from the direct physical effect of comfort feedback when used to fine-tune building controls but also through occupant empowerment. This has the effect of promoting thermal acceptability over a wider range of temperatures, thus facilitating more energy-efficient operation and increases in building performance ratings.
- *Assessing impact of energy-efficient control strategies*: As the comfort tool provides both real-time feedback and historic reporting on industry standard comfort metrics, advanced building control strategies can be assessed, such as wider operating temperature bands, adaptive comfort setpoints that more closely reflect ambient conditions and demand response initiatives that may give priority to less favourable comfort conditions for a brief reduction in energy demand.
- *Raising energy awareness*: As occupants are informed of key energy performance metrics, electricity price tariffs and recommended actions for saving energy, an increase in energy awareness is achieved. This can assist in provoking thought on energy efficiency measures and encouraging energy saving behaviour.

In trials of the system at the CSIRO Newcastle Energy Centre, the tool provides additional functionality to inform staff when the building is in natural ventilation mode and windows should be opened to enable the flow of outside air into the building.

Automated building control techniques

HVAC control in a typical commercial building is carried out by a building management system – a computer program that measures and adjusts chiller, heater and air handling unit operation to regulate the temperature for building occupants.

As we seek to improve building energy performance, an advanced approach needs to be adopted that optimizes building operation based on a simple high-level goal – namely judicious use of resources to provide appropriate environmental conditions. Resources include, though are not limited to, energy use, financial cost and greenhouse gas emissions. Appropriate environmental conditions differ, depending on the use of a building. In our research, we have focused on occupant thermal comfort as a metric; however, other metrics such as occupant productivity may be appropriate.

Having considered the various types of resource usage and desired environmental conditions, the role of an advanced building control system is to allow an appropriate balance to be found between what are inevitably competing goals. Finding an optimal balance requires an advanced building controller to operate in a fundamentally different way to a conventional system, specifically:

- An awareness of different energy sources and implications of their usage. For example, a building may utilize staged electrical chillers for cooling and natural gas-based cogeneration with supplementary boilers for heating. Different fuel types have different cost and greenhouse gas implications, while the particular plant items that are utilized at different load levels operate with different efficiencies.
- Use of forecasting to move away from a reactionary control philosophy. As an example, many buildings in temperate climates will operate in heating mode in the morning followed by cooling mode later in the day. By taking into account anticipated weather and thermal loads later in the day, heating can be appropriately limited, thereby reducing both heating load and the subsequent cooling load.
- Including the building occupants. Despite advances in research in thermal comfort, the best measure will always be feedback from the building occupants themselves – dress, physiological differences, work pattern and other factors mean that although an aggregate of the preferences of a large group of people may be well represented by comfort models, individuals will always differ. Responding to actual user comfort information at zone level provides the opportunity to drop below the theoretical 5% lower bound on PPD. The challenge here is how to inform users of HVAC operation status and obtain comfort feedback in a non-intrusive manner.

CSIRO RESEARCH EXPERIENCES IN COMFORT CONTROL

The CSIRO research team has carried out a number of building energy management trials to assess the likely benefits achievable through the widespread adoption of advanced building management techniques.

Seasonal thermostat adjustment

The *Smart Thermostats* trial was designed to explore the relationship between zone setpoint temperatures and building energy consumption. The key question was 'what level of energy savings can be achieved through changes to setpoint temperatures, such as seasonal setpoint reset?'

The trial site was chosen to be representative of Australian commercial building stock and involved detailed experimentation on an 11-floor office building in Melbourne. The building had a total floor area of around 10,555m^2 and an HVAC system comprising two chillers (a screw compressor and a centrifugal compressor with capacities 780 and 600kW thermal, respectively), two boilers (each around 700kW thermal) and 11 air handling units – one on each level. The building uses a constant-volume air system, including an economy cycle that uses outside air when appropriate.

To facilitate the trial, additional monitoring equipment was installed, allowing the recording of:

- all building zone temperatures, around six per level and 68 in total
- ambient temperature conditions
- current consumption (amps) of each individual chiller and
- current, voltage and power of the total building HVAC system.

The inclusion of full electrical measurements at the building mechanical services board allowed assessment of the full impact of experimental trials, including the effects on chillers, air handling units, water circulation pumps, cooling towers and all other HVAC equipment.

Through the trial, multiple methods were utilized to determine the relationship between building zone temperatures and energy consumption. One such method was to identify conditions where the HVAC system was operating under reasonably steady-state conditions. The resulting power demand data points are plotted as a function of external (ambient) temperature in Figure 4.

There is a considerable spread in these data due to other factors that also influence power consumption, including solar radiation, operational differences throughout the day and the use of economy mode at low external temperatures. However, the general trends are certainly clear, and we see a 10–20% change in total HVAC power demand for a 1°C change in zone temperature. A similar result was also obtained through comparison of daily data and using a detailed computational model of the building thermal dynamics.

Short-term demand management thermostat adjustment

Further research was conducted on the commercial office building described above to address a second question, 'to what extent can building energy consumption be time

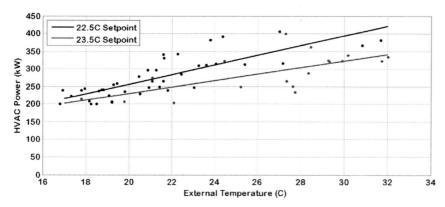

Figure 4 | Influence of external temperature and building setpoint temperature on HVAC power consumption

shifted to facilitate integration with renewable energy sources, electricity network demands and to take advantage of energy pricing structures?'.

These experiments were performed by manipulating zone temperature setpoints, for short periods of time, to determine thermal response characteristics. The building fabric (walls, floors, furniture) was found to result in dominant thermal time constants of around 1.5 hours. These slow time constants mean that the HVAC system can modulate energy usage to smooth out fluctuations from renewable generation without having an impact on thermal comfort. This result was largely as expected, as similar results have been observed in many other buildings. However, looking in more detail at the different zone temperatures in the building yielded some interesting behaviours.

Figure 5 shows one such experiment where an HVAC load reduction was desired for 2.5 hours from 1:45pm to 4:15pm. One standard method of minimizing building user discomfort during load reduction is to initially reduce setpoints slightly to pre-cool the building fabric. In this case however, the HVAC system was already operating at full load, so although reducing setpoints allowed the temperatures

in some zones (such as T_{Zone22}) to reduce, others (such as T_{Zone42}) rose as cool air was diverted elsewhere.

Results such as this provide the impetus that advanced HVAC control must actively balance resource usage and conditions down to zone level – high-level setpoint adjustments are not sufficient.

Multi-objective HVAC control trials

Building on the experience gained through many HVAC monitoring and control projects, we are now trialling an advanced HVAC control system at a Newcastle (Australia) site. In addition to conventional chillers for cooling, this site uses a cogeneration plant to provide heating and has substantial on-site renewable generation.

The control system has been designed to optimize HVAC operation to balance (i) running costs, (ii) greenhouse gas emissions and (iii) occupant thermal comfort. User comfort is assessed via thermal comfort models based on measured temperatures and humidity and nominal values of other factors (airspeed, clothing and activity levels).

Building users are advised of the current HVAC operational state via the comfort tool icon in the system tray of their computer and can submit comfort feedback via a

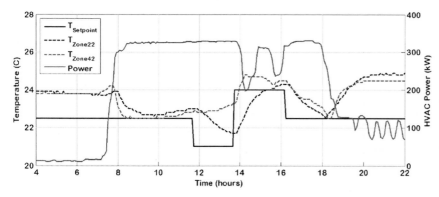

Figure 5 | Changing the temperature setpoint – zone responses and HVAC power

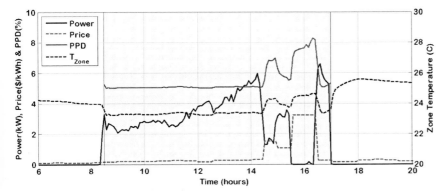

Figure 6 | Performance of the advanced HVAC controller being tested in Newcastle, Australia

(user initiated) survey function. This user feedback is used to calculate an offset map for each HVAC zone – capturing user comfort preference – which is added to the computational thermal comfort model to reflect local user preferences.

A typical data set for one of the zones in this system is shown in Figure 6. This figure shows HVAC power, electricity tariff ($/kWh based on a real-time pricing scenario), estimated thermal comfort of building occupants (PPD) and measured zone temperature. Operational hours of the building are from 8:30am to 5:00pm, as shown by the shaded region of the figure, outside of which thermal comfort does not need to be maintained.

Although there is no explicit startup/shutdown optimization in the control scheme, the advanced controller has determined an appropriate operation schedule that has achieved this through seeking to minimize greenhouse gas emissions and energy costs. For the first part of the working day, operation appears similar to a conventional HVAC system.

However, for the real-time pricing electricity tariff that we have used, there is a substantial price spike during the afternoon, and we see the controller attempting to balance the conflicting goals of minimizing energy costs while maintaining comfort. This initially leads to a deterioration of comfort and ultimately the HVAC system is completely shut down briefly during the (very severe) price peak of over $3/kWh.

To date, results from this advanced HVAC controls trial are yielding energy and greenhouse gas savings of around 30% compared with the existing building controls. This has been achieved without compromising occupant thermal comfort levels.

Multi-objective HVAC control trials with direct occupant comfort input

The integration of behaviour-reliant technologies into HVAC automation introduces a new level of both functionality and complexity. Methods need to be developed for (non-intrusively) assessing and steering behavioural

preferences and incorporating these into building controls. Unlike conventional building controls that are largely fixed at design time, the number and locations of building users are constantly in a state of flux making scalability and adaption to user preferences a necessity.

For the trials currently under way in Newcastle, Australia, the comfort polling application (Figure 3, in the section Behavioural change centric techniques) is installed on personal computers of building users. This provides access to real-time comfort feedback to HVAC control system operation via the user-initiated survey function.

To reduce the perceived intrusiveness of user feedback, the advanced HVAC controller was implemented with a PMV-PPD model, configurable for each zone based on anticipated usage (Figure 7). Consequently, user feedback is only expected (and needed) when users are uncomfortable, likely reflecting a mismatch with the PMV-PPD model.

The challenge for control algorithms is to learn over time how user comfort deviates from the model. This involves appropriate parameterization of user preferences, fine

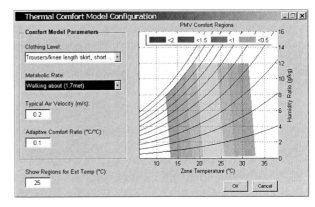

Figure 7 | Zone configuration window for the occupant comfort model of the advanced HVAC controller being tested in Newcastle, Australia

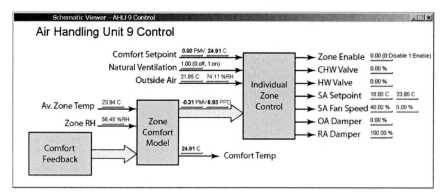

Figure 8 | Engineering schematic screen showing PMV-based zone control on the advanced HVAC controller being tested in Newcastle, Australia

enough resolution of user preferences and techniques to generalize preferences to operating conditions that have not been encountered previously.

Importantly, the control methodology for the advanced HVAC controls trial in Newcastle is based on directly managing occupant thermal comfort via PMV setpoints rather than the traditional temperature-based approach. A screenshot of a zone control engineering panel for this system is shown in Figure 8. The 'measured' PMV for each zone is determined from the theoretical PMV-PPD and adjusted based on user comfort feedback as previously described.

CONCLUSION

Pathways to deep emission reductions in commercial buildings will require increased consideration of both (i) bioclimatic architectural principles and (ii) utilization of renewable

energy technologies. These approaches are expected to result in reduced reliance on fixed indoor comfort conditions and a shift towards adaptive comfort control.

Fundamental to the cost effectiveness of these improvements will be integrating advanced automation of HVAC systems while responding to and managing occupant preferences and behaviour. Trials that demonstrate the feasibility of a range of different approaches are currently under way. These approaches are discussed in this article and some early results are presented.

It is our thesis that substantial building sector energy and emission reductions are available through advanced HVAC controls, that low emission HVAC technologies will need advanced control to be cost effective, and that both will only reach their full potential when coupled to behavioural techniques to manage the expectations and perceptions of building users.

References

ANSI/ASHRAE Standard 55, 2004, *Thermal Environmental Conditions for Human Occupancy*, Atlanta, GA, American Society of Heating, Refrigerating and Air-Conditioning Engineers.

Arens, E., Turner, S., Zhang, H. and Paliaga, G., 2009, 'Moving air for comfort', *ASHRAE Journal*, 51(5), 18–29.

Bordass, B., Leaman, A. and St. Willis, 1994, 'Control strategies for building services: the role of the user', *Proceedings of the BRE/CIB Conference on Buildings and the Environment, UK*, 16–20 May.

Brager, G.S., Paliaga, G. and de Dear, R., 2004, *Final Report: ASHRAE RP-1161*, UC Berkeley, Center for Environmental Design Research.

de Dear, R. and Brager, G. 1998, 'Developing an adaptive model of thermal comfort and preference', *ASHRAE Transactions* 104(1a), 145–167.

Henning, H.-M. (ed), 2007, *Solar Assisted Air-Conditioning in Buildings; A Handbook for Planners*, New York, NY, Springer-Verlag Wien.

ISO, 2005, 7730:2005, *Ergonomics of the Thermal Environment – Analytical Determination and Interpretation of*

Thermal Comfort Using Calculation of the PMV and PPD Indices and Local Thermal Comfort Criteria, Geneva, International Organization for Standardization.

White, S.D., Kohlenbach, P. and Bongs, C., 2009, 'Indoor temperature variations resulting from solar desiccant cooling in a building without thermal backup', *International Journal of Refrigeration* 32, 695–704.

Wilkenfeld and Associates, 2002, *Australia's National Greenhouse Gas Inventory, End-Use Allocation of Emissions*, Canberra, Australian Greenhouse Office.

ARCHITECTURAL
SCIENCE
REVIEW

Hybrid buildings: a pathway to carbon neutral housing

Peter W. Newton* and Selwyn N. Tucker
Swinburne University of Technology, Hawthorn 3122, Victoria, Australia

In the residential sector, there is growing interest in the concept of carbon neutral and net zero energy housing within the context of emerging climate change mitigation and energy security strategies. A hybrid building represents a new class of dwelling capable of achieving net zero energy, carbon neutral or zero carbon status. This article reports on the carbon footprints of alternative configurations of a hybrid building, where variations in performance are explored across different types of residential structure (detached, medium density, high-rise), different energy ratings of the shell, number and mix of domestic appliances in use, and type of distributed or local energy generation technology employed. Hybrid building pathways to zero carbon housing are identified, delivering average savings of approximately 11 tonnes CO_2-e per year per dwelling compared with new detached project homes designed to current 5-star energy standards.

Keywords: Carbon neutrality; distributed energy generation; energy efficiency; greenhouse gas emissions; housing; sustainable cities; zero carbon

INTRODUCTION

Mitigating climate change that involves temperature increases of more than 2°C requires more than halving greenhouse gas emissions by the middle of this century – a significant challenge to governments, industry and the community, given the forecast growth in energy demand over that period.

All sectors of the economy and society must contribute to this challenge, including the housing sector, given that it is responsible for approximately 10% of Australia's total greenhouse gas emissions.

Decarbonizing the housing sector needs to become a key goal within a national policy to reduce carbon emissions, and hybrid buildings provide a technical pathway towards achieving that objective.

Hybrid buildings are defined here as residential buildings that have the capacity to supply, in total, the annual operating energy requirements of their occupants by providing locally generated (low or zero emission) energy to the grid at times of generating energy, which is surplus to its occupants' immediate demands and receiving energy back from the grid if the dwelling is unable to generate sufficient energy for autonomous operation. Operating energy includes energy for heating, cooling, lighting and domestic appliances (built-in and plug-in). Local energy is supplied by a number of distributed generation technologies, both low emission and zero emission. Local energy generation technologies examined include those that can operate autonomously for

a single residential property (e.g. photovoltaics) or can supply energy to individual dwellings from a generation unit that has the capacity to serve a precinct.

The built environment sector has been identified as the most prospective for significant reductions in energy use (McKinsey & Company, 2008) and clearly there are multiple routes to effect this reduction. Energy efficiency and technology substitution for energy generation are principal among these. The Energy Efficiency and Greenhouse Working Group (2003) in Australia estimated that energy consumption improvements of 15–35% could be achieved under the conservative assumptions that only existing technology was used and that the change would pay for itself within 4 years. Using more optimistic assumptions of new technology application and longer payback periods, energy reductions exceeding 70% were shown to be viable. Energy efficiency of itself, however, will not deliver a carbon neutral or zero carbon future for the housing sector.

There is uncertainty about the role that building- and household-oriented energy efficiency initiatives and new low emission and renewables-based distributed energy generation industries can play in achieving Australia's greenhouse emission targets within the Carbon Pollution Reduction Scheme (CPRS), which currently excludes a role for the housing sector. The CPRS potentially places Australia at odds with other countries such as the United Kingdom (Department of Communities and Local Government, 2006) that are actively pursuing policies and

*Corresponding author: *Email:* pnewton@swin.edu.au

ARCHITECTURAL SCIENCE REVIEW 53 | 2010 | 95–106
doi:10.3763/asre.2009.0052 ©2010 Earthscan ISSN: 0003-8628 (print), 1758-9622 (online) www.earthscan.co.uk/journals/asre

programmes to deliver carbon neutral built environments, and it suggests that the voluntary greenhouse gas savings from housing 'will simply subsidize big industrial polluters' (Millar, 2009, p1). This leaves a gap that needs to be closed in a transition to carbon neutral and zero carbon housing.

The study described in this article explores the extent to which hybrid buildings can contribute to decarbonizing the built environment, as measured by the following key potential outcomes:

- *Net zero energy building*: Supplies as much energy to the grid over the course of a year as it uses, without any reference to carbon emissions. This class of building does not preclude use of low emission, local energy generation technologies (also termed grid neutral building (Department of General Services, 2008)).
- *Carbon neutral building*: Generates sufficient surplus CO_2-e free energy over the course of a year that balances any purchase of grid energy (primarily fossil fuel based). This recognizes that a single dwelling/household may be unable or unwilling to generate sufficient CO_2-e free energy to be classed as zero carbon.
- *Zero carbon building*: Uses carbon free energy over the entire year, sufficient in quantity to supply all the household energy needs (both dwelling operations and appliances to match any lifestyle).

Connection to the grid in all three cases is primarily in order to supply energy that is surplus to household needs, and for periods of demand when local energy systems may be inoperable (due to diurnal or wind impacts or mechanical breakdown of the distributed generation system). Connection to the grid also provides the opportunity for local energy generation to aid in reducing the growing problem of mid-afternoon summer peak demand for air-conditioning.

To date, the most significant advance towards a reduction of energy use in Australian housing has been the introduction, in 2003, of the National Home Energy Rating Scheme (NatHERS). It specifies for each of Australia's climate zones the band of performance in operating energy for space heating and cooling required to achieve a specified star rating (see Figure 1). The minimum star rating assigned in 2003 was 5 stars. On 1 May 2009, the Council of Australian Governments agreed to move to a 6-star rating beginning 1 May 2011, notwithstanding findings established and accepted for some time (Horne *et al.*, 2005) that Australia's 5-star standard was of the order of 2–2.5 stars below comparable average international levels of performance of the residential building shell.

The focus for this article is on energy and carbon-based analyses of alternative configurations of a hybrid building, where variations in performance are explored across different types of residential structure (detached, medium density, high-rise) and floor area, different energy ratings of the shell, the number and mix of domestic appliances in use, and type of distributed generation technology employed. The most prospective intervention points for delivering carbon neutral and zero carbon residential development are identified.

METHOD

Significant innovation is required for a sustainability transformation of the residential sector of our cities. Here we need to be able to draw from a pipeline of innovative (or historically proven but overlooked) technologies, products and processes relating to key infrastructures – water, energy, transport, communications and buildings – that can be substituted as existing applications show signs of failure. Newton (2007) – see also Newton and Bai (2008) – has proposed a three-horizon system of innovation capable of being applied to technology, design and urban development. Figure 2 illustrates the concept in relation to the evolution of effective technical solutions.

Horizon 1 solutions are those where the technology is commercially available and has a demonstrated level of

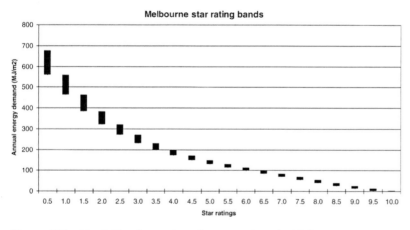

Figure 1 | Residential heating and cooling star ratings for Melbourne
Source: Newton and Tucker (2009)

performance in cost and environmental terms that is superior to products currently in the marketplace and where there should be immediate substitution. The compact fluorescent tube and energy rated appliances are classic examples. In some cases this represents improved product efficiency or product evolution.

Horizon 2 solutions involve more innovation and although examples are in operation they not widespread, e.g. 7 star energy rated housing and water-sensitive urban design. They are associated with better-performing processes or products that have the scope to be applied more broadly or in new combinations, but where there may be a need for some examination of how they would perform in new locations or with modified functional settings.

Horizon 3 solutions are innovations, which for the most part currently reside in research laboratories as prototypes, but whose sustainability impact can be truly transformational. The challenge is to get a real-world application so their performance can be assessed, and if field performance matches the promise of the laboratory, then they become Horizon 2 innovations and should be adapted more widely. The solar hydrogen fuel cell is a good example of a Horizon 3 innovation.

Hybrid building represents an opportunity for integrating innovations from across all three horizons, from the incremental Horizon 1 to the more transformative Horizons 2 and 3. The first steps towards Horizon 2 and 3 futures need to be put in place now, or else there is the prospect of getting 'caught short' and having to pursue suboptimal solutions because of the lack of time available to respond.

The window of opportunity for making a successful sustainability transition in the 21st century in relation to energy is beginning to close rapidly. Examples of energy innovation across the three horizons include:

- *Horizon 1*: Compact fluorescent lighting, 5 star energy rated buildings, gas-boosted solar hot water heating
- *Horizon 2*: LED lighting, 7 star rated buildings, photovoltaic local electricity generation
- *Horizon 3*: Smart lighting (sensors), 10 star rated buildings, solar hydrogen fuel cell.

Energy and carbon calculator

All the calculations in this article were done using an Excel spreadsheet, especially set up to facilitate scenario selection. Each of the categories of dwellings, heating and cooling, hot water, cooking, plug-in appliances and common area services were set up in separate blocks to enable index selection from a series of drop-down options on the scenario worksheet. Results are displayed in tables and charts equivalent to those displayed in Table 1 and Figure 9.

Dependencies such as heating and cooling for different dwelling types and sizes were linked to automatically adjust demand, and similar links provided adjustment to demands for energy and resulting CO_2-e emissions when technologies such as ground source heat pumps (GSHP) and gas combined cooling, heating and power (CCHP) provided energy for multiple uses such as heating and hot water as well as electricity generation.

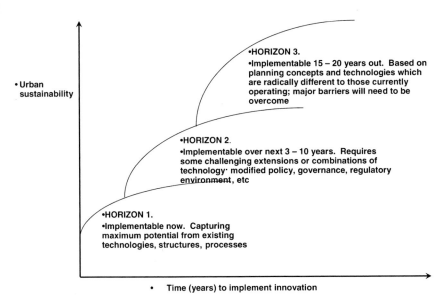

Figure 2 | Three horizons of technical innovation
Source: Newton (2007)

Table 1 | Scenarios for assessing transition to zero carbon dwellings

Attribute	Scenario 1	Scenario 2	Scenario 3	Scenario 4	Scenario 5
Dwelling type	Detached single storey	Detached single storey	Detached single storey	Detached single storey	Detached single storey
Star rating	2.5 star	5 star	2.5 star	5 star	7 star
Space heating and cooling	Electric heating and cooling	Gas ducted and electric evaporative	Gas ducted and electric evaporative	Gas ducted and electric evaporative replaced by GSHP	Electric reverse cycle replaced by GSHP
Hot water	Electric	Gas – storage	Solar thermal – gas boost	Solar thermal – gas boost replaced by GSHP	Solar thermal – gas boost replaced by GSHP
Cooking	Electric cooktop, electric oven, microwave	Gas cooktop, electric oven, microwave	Gas cooktop, gas oven, microwave	Gas cooktop, gas oven, microwave	All microwave
Lighting	All halogen	Average mix	All compact fluorescent	All compact fluorescent	All compact fluorescent
Appliances	Average performance affluenza	'Best of breed' basic	'Best of breed' basic	'Best of breed' basic	'Best of breed' basic
Local generation 1	None	None	Solar – photovoltaic 4500W	Ground source heat pump – 14kW thermal	Ground source heat pump – 14kW thermal
Local generation 2	None	None	None	Solar – photovoltaic 1500W	Solar – photovoltaic 3000W
Local generation 3	None	None	None	Wind turbine	None
Energy used by consumption (MJ/year)	117,894	84,866	151,117	83,262	37,177
(MJ/m²/year)	683	492	876	483	216

Energy generated by local energy generation (MJ/year)	0	33,726	80,954	40,515
(MJ/m^2/year)	0	196	469	235
Energy supplied by grid (MJ/year)	117,894	117,391	2307	−3338
(MJ/m^2/year)	683	680	14	−19
CO$_2$-e emitted by consumption (kg/year)	47,289	12,096	8291	7584
(kg/m^2/year)	274	70	48	44
CO$_2$-e saved by local generation (kg/year)	0	9181	8519	8923
(kg/m^2/year)	0	53	49	52
CO$_2$-e net emitted by the grid supply (kg/year)	47,289	2915	−227	−1339
(kg/m^2/year)	274	17	−1	−8
Annual equivalent cost ($)	12,771	8363	5994	5551
Net zero energy target	×	×	×	✓
Carbon neutral target	×	×	✓	✓
Zero carbon target	×	×	×	✓

Metrics

A variety of metrics for measuring the consumption of energy and production of greenhouse gas emissions are available but the principal ones used are energy (electricity) in MJ/year (for comparison purposes rather than kWh/year), energy (gas) in MJ/year, electricity generation emissions in kg CO_2-e/year and gas emissions in kg CO_2-e/year. Total emissions for dwellings are in tonnes CO_2-e/year.

All the energy consumed is as metered at the dwelling, whether electricity or gas. This is termed 'delivered energy'. The conversion factors for the energy used to the greenhouse gases emitted are those provided by the state government for usage of delivered electricity and gas in the State of Victoria (Sustainable Energy Authority Victoria, 2002, p6). Thus, for average Victorian electricity, which is predominantly generated from brown coal, 1MJ of delivered energy consumed for heating and cooling produces 0.4kg CO_2-e, and for Victorian gas, 1MJ of delivered energy consumed for a similar end use produces 0.052kg CO_2-e. For green power, there are zero emissions.

The energy prices used in this study are the 2009 retail prices of a Melbourne energy supplier as regulated by the Victorian state government and published from time to time in the *Victoria Government Gazette*. Rebates and subsidies, including renewable energy certificates, are not included in this study because they are changeable and relatively short-lived. While feed-in tariffs can affect whether to invest in local energy generation, the current flux in this area of policy has meant that feed-in tariffs have been ignored here.

In this study, cost is the sum of the annual equivalent cost (AEC) of the purchase and installation costs plus the annual operating costs including energy and maintenance costs.

Dwelling types and energy ratings

The alternative forms of dwellings investigated are detached single storey, detached two storey, medium density walk-up flat (i.e. middle floor apartment, no lift), and high-rise apartment (i.e. with lift). The alternative performance (heating and cooling) levels of each were 2.5-star performance, representing existing housing stock, 5-star performance, representing current standard, and 7-star performance, indicative of likely future standard. The available sizes and types of dwellings for which heating and cooling assessments could be made (Tony Isaacs Consulting, 2007) were typical of their type currently entering the property market, that is, 230, 302, 109 and 110m^2, respectively, of gross floor area. The net conditioned floor area (NCFA), which is the basis for calculating the energy required for heating and cooling, can be considerably less (e.g. 173m^2 (25% less) and 237m^2 (22% less)) for the detached single and two storey houses, respectively. The gross floor area and NCFA for medium density and high-rise apartments are the same, primarily due to an absence of unconditioned garage space in the dwelling envelope. The unconditioned floor areas include space such as that for garages and verandas. All energy metrics per unit area are per square metre of NCFA.

The approaches used for estimating heating and cooling loads for each of the 3-star ratings for each of the four dwelling types were the same as those used in rating the operating energy performance of residential buildings (CSIRO's Accu-Rate residential energy rating tool; www.nathers.gov.au/about/index.html), which models for all day occupancy. The energy used for heating and cooling was provided by the following range of equipment and energy sources: gas ducted heating, electric heating, electric reverse cycle heating, electric evaporative ducted cooling and electric reverse cycle cooling. The efficiencies were obtained from the Department of the Environment, Water, Heritage and the Arts (2008) report on energy use in the Australian residential sector. Heating and cooling energy demand necessary to provide occupant thermal comfort and solar energy generation potential was based on the climate characteristics of Melbourne (i.e. Australia climate zone 6, mild temperature, at 38°S latitude).

Domestic appliances

The appliances used in this study are those typically found in dwellings and are designed for domestic use:

- *hot water* – gas storage, gas instant, electric storage and solar thermal
- *built-in appliances* – gas cooktop, electric cooktop, electric oven, gas oven, microwave oven, incandescent lighting, halogen lighting, compact fluorescent lighting, LED lighting and common area energy (class 2 buildings)
- *plug-in appliances* – refrigerator, freezer, dishwasher, washing machine, clothes dryer, television, computer, home entertainment systems, set-top box, games, electric kettle, small miscellaneous and other standby equipment.

For analytical purposes, appliances are characterized in two key respects: operating energy performance, where there is a distinction made between 'average' performance (Department of the Environment, Water, Heritage and the Arts, 2008) and 'best of breed', and range of appliances, differentiating between a 'basic' and an 'affluenza' set, where an affluenza set of appliances highlights the accumulation of appliances and high usage by an increasing proportion of Australian households, for example, multiple flat screen televisions, home entertainment systems, refrigerators and lighting, pools and spas (Hamilton and Denniss, 2005).

For built-in appliances, a number of alternative scenarios are derived: cooking, where a number of different combinations of appliances are represented (e.g. all-gas, all-electric, mixture and microwave only), and lighting, where different technologies are featured (e.g. all-incandescent, all-halogen, all-LEDs or common mix as defined by Department of the Environment, Water, Heritage and the Arts (2008)).

Local energy generation

Local (or distributed) energy generation encompasses a suite of zero emission and low emission technologies that aim to reduce reliance on a centralized energy supply, reduce emissions and improve energy use efficiency. It involves relatively small capacity (<30MW) units typically sited close to the point of consumption (Jones, 2008).

In the present study, both zero emission and low emission local energy technologies are examined. The zero emission technologies considered are solar photovoltaic, wind turbine and solar hydrogen fuel cell. The low emission technologies considered are ground source heat pump (heating and cooling), gas fuel cell and gas reciprocating engine CCHP (heating and cooling). The hot water technologies considered are solar gas boosted and solar electric boosted.

Figure 3 shows the annual CO_2-e generated, saved and produced by the local energy generation technologies. The plant sizes have been set by what is typical of the installations for residential applications, with the result that the capacity of the low emission technologies is much higher because they are designed to supply, from an external precinct energy supplier, close to 100% of locally generated electricity demanded by a typical household.

Low emission local energy generation consumes significant amounts of energy to deliver electricity and heating (including hot water heating) with the advantage of their ability to deliver electricity direct from gas and heating and cooling in a distributed system (i.e. close to the end consumer). Solar hot water systems also constitute a class of local generation technologies capable of delivering significant savings in emissions. The zero emission technologies could be configured to supply much more energy per dwelling but such decisions constitute individual household choices influenced by plant size, available space (area and position/access/orientation), costs and rebates.

Payback periods (without consideration of rebates or subsidies) for the various local energy technologies at January 2009 prices are long (20+ years) with only the high capacity precinct installations and solar hot water systems having a payback period of about 10 years or less. The introduction of a carbon price and a reduction in the future capital costs of local energy technologies (including possible subsidies), which could accompany an increase in local demand and supply, would further reduce a payback calculation, but have not been factored into these analyses.

RESULTS AND DISCUSSION

Dwelling type
Four dwelling types representative of those being currently built were selected for analysis. All performed at an annual operating energy level equivalent to a 5-star energy rating (equates to new project home offerings that meet the current operating energy standard for housing), while featuring different floor spaces reflective of what is typically offered to the market and with a mix of building materials.

Operating energy performance of the building shell (heating and cooling) plus appliances was modelled for all four types under grid supplied energy scenarios to compare energy demands. Heating and cooling systems plus appliances are common across detached and medium density dwellings but vary for high-rise apartments, given that, for a majority of such high-rise developments, electricity represents the dominant energy source for space heating and cooling and cooking.

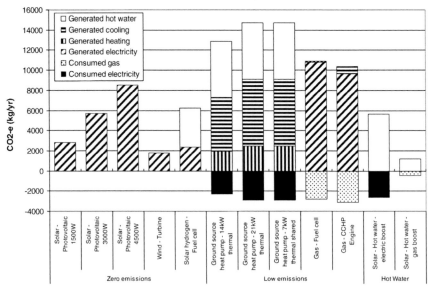

Figure 3 | CO_2-e from energy used to generate local energy and CO_2-e saved by local energy technologies

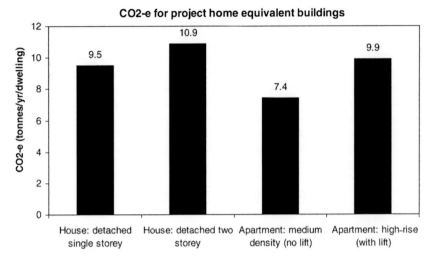

CO2-e for project home equivalent buildings

Figure 4 | Total CO_2-e emissions for project home equivalent dwelling types

The total CO_2-e emissions are shown in Figure 4, with medium density housing having the lowest emissions and the emissions of the high-rise exceeding those of the single storey house and still within 10% of those of the two storey detached house, due to the additional energy demand of the common area services (lift, pool, car park, entry and corridor lighting) and the energy for appliances being primarily sourced from electricity.

With the CO_2-e emissions resulting from the variable energy demands being similar, further analysis of the options for local generation for various scenarios of shell efficiency and appliances was restricted to options involving single storey detached houses, which continue to be the dominant class of housing built in Australia.

For a detached single storey dwelling (in Melbourne), a transition from 2.5 to 5.0 star energy rated housing translates to a 56% reduction in annual energy use for heating and cooling from 65,516MJ/year ($379MJ/m^2$/year) to 28,894MJ/year ($167MJ/m^2$/year). A further transition from a 5.0 to a 7.0 star rated house saves a further 18% energy. The overall shift from a 2.5 star rated house (considered to be representative of stock built prior to the introduction of home energy ratings in 2004) to a 7.0 star rated house delivers a 74% reduction in annual energy used for space heating and cooling from 65,516MJ/year ($379MJ/m^2$/year) to 17,216MJ/year ($99MJ/m^2$/year), an energy saving of 48,300MJ/year ($280MJ/m^2$/year) per detached dwelling.

Domestic appliances
For domestic hot water heating capable of delivering total household demand for a detached single storey family house, annual energy consumption ranges from 20,973MJ/year for gas storage to 6581MJ/year for solar thermal electric boost. The picture changes completely with respect to CO_2-e emissions from hot water heating appliances, where the range extends from 5599kg/year for electric storage to

441kg/year for solar thermal gas boost, a reduction of 92% as clearly shown in Figure 5. A shift from coal-based electricity to gas represents an intermediate energy transition en route to renewables. The solar thermal calculations assume that the boost energy is the same as the grid energy that the solar thermal replaces; for example, the solar thermal component with electric boost reduces emissions compared with an electric storage system.

Comparison of a basic set of household plug-in appliances that have 'average' energy performance vs 'best of breed' performance reveals an average annual energy consumption of 9749MJ/year as opposed to 6998MJ/year, a difference of 28%. In greenhouse gas terms, as shown in Figure 6, the difference is 3910kg CO_2-e vs 2807kg CO_2-e, also a difference of 28% (due to the fact that all appliances are electric). The impact of lifestyle (the affluenza scenarios) on greenhouse emissions is evident, with a 56% increase in CO_2-e for the best-of-breed/affluenza appliance scenario compared with the best-of-breed/basic option.

For cooking, the greenhouse gas implications of different kitchen set-ups range from: 914kg/year (all electric), through 327kg/year (gas appliances plus microwave) to 259kg/year (all microwave), representing a capacity for CO_2-e reductions of the order of 72% (Figure 7). All electricity is assumed to be supplied by the grid.

For lighting, the greenhouse gas implications of different set-ups range from 15.8kg/year for all halogen to 1.7kg/year for all compact fluorescents (compact fluorescents may have been under-specified (Department of the Environment, Water, Heritage and the Arts 2008, p249)), but the indicative potential for CO_2-e reductions is of the order of 89% (Figure 8).

The standby energy for the sets of appliances used in this study varies from 14% of total energy consumption for a 'best of breed' set of appliances to 17% for a set of appliances with average performance.

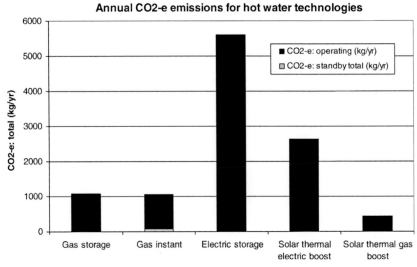

Figure 5 | Annual CO$_2$-e emissions for hot water technologies

Local energy (distributed) generation

The annual average energy demand per dwelling in Melbourne (for space heating and cooling, hot water heating plus domestic appliances) is 75GJ. Local energy generation technology options will provide outcomes generally well short of total energy demand. However, with a reduction in energy demand and a combination of local generation technologies, it is possible to get to net zero energy, carbon neutral and zero carbon solutions. Given the significant number of dwellings across Australia that will be required to reduce their carbon footprint, and with the current glacial rate of change to the proportion of green energy in the national grid (currently less than 5%), this study sheds some light on the path that individual property owners and developers could take towards a low or zero carbon future for their housing. At present, however, most Australian governments, industries and communities lack the information to make informed decisions.

Hybrid buildings

An extensive range of traditional and hybrid building scenarios have been subjected to modelling, whereby various combinations of building shell efficiency, appliance efficiency and local energy generation options have been jointly explored by the energy and carbon calculator. These are extensively discussed in the full report by Newton and Tucker (2009).

A positive finding overall is that significant greenhouse gas reductions can be achieved via all the distributed generation technologies examined. Large gas users such as CCHP,

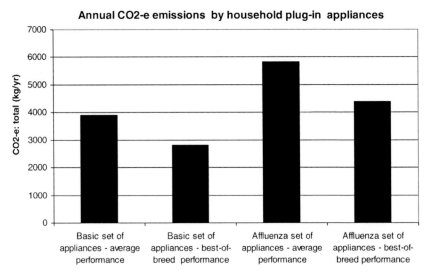

Figure 6 | Annual CO$_2$-e emissions for appliance scenarios

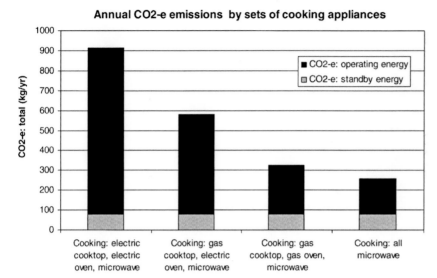

Figure 7 | Annual CO_2-e emissions for cooking scenarios

however, will find it difficult to deliver carbon neutral outcomes and impossible to deliver zero carbon outcomes.

The five scenarios presented here (summarized in Table 1 and Figure 9) represent a wide spectrum of housing outcomes. At one extreme we have the most profligate scenario (from an energy and carbon perspective) whereby the dwelling has a poorly performing building shell constructed before the introduction of any building energy regulation and which is reflected in significant demands on energy for space heating and cooling, a set of domestic appliances that have 'average' energy efficiency and are reflective of an 'affluenza' lifestyle, total reliance on the grid for all its energy – and a carbon footprint approaching 50 tonnes CO_2-e per year. At the other end we have the zero carbon

house, a net contributor of carbon-free renewable energy to the national grid over and above what is required to deliver annual energy requirements to the occupants of that dwelling.

Net zero energy, carbon neutral and zero carbon housing outcomes have been demonstrated as possible via carefully tailored combinations of local energy generation (providing electricity from renewable sources) to suit low energy demand shell and appliances. This transition is difficult if not impossible with 2.5 star rated dwellings, indicating a necessity for upgrading the energy efficiency of the shell as a key step in the process. All transitions from current 5 star project housing come at an additional AEC (see Table 1), but could be expected to be significantly offset once a carbon tax is introduced.

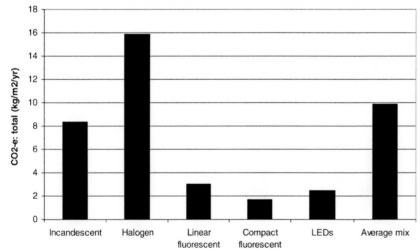

Figure 8 | Annual CO_2-e emissions for lighting technologies

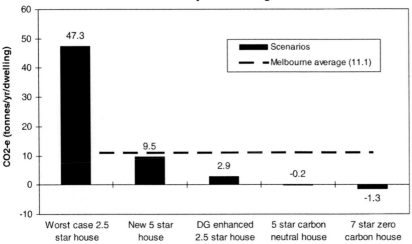

Figure 9 | CO_2-e emissions for scenarios examining transition to zero carbon housing

What has been designated as the base case house – new 5 star detached (see Figure 9), which is representative of new grid connected project homes being marketed at present – generates approximately 9.5 tonnes of CO_2-e annually in order to supply the comfort and amenity expected by Australian households. A transition pathway to zero carbon housing has been demonstrated that is also capable of exporting the excess 'green' electricity the hybrid building generates using distributed generation renewable technologies to the grid (thereby removing a further 1.3 tonnes of CO_2-e annually). The zero carbon house is capable of delivering a net saving of CO_2-e per dwelling of approximately 11 tonnes annually.

As far as CO_2-e emissions and the AECs are concerned, comparison of scenarios 1 and 2 (i.e. worst case vs current project home) reveals a reduction in CO_2-e of 38 tonnes per year and a cost saving of approximately $8000. To make the transition from the 5 star project home, which generates 9.5 tonnes of CO_2-e per year, to a zero carbon house incurs an AEC increase of approximately $600, excluding subsidies, rebates, carbon price impost and feed-in payments.

CONCLUSIONS

Hybrid buildings are currently located at the foot of the innovation-diffusion S-curve. In this article, the concept has been articulated and subjected to a 'virtual' performance assessment. It has been demonstrated that hybrid buildings will enable a transition to zero carbon housing – a necessary response by the housing sector to greenhouse gas mitigation in the 21st century. There are challenges, however.

More than 95% of Australia's housing stock would reflect an (operating) energy rating of 2.5 stars or less. Modelling undertaken in this study suggests that such housing, together with a worst case set of appliances and use, can be responsible for generating levels of CO_2-e exceeding 45 tonnes per detached

dwelling per year. This combination of poorly performing stock plus appliances constitutes the greatest challenge for transition to a carbon neutral or zero carbon housing sector.

A transition of the housing stock built before the 2003 introduction of a national 5 star energy rating system to carbon neutral or zero carbon status will require all of the following interventions:

- an upgrade of the building shell to at least a 5 star (and preferably 7 star) rating
- utilization of 'best of breed' appliances
- application of local energy generation (low emission or zero emission) provided on site or accessed from a local precinct supplier, given the negligible extent to which the national grid is drawing on renewable energy sources.

New (single storey detached 5 star) project homes are typically responsible for 9.5 tonnes of CO_2-e emissions per year. New double storey detached and high-rise apartments have larger carbon footprints (of the order of 10.9 and 9.9 tonnes per year, respectively). Medium density housing represents the best outcome from a greenhouse gas perspective (7.4 tonnes per year) and should become the principal vehicle for the intensification of urban development in Australian cities.

Pathways for achieving zero carbon housing for contemporary 5 star project built homes have been identified. In addition to the 5 star energy-efficient shell, they require:

- solar hot water systems
- 'best of breed' appliances
- local energy generation tailored to household demand.

Transformations of the type envisioned in this article are unlikely to progress, however, without engagement by the key stakeholders involved in the housing energy transitions arena. They include:

- *Distributed energy generation and renewable energy industries*: They offer a range of available technologies, but information shortfalls exist in relation to cost and performance over a scale of applications ranging from building to precinct. As an emerging green industry for the 21st century, distributed generation currently lacks scale economies that can deliver downward pressure on prices and currently there is uncertainty over the attractiveness to households and investors of a community-scale energy industry.
- *Energy regulators*: Key here is their attitude towards building and precinct level local energy generation; agreements on gross vs net feed-in tariffs; and the availability of infrastructure that would enable the emergence of an intelligent green grid.
- *Design professions*: Architects need to be aware of the requirements of distributed generation technologies (effectively a new building element) at an earlier stage of the design process than with conventional energy supply. Urban planners also need to be aware of the added space (area) requirements of renewable energy generation compared with the grid (Newton and Mo, 2006).
- *Property developers*: Principal uncertainties involve their understanding of the benefits and costs of installing specific local energy generation facilities.
- *Energy distributors*: This stakeholder group requires knowledge of local energy generation options that can

assist their decision making in what role distributors may play in community-scale initiatives.

- *Energy generators*: This centralized, fossil fuel-based industry is rapidly making assessments of and potential responses to the impacts that carbon pricing will make, as well as examining the most eco-efficient options for meeting peak demand for energy.
- *Housing industry and its associations*: This group has been historically resistant to any innovation that has some upfront capital cost impost on housing. Issues of lifetime costing and split incentives represent two key policy areas where the industry sector needs to identify pathways to encourage investment in housing innovation.
- *Housing consumers*: All consumers need to become more informed about the costs and benefits of energy efficiency and local energy generation as it applies to existing as well as new housing.
- *Government*: From an energy perspective, governments need to identify the most cost-effective ways to provide incentives for and/or regulate efforts made to reduce the levels of CO_2-e emissions across the built environment. This will involve a re-examination of building codes and planning regulations to the extent that they currently inhibit local energy generation.

To exclude the housing sector from any carbon pollution reduction initiative would represent a mistake of monumental proportions.

References

Department of Communities and Local Government, 2006, *Building a Greener Future: Towards Zero Carbon Development*, London. Available at: www.communities.gov.uk/documents/planningandbuilding/pdf/153125.pdf [accessed 12 June 2009].

Department of General Services, 2008, *Grid Neutral. Electrical Independence for California Schools and Community Colleges*, State of California, Sacramento.

Department of the Environment, Water, Heritage and the Arts, 2008, *Energy Use in the Australian Residential Sector 1986–2020*, Canberra, Department of the Environment, Water, Heritage and the Arts.

Energy Efficiency and Greenhouse Working Group, 2003, *Towards a National Framework for Energy Efficiency: Issues and Challenges*, Discussion paper. Canberra, Energy Efficiency and Greenhouse Working Group. Available at: www.nfee.gov.au/about_nfee.jsp?xcid=64 [accessed 12 July 2006].

Hamilton, C. and Denniss, R., 2005, *Affluenza: When Too Much Is Never Enough*, Sydney, Allen & Unwin.

Horne, R., Hayles, C., Hes, D., Jensen, C., Opray, L., Wakefield, R. and Wasiluk, K., 2005, *International Comparison of Building Energy Performance Standards*, report prepared for Australian Greenhouse Office, Melbourne, RMIT University.

Jones, T., 2008, 'Distributed energy systems', in P.W. Newton (ed), *Transitions: Pathways Towards Sustainable Urban Development in Australia*, Melbourne, CSIRO Publishing and Dordrecht, Springer.

McKinsey & Company, 2008, *An Australian Cost Curve for Greenhouse Gas Abatement*, Sydney, McKinsey & Company.

Millar, R., 2009, 'State emission cuts "futile"', *Age* 23 March, 1.

Newton, P.W., 2007, 'Horizon 3 planning: meshing liveability with sustainability', *Environment and Planning B: Planning and Design* 34, 571–575.

Newton, P.W. and Bai, X., 2008, 'Transitioning to sustainable urban development', in P.W. Newton (ed), *Transitions: Pathways Towards Sustainable Urban Development in Australia*, Melbourne, CSIRO Publishing and Dordrecht, Springer.

Newton, P.W. and Mo, J., 2006, 'Urban energyscapes. Planning for renewables-based cities', *Australian Planner* 43(4), 8–9.

Newton, P.W. and Tucker, S.N., 2009, *Hybrid Buildings: Pathways for Greenhouse Gas Mitigation in the Housing Sector*, Melbourne, Institute for Social Research, Swinburne University of Technology.

Sustainable Energy Authority Victoria, 2002, *Calculating Energy Use and Greenhouse Emissions, Module 3, Energy and Greenhouse Management Toolkit*, Melbourne, State Government of Victoria.

Tony Isaacs Consulting, 2007, *Costs for Achieving 5, 6, 7 and 8 Star Fabric Ratings in New Victorian Houses*, report prepared for Department of Sustainability and Environment, Melbourne.

ARCHITECTURAL
SCIENCE
REVIEW

The role of rainwater tanks in Australia in the twenty first century

Ted Gardner* and Alison Vieritz

Department of Environment and Resource Management, Queensland Government, Meiers Road, Indooroopilly, QLD 4068, Australia

This overview of rainwater tanks in the Australian urban landscape shows that even small tanks (e.g. 5kL) can be very effective in supplying non-potable water to a detached dwelling and reducing mains water use. However this self-sufficiency comes at an energy cost compared with reticulated mains supply. Public health is another core performance criterion, and risk assessment research suggests that zoonotic pathogens occur at concentrations that will adversely impact on public health if rainwater is ingested without disinfection. However epidemiological studies do not support this predictions. The quality of rainwater in Australian cities is likely to meet ADWG (2004) on all chemical criteria unless exposed lead flashing on the roof contaminates the collected rainfall. Changes in state regulation have largely mandated internally plumbed tanks and this has led to a change in the *hydro social contract* where householders are now expected to take on some responsibility for their water supply. The results from social/market research in SEQ is not encouraging that new householders understand this change in their responsibilities. We conclude the overview with a brief economic assessment, and report that small internally plumbed rainwater tanks connected to large roof areas can supply water at a levelised cost ($/kL) competitive with the future mix of mains water supplies.

Keywords: Chemical contaminants; energy; first flush devices; guidelines; levelized cost; microbiology; models; potable substitution; rainwater; sociology

INTRODUCTION

Drought is changing the urban water cycle in the 21st century. South East Queensland (SEQ) has just gone through the worst drought on record (120 years) providing ample evidence that the water infrastructure in SEQ is inadequate. Without significant rainfall runoff, the three major reservoirs that supplied SEQ were predicted to run out of water in late 2009 unless other water supply steps were taken (Gardner and Dennien, 2007).

SEQ was not alone in this water supply deficit. For example, in the mid-1970s, runoff to Perth's surface water reservoirs, Western Australia, was approximately halved compared with the prior 60-year average, in response to a 20% drop in rainfall (Water Corporation of WA, 2009). This behaviour persists to the present (Figure 1). Such data also demonstrate the strong non-linearity between rainfall and runoff in Australian catchments (Chiew, 2006).

Currently, the Murray Darling basin (the food bowl of Australia) is experiencing its worst drought on record due to rainfall deficits in the major reservoir catchment in northern Victoria and the Snowy Mountains. The result is that irrigation allocation has decreased from 12,000GL to less than 2000GL per year. Concurrent with this agricultural drought is a severe reduction in inflows in the mountain eucalypt catchments supplying Melbourne, as well as in the Mt Lofty ranges supplying half of Adelaide's water.

Most of the water authorities have responded to this with large expenditure on climate-independent water sources such as the following: desalination plants (Table 1); pipelines (e.g. Victoria, Queensland (QLD) and New South Wales (NSW)); purified recycled water (QLD); stormwater harvesting; domestic and commercial water conservation through appliance changes such as shower roses, taps and washing machines; new dams (especially QLD); and rainwater tanks (especially QLD and NSW).

This article will focus on the adoption and use of rainwater tanks and cover their hydrology (at three scales: household, cluster and suburb), energy costs, health issues, sociological aspects and economics.

HYDROLOGY OF THE RAINWATER TANK

When compared with dams, rainwater tanks have the following two advantages.

*Corresponding author: *Email:* Ted.Gardner@derm.qld.gov.au

doi:10.3763/asre.2009.0074 ©2010 Earthscan ISSN: 0003-8628 (print), 1758-9622 (online) www.earthscan.co.uk/journals/asre

earthscan

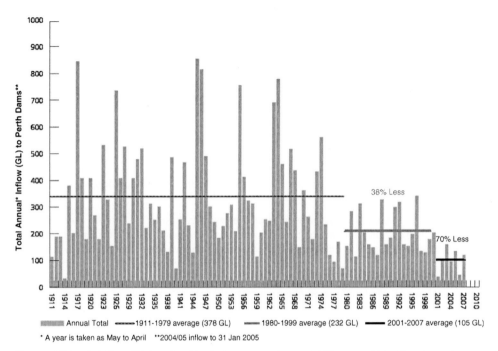

Figure 1 | Yearly inflow (GL/year) to Perth dams over the past 100 years. Note the steep decrease in the middle of the 1970s and another steep decrease in the early 2000s
Source: Water Corporation of WA (2009)

Rainwater tanks are located at the right end of the rainfall gradient. A strong rainfall gradient exists running from east to west along the east coast due to the Great Dividing Range, especially in SEQ. Since most of the population lives within 80km of the coastline, urban rainwater tanks can take advantage of the higher rainfall, whereas many of our large dams are located inland of the Great Dividing Range, where rainfall is substantially less than that on the coast. For example, annual rainfall over the 1890–2008 period averaged 969mm for Brisbane on the coast and 788mm for Esk at the western boundary of Lake Wivenhoe, the largest urban water supply reservoir in SEQ (Figure 2).

Table 1 | Desalination plants planned in Australia and their expected impact on supplying urban water demand

Location	Expected Supply of Desalination Water (GL/year)	% of Water Demand Supplied
SEQ	45	10
Perth	47 + 47*	35
Melbourne	150	35
Sydney	180	30
Adelaide	50 + 50*	50

*Initial plant size has been doubled.

Roofs are better than rural catchments at conveying rainwater to water storages. Rain tank catchments, usually house roofs, are 100% impermeable and as such shed the majority (>90%) of incident rainfall. In comparison, not only do rural catchments show a strong non-linearity between annual rainfall and annual runoff, but also they show a high rainfall threshold before runoff commences. For example, in the case of the Somerset catchment, one of the largest SEQ dam catchments, this threshold is about 600mm/year (Figure 3). In contrast, runoff from roofs occurs after the first millimetre or so of rainfall.

Case study at house scale using large tanks: healthy home

Large tanks have been shown to significantly contribute to household water supply self-sufficiency even in drought years. A sustainable home, 'Healthy Home', was built on the Gold Coast in 1999. Its focus was to be healthy (low out-gassing materials), energy efficient (insulation, ventilation and solar shading devices), largely self-sufficient in energy (solar hot water system (HWS) and grid-connected photovoltaics (PV)) and water (rainwater and greywater) (Gardner *et al.*, 2003). One major water innovation was a 25kL concrete rainwater tank installed in the ground beneath the house; it was built on piers less than 1m high (Figure 4).

The tank was connected to council mains via a trickle top up float valve installed in such a way as to ensure that backflow of rainwater into council mains water was highly

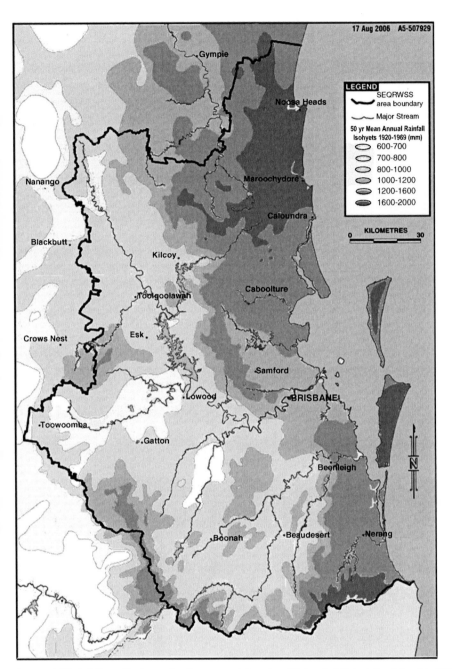

Figure 2 | Rainfall gradient running from coastal region (high rainfall) to inland (low) in SEQ
Source: Queensland Department of Natural Resources and Mines (2006)

unlikely to occur. Because the house was located in a reticulated water supply area, Gold Coast City Council permission was requested to connect the tank to all household taps, as well as the tank to council mains.

The results from 4 years of monitoring (2000–2003) showed that water self-sufficiency averaged 45%, even though 3 of the 4 years were drought years, ranging from 6 to 26 percentile rainfall years, with rainfall well below the long-term average of 1460mm/year. Using simple water balance modelling, the self-sufficiency percentage was expected to increase to 65% in an average rainfall year (1460mm/year) (Gardner *et al.*, 2008).

These simple results were among the first in Australia to clearly demonstrate that the hydrological response to drought is very different in impervious (i.e. house roofs) and pervious (i.e. agricultural and forested catchments) and that reduced

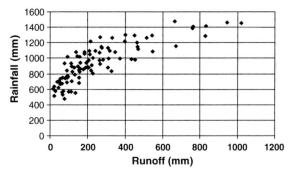

Figure 3 | The modelled relationship between runoff and rainfall for the Stanley River, at Somerset dam, SEQ over the period 1900–1996. *Data from Water Science Modelling Group, DERM, QLD*

yearly rainfall can still provide significant and viable water supply in urban areas.

Reduced energy use was another major objective of the Healthy Home study and the combination of natural ventilation of the house, solar hot water and grid-connected PV resulted in a net energy use of about 50% of that of a typical Gold Coast detached residency of 25kWh/household (hh)/day (Gardner *et al.*, 2006). However, a closer examination of the rainwater and greywater systems, which depended on small electric pumps and UV disinfection units for their successful functioning, identified an average energy use of 4.3kWh/day, compared

with a water and sewage grid value of about 0.6kWh/day (Gardner *et al.*, 2006). Clearly, the aim of water self-sufficiency appears to have been realized at a significant energy and hence greenhouse gas penalty, and this issue will be discussed in more detail later in this article.

Case study at cluster scale using large tanks: Payne Road Development

During the monitoring period of the Healthy Home, rainwater tanks became more popular in urban developments that focused on the urban sustainability market, or were required to gain council planning approval because of stormwater requirements (large tanks are effective stormwater *detention* and *retention* devices), or because of difficulty in connecting to council water supply and sewerage services. The Payne Road Development in Brisbane was one such example where a 22 lot development was approved on the condition that large 20kL rainwater tanks (supplemented indirectly from council mains top up supply) as well as greywater treatment and irrigation, and off peak discharge of sewage into council mains were installed at each house.

Figure 5 shows the hydraulic circuit of Payne Road where individual rainwater tank overflows were routed to two large communal tanks of 75kL each; these tanks store the excess rainwater during wet times and supply water during times of rainfall deficit. The communal tank was connected to council water mains to ensure supply continuity, as well as

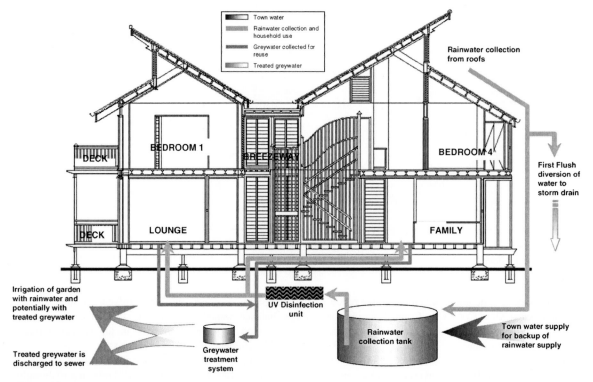

Figure 4 | Schematic of the Healthy Home at the Gold Coast, QLD, showing the rainwater and greywater systems
Source: Gardner *et al.* (2003)

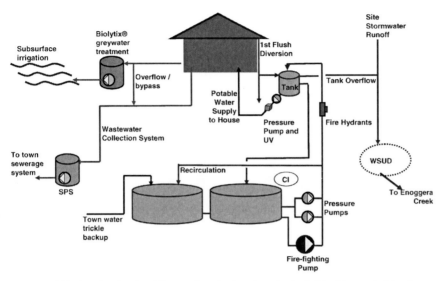

Figure 5 | Hydraulic circuit of Payne Road, showing the individual household rainwater tanks connected to a pair of large (75kL) communal tanks. A local reticulation system supplies both 'top up' to the household tanks, and fire-fighting flows. A greywater system was installed in each home with subsurface irrigation of the treated water
Source: Gardner *et al.* (2006)

to provide fire fighting flows required by state legislation (15L/s from two hydrants with 10m residual head after meeting peak daily flow; Queensland Department of Natural Resources and Water, 2007). These flows were implemented using a diesel pump (28kW) connected to a 100mm ring main, and became operational if the ring main pressure decreased below 200kPa. The ring main is pressurized by a 0.75kW electric pump to supply trickle top up water to the individual tanks on an as-needed basis. Taken overall, this system solved the two major problems of using rainwater tanks for the main supply in urban areas, and was considered to be ground-breakingly innovative at its implementation date (2005).

The water, energy and nutrient cycle of the water and greywater system at Payne Road have been monitored since mid-2006 for six houses. House and allotment package sales were slow because of general market conditions and asking prices; however, all 22 lots have now been sold. Overall, 88% of the water use supplied to all household taps and appliances was sourced by rainwater with the remainder from council mains top up. Of the 88%, 13% was calculated to be supplied by *rainwater* stored in the communal tank (Gardner *et al.*, 2006; Beal *et al.*, 2008).

Similar to the Healthy Home study, these results were obtained during unusually low rainfall years (4 percentile and 14 percentile rainfall), testifying yet again to the water supply reliability of combining large 20kL rainwater tanks connected to large roof areas (200–300m^2), and end uses with regular daily demands such as toilets and washing machines.

Case study at suburban scale using small tanks
Small tanks have been shown to significantly reduce household mains water use.

In January 2007, the Queensland Development Code (QDC) (Queensland Department of Infrastructure and Planning, 2008) introduced three mandatory policies (MP), which involved alternative urban water sources and sustainable building proformance criteria (QDC MP4.2). QDC MP4.2 applied to detached and attached dwellings and required the house owner to install a 5kL tank connected to an at least 100m^2 roof area to supply water to the toilet, cold water laundry and an external tap with the objective of reducing potable water demand by 70kL/hh/year (42kL/hh/year for attached dwellings). The regulation allows recycled water, either treated sewage effluent or treated stormwater, to be used as a substitute for rainwater but this option would normally require installation of a third pipe at the developer's expense. Consequently, most new homes, constructed post January 2007, have rainwater tanks installed by the builder with the additional cost (about $4000) passed onto the home buyer. Given there are about 20,000 new homes built in SEQ each year, the overall cost to society is about $80m/year. The question arises as to the actual water savings achieved, as this assumption is built into the South East Queensland Water Strategy (Queensland Water Commission, 2008) and supplies almost 10% of the predicted water demand in 2056 (about 1,000,000ML/year).

To explore the likelihood of these savings, a large ($n >$ 20,000) 'paired' statistical study has been initiated in SEQ where council-billed water use data are being compared in detached dwellings built before and after QDC MP4.2 became operational. Figure 6 shows some preliminary results from Beal *et al.* (2009) for Caboolture, with severe water restrictions, where no statistically significant savings

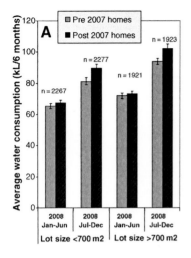
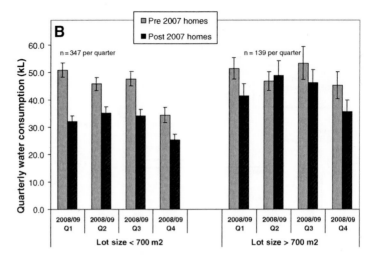

Figure 6 | Comparisons of total household water use for detached dwellings constructed pre-2007 (tank-free) and post-2007 (tank-mandated) in the Caboolture Shire (Figure 6a) and Gold Coast City Council areas (Figure 6b). The data are also separated into allotment size less than and greater than 700 m^2
Source: Beal *et al.* (2009)

were identified, and the Gold Coast, where water restrictions eased in mid-2008 and where savings ranged from 25 to 52kL/hh/year, presumably reflecting the ability of non-tank owners (i.e. in pre-2007 homes) to water their gardens in the last two billing quarters. A much more detailed data analysis is underway using the Australian Bureau of Statistic's demographic and other biophysical data such as lot size, people per dwelling, irrigation demand and pre-2007 house owners installing tanks under the Queensland Government Water Wise rebate scheme (Spiller, 2008) to help ensure that 'like is being compared with like'.

NSW implemented a similar scheme (BASIX) in 2004 whereby new residential dwellings were required to use 40% less mains water and produce 40% fewer greenhouse gas emissions (www.basix.nsw.gov.au/information/index. jsp). Approved potable water saving measures that were used included rainwater tanks, water-efficient native gardens, 3-Star household water fixtures and appliances and recycled water for non-potable uses such as a third pipe system.

The method used to validate the water savings was compared with the NSW water use benchmark of 90kL/pp/year, which equates to 248L/pp/day. This figure is then compared with the actual water use of the BASIX compliant dwellings (NSW Department of Planning, 2008). Over the 3 years from June 2005 to June 2008, 42,600 single dwelling detached homes were granted development approval in NSW (NSW Department of Planning, 2009) and a subset (834) were examined in detail by combining their water billing record with a telephone survey of occupancy per house, etc. for the 'water year' 2007/2008 (NSW Department of Planning, 2008). Overall, the actual water use was 192kL/hh/year compared with a BASIX benchmark (i.e. nil intervention) of 324kL/hh/year (based on an occupancy for the houses of

3.6 persons per house), thereby returning an average mains water saving of 41%. In fact, 61% of the surveyed population actually achieved savings of greater than 40% (Sullivan and Wilson, 2009).

Of course, it cannot be claimed that *all* of this water saving is due to rainwater tanks, although 96% of homes had installed tanks (with a medium size of 5kL) connected to an average 230m^2 of roof, and then plumbed to the garden (98% of homes), toilet (91% of homes) or laundry (82%) (NSW Department of Planning, 2009).

Extending our knowledge of tank water supply impacts using models

Using empirical data to measure potable water savings by rainwater tanks will always be limited by the specificity of tank size/connected roof area/end uses in the sample, as well as the rainfall in the years of observation. Consequently, water balance models are very attractive tools to explore rainwater tank hydrology in any area of Australia. One comprehensive example is the work of Coombes and Kuczera (2003a), who used a model called PURRS (Probabilistic Urban Rainwater and Wastewater Reuse Simulator) operating at a small time step of 6 minutes to explore the effect of tank size (kL), connected roof area (m^2) and people per dwelling on rainwater supplied in the capital cities of Adelaide, Melbourne, Sydney and Brisbane.

The results for a combination of 5kL, 150m^2 roof and three residents per dwelling are given in Table 2 assuming that the end uses include the toilet, laundry, hot water system and outdoor uses. Predicted supply ranges from 42kL/hh/year in Adelaide to 90kL/hh/year in Brisbane, with the order largely following the variation in annual rainfall between cities (small in Adelaide and large in Brisbane).

Table 2 | PURRS analysis of rainwater yield from 5kL tanks for four Australian capital cities

Location	Rainfall (mm/year)	Internal Use Assumed (kL/year)	External Use Assumed (kL/year)	Rainwater Tank Yield (kL/year)
Adelaide	520	173	146	42
Melbourne	665	157	81	52
Sydney (North Ryde)	960	243	95	71
Brisbane	1110	126	126	90

Note: The analysis assumed that the tanks were connected to $150m^2$ roof for dwellings with three residents using the rainwater for the toilet, laundry, hot water system and external end uses.
Source: Coombes and Kuczera (2003a)

However, all models are sensitive to the assumptions used and in this case the assumption of external use creates a large, albeit seasonal demand, which maximizes the rainfall catch by a tank because of the increased frequency of pre-rainfall 'air void' in the tank. This is of course a very desirable outcome in terms of both storing more rain and reducing the stormwater runoff from impervious urban areas, which is required under water-sensitive urban design performance criteria (Queensland Department of Infrastructure, 2007).

However, external water use is very responsive to the behaviour of residents who generally overirrigate their gardens and under-water their lawns and schedule the watering on the basis of their perception of the weather (number of rainfall days and temperature) rather than on a rational soil/water balance model customized to a given soil texture (Devi, 2009). Consequently, rainwater tank models are least accurate when they use soil water balance models to predict domestic irrigation demand. However, internal water use is a different matter and detailed end use measurements (e.g. Loh and Coghlan, 2003; Willis *et al.*, 2009) have provided data that can be used with confidence in rainwater tank models.

One example of an application is shown in Figure 7, where the effect of end use and connected roof area is explored for a 5kL tank in the Pimpama-Coomera area, located between Brisbane and the Gold Coast with an average rainfall of 1320mm/year. The results were calculated using a daily time step model called Rainwater TANK (Vieritz *et al.*, 2007), which allows the user to define the end use combinations.

Figure 7 clearly demonstrates the catch (i.e. yield) value of increasing the internal demand, with $100m^2$ of the roof predicted to supply between 38kL/hh/year, used for the toilet alone, and 70kL/hh/year if the tank is connected to the toilets, laundry, hot water and bathroom shower and basin. Moreover, if the connected roof area increases to $200m^2$, readily achieved in BASIX-compliant homes for example, the maximum yield increases to 100kL/hh/year.

Marsden Jacob Associates (2007a) also constructed a credible daily water balance model assuming that rainwater supplied all internal end uses (but excluding cold water to the kitchen and bathroom) and external demands, as well as a scenario that considered only external garden use.

A summary of their water balance results is shown in Figure 8, where annual tank yield is shown as variations from a base case (5kL tank, $125m^2$ connected roof, 900mm/year rainfall, temperate climate) which is estimated to supply 71kL/hh/year. Their sensitivity analysis showed that the connected roof area has the single greatest impact on annual tank yield, followed by tank size, annual rainfall and the number of occupants in the house.

The pattern of rainfall (i.e. tropical to Mediterranean) had relatively little effect on tank yield because of the assumed high level of indoor use. However, if only external use is considered, the quantity of rainfall (mm/year) became much less important than the timing of rainfall, which determined the degree of matching between supply (seasonal rainfall) and irrigation demand (data not shown).

For a particular location such as Brisbane (assumed rainfall of 1200mm/year), a 5kL tank and $200m^2$ of connected roof could supply 99kL/hh/year for internal and external

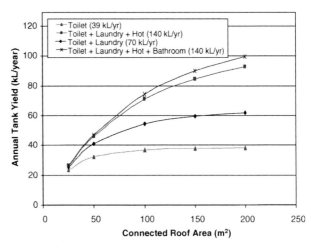

Figure 7 | Modelled long-term rainwater supply per household for a 5kL tank connected to different roof areas and different internal end uses in the Pimpama-Coomera region of SEQ. The yield was predicted by the Rainwater TANK model
Source: Vieritz *et al.* (2007)

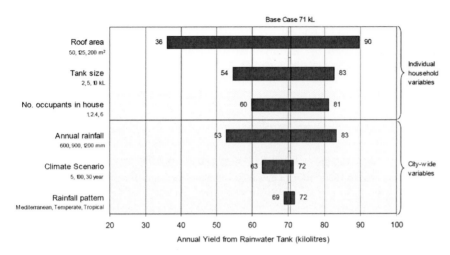

Figure 8 | Predicted annual rainwater tank yield varied by key factors – tank plumbed for both indoor and outdoor use
Note: The line dissecting the graph (71kL/year) relates to the 'base case', that is, a property with 125m² roof connected, 5kL tank and average 2.4 occupants, and a location with an average rainfall of 900mm (based on the 100 year record) and a temperate climate. Low and high variations to yield are based on the low and high estimates described on the vertical axis.
Source: text and figure from Marsden Jacob Associates (2007)

uses, decreasing to 79kL/hh/year for outdoor use only. These data support the SEQ Regional Water Supply Strategy assumption of 70kL/hh/year from rainwater tanks (Queensland Water Commission, 2008) albeit with fewer internal end uses allowed. For example, connection to the hot water system is not allowed in SEQ. For Adelaide with the lowest rainfall (560mm/year) of any Australian capital city, equivalent tank supply results were still very encouraging with supplies of 73 and 47kL/year predicted for indoor/outdoor and outdoor-only uses, respectively.

The interaction between tank size, connected roof area and demand is both subtle and complex but, reduced to its fundamentals, requires an 'air gap' to pre-exist in the tank for as many rainfall events as possible. The *regular water use* accompanied by internally plumbed connections will maximize the size and frequency of this pre-event 'air gap' and thereby *maximize the rainfall catch*. And it is for this reason that small tanks, for example, from 2 to 5kL, can still supply significant amounts of water for detached dwellings built on space challenged allotments (e.g. <600m²) typical of new urban subdivisions.

ENERGY COSTS OF RAINWATER TANKS

How does the energy costs of rainwater tanks compare with traditional water sources and desalination? There is a traditionally accepted view that centralized water and sewerage services are inefficient compared with decentralized services on energy and economic grounds because of the large transport distances, and the associated big pipes and pumps. Figure 9 shows the results of the most rigorous energy analysis for capital cities undertaken to date

(Kenway *et al.*, 2008) and specific energy for water supply pumping ranges from 0.07kWh/kL for Brisbane to 1.82kWh/kL for Adelaide, reflecting the large distance from the Murray River (84km) that supplies over 50% of the water consumed in Adelaide. If water treatment is added in, the specific energy range increases from 0.7kWh/kL for Brisbane to 1.9kWh/kL for Adelaide.

These then are the traditional yardsticks against which decentralized water supply sources may be compared, and available results for rainwater pumps are not particularly encouraging. For example, Figure 10 compares the energy

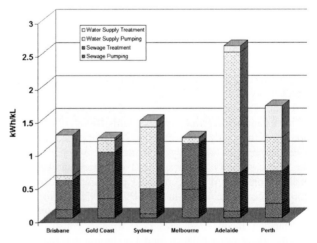

Figure 9 | Specific energy (kWh/kL) for the treatment and reticulation of water and sewage in Australian capital cities
Source: Kenway *et al.* (2008)

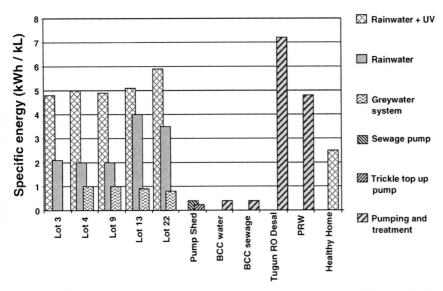

Figure 10 | Specific energy use for Payne Road rainwater pumps and disinfected rainwater compared with centralized services from Brisbane City Council (BCC). Also shown are specific energy use for future centralized supplies including Tugun sea water desalination and the Western Corridor Purified Recycled Water scheme
Source: Beal *et al.* (2008) and Queensland Water Commission (2008)

use by rainwater (and other pumps) at the Payne Road development in Brisbane where all (22) homes will be supplied from 20kL individual rainwater tanks topped up from a large 150kL communal tank system connected to council mains (Beal *et al.*, 2008). Specific energy for the submersible rainwater pumps ranges from 2 to 4kWh/kL, with a weighted average of 2.3kWh/kL. If energy use from the UV disinfection units is included to compare *like with like*, that is, potable mains water, then specific energy increases to about 5kWh/kL. In comparison, potable water is supplied to houses in Brisbane at an average specific energy of 0.7kWh/kL (Figure 9), which clearly identifies rainwater pumps as having a substantial energy disadvantage.

One might argue that future homes in SEQ will be supplied from a centralized supply; however, the QDC MP4.2 effectively mandates 5kL tanks with some internal plumbing. Energy modelling suggests that, by 2056, these mandated tanks could produce almost 20% of the total greenhouse gas emissions associated with the regional water supply due to the operation of the water pumps (Hall *et al.*, 2009). However, there are other data that suggest that rainwater pumps may not be quite as inefficient on both relative and absolute comparisons. Figure 10 for example shows that the specific energy for the Tugun reverse osmosis desalination plant is similar to that of the disinfected rainwater at the Payne Road development, while other potable water sources (purified recycled water) will use considerably more energy than the existing water supply systems (based on Wivenhoe, Somerset and Pine River dams). In the

future, a weighted diverse water supply is likely to consume 1.2kWh/kL (Claydon, 2008). These results, of course, are not unique to QLD as all of the capital cities of Australia are actively pursuing climate-independent water supplies based largely on desalinating sea water using reverse osmosis membrane technology.

More importantly, other studies on rainwater pumps have reported more optimistic figures ranging from 1.3kWh/kL for the Ecovillage at Currumbin, QLD (Hood *et al.*, 2010) to 0.8–1.7kWh/kL for rainwater pumps installed in a range of Sydney dwellings (Retamal *et al.*, 2009), noting however that in all cases the water was not disinfected. Some of the reasons for such large differences in specific energy are due to the end uses (e.g. toilet vs garden), the type of house construction (multi-level vs single storey), the use of pressure vessels to reduce pump start ups, the adoption of mains switching valves vs direct trickle top up, the plumbing used inside the house (e.g. 12 vs 20mm piping), the pressure settings on the pump controller, and of course the hydraulic characteristics of the pump itself.

It is evident that domestic rainwater systems were not designed with energy efficiency as a prime performance criterion, but there is no reason to believe that clever technology such as the variable speed pump controller and on demand UV disinfection, combined with simple engineering, for instance a header tank for 'long duration' end uses such as toilet cistern filling, cannot deliver household rainwater systems that equal or exceed the energy efficiency of the future 'combined source', potable water supply.

HEALTH ISSUES WITH USING RAINWATER TANKS

How safe are rainwater tanks for potable use? How can they be made safer? As rainwater tanks become more ubiquitous because of rebates or regulation (e.g. BASIX or QDC MP4.2), the incidence of deliberate and accidental ingestion of rainwater is likely to increase. In SEQ for example, over 50,000 tanks have been installed under QDC MP4.2, while a market research type survey identified that over 20% of these mandated tank owners 'often or sometimes' used the rainwater for drinking and/or cooking (Gardiner, 2009). To these numbers must be added the 'tank rebators', who chose to install a tank (largely for garden irrigation) during the SEQ drought, of which almost 30% use rainwater 'often or sometimes' for drinking and/or cooking (Gardiner, 2009). By the time the rebate was discontinued in December 2008, the number of tank rebators had swelled to over 263,000. However, very little research has been undertaken on their chemical and microbiological safety.

Rainwater microbiological quality

The delivery of high-quality sanitation and supply of pathogen-free drinking water have largely been responsible for the increase in longevity, from 47 years to 81 years for people (Hassed, 2002) over the past century or so; hence, it is with some caution that urban water experts are advocating a return to decentralized technologies. A limited number of studies in New Zealand (Simmons *et al.*, 2001) have identified pathogenic *Salmonella* and *Campylobacter* bacteria occurring in peri urban tanks, while epidemiological studies in Adelaide (Heyworth *et al.*, 2006) showed no statistical difference in the incidence of gastroenteritis in early age school children who came from homes where rainwater was or was not used for cooking and drinking. Adelaide is particularly interesting in that 37% of householders have rainwater tanks, of which 28% use rainwater for drinking and/or cooking (Australian Bureau of Statistics, 2007).

The problem with assessing the potential health risk of this practice is that conventional microorganisms used to assess faecal contamination such as *Escherichia coli* are indicators and not (usually) pathogens. Furthermore, *E. coli* is a ubiquitous gut-dwelling bacterium and its presence in rainwater tanks is not unusual. Recently, advances in molecular biology techniques (polymerase chain reaction or PCR) have allowed actual pathogens to be identified (i.e. presence/absence) and enumerated in environmental waters (i.e. organisms per 100mL of water sample; Ahmed *et al.*, 2008) at cost-effective prices, providing the opportunity to quantify the infection risk from ingesting rainwater either by accident (e.g. showering) or by intent (i.e. drinking).

Table 3 shows the results of sampling 64 tanks, 84 including multiple samplings, in SEQ during the 2007/2008 wet season and the listed bacterial (e.g. *Salmonella*) and protozoan (e.g. *Giardia*) pathogens were enumerated using real-time PCR (Ahmed *et al.*, 2009). Using a combination of estimated ingested volume by liquid and aerosols, fractions of organisms that are both viable and infective, and fraction of the total human population exposed to the pathogens (e.g. 6% for drinking and 30% for hosing), Ahmed *et al.* (2009) were able to calculate the likely incidence of giardiasis and salmonellosis on a yearly basis. The results are shown in Table 4 and indicate that infection risk from accidentally ingesting aerosols by hosing or showering is negligibly small (<1 infection per 10,000 people per year). However, if the undisinfected rainwater is ingested by drinking, then the gastrointestinal diseases of salmonellosis and giardiasis will be strikingly high with infection incidence ranging from 44 to 520 cases per 10,000 people per year.

Unfortunately (or perhaps fortunately), these predictions were not supported by the incidence of these diseases reported in the Notifiable Diseases Surveillance System Database (http://www9.health.gov.au/cda/Source/CDA-index.cfm). A number of explanations are possible including the following: the naturally high incidence of gastroenteritis in the community, for example, 8000 cases per 10,000 people per year (Hellard *et al.*, 2001) masking the actual diseases; the fact that giardiasis is not a notifiable disease in QLD; a much lower ratio of viable organisms to gene copies than was assumed in the analysis; or more likely, that pathogens do not occur at concentrations reported in Table 3 for 365 days of the year, as was assumed in the risk model calculations.

This latter explanation is being pursued by a longitudinal study using fortnightly sampling over several months, and

Table 3 | Quantitative PCR* results of selected pathogens found in rainwater tanks in a study in SEQ

Target Pathogens	PCR-Positive Results	Gene Copies/100mL	Infectious Units/100mL
Campylobacter jejuni	1	-	
Legionella pneumophila	8	6–17	6–17
Salmonella spp.	17	6.5–38	6.5–38
Giardia lamblia	11	0.9–5.7	0.06–0.36

*Polymerase chain reaction
Source: Ahmed et al. (2009)

Table 4 | Predicted infection risk per year from ingesting or inhaling rainwater in SEQ

Risk Scenario	Potential Pathogen Exposure	No. Events/ Year	Infection Risk per Year (No. per 10,000 Brisbane Persons per Year)
Drinking ingestion	Salmonella	365	44–250
Drinking ingestion	Giardia	365	85–520
Hosing ingestion	Salmonella	104	0.06–0.34
Hosing ingestion	Giardia	104	0.11–0.72
Showering inhalation	Legionella	365	0.013–0.035
Hosing inhalation (small aerosols)	Legionella	104	0.01–0.03
Hosing inhalation (large aerosols)	Salmonella	104	0.1–0.7
Hosing inhalation (large aerosols)	Giardia	104	0.2–1.4

Source: Ahmed et al. (2009)

Table 5 | Selected chemical and microbiological quality of rainwater measured in tanks at Payne Road over a 30-month period

Parameter	Units	Untreated Rainwater from Tanks			
		n	Average	Min.	Max.
pH	–	26	6.2	4.6	7.8
Electrical conductivity	µS/cm	26	97	16	316
Langelier index	–	6	−5.0	−6.03	−4.1
True colour	Hazen units	25	15	0.2	190
Hardness	mg/L	26	24	6.6	94
E. coli	cfu/ 100mL	29	14000	680	48000
Total Legionella spp.	cfu/ 100mL	27	58	10	700

Source: Beal et al. (2008)

until this pathogen issue is resolved, it would seem prudent to disinfect rainwater before drinking it. This could involve filtration using under-sink units, using UV disinfection units or more simply by boiling the water.

Rainwater chemical quality

Similar to microbiological quality, there have been relatively few studies on the chemical composition of rainwater in Australia and its likely effect on human health (but see Chapman et al., 2008a and Magyar et al., 2007). Table 5 reports traditional criteria (chemistry and microbiology) for a series of rainwater tanks at Payne Road, Brisbane (Beal et al., 2008). Although most values reported are acceptable, including a very low salinity of $\leq 100 \mu S/cm$, the parameter values of concern are the Langelier Index, colour and the microbiology, especially Legionella pneumophila. The Langelier index is a measure of corrosion and scaling potential in the household plumbing, and the value of −5 indicates that corrosion of the copper and brass fittings is highly likely unless steps are taken to increase the alkalinity level – marble chips (calcium carbonate) suspended in the tank is one solution.

Colour is usually an aesthetic issue with mains tap water having a value of ≤ 5 hazen units. However, one house consistently returned a value of >150 hazen units because of a combination of leaf drop on the roof, leaf gutter guards but no barrier screens on the downpipes, and a 'wet downpipe' system that became waterlogged as the drainage holes got blocked with decomposing tree litter. As tank water at Payne Road is designed to supply all household uses, the colour problem became so unacceptable that the householder disconnected their household plumbing from their tank. This illustrates how important it becomes to install preventative measures, especially for tree litter management, where site access is difficult particularly for multi-level homes on steep allotments. Guidelines on tank and roof maintenance are readily available (e.g. EnHealth Council, 2004; Chapman et al., 2008b).

The other issue of tank water quality is atmospheric and roof sourced chemical contamination. It is generally accepted that houses located near freeways and industrial areas are more likely to suffer from organic chemical contamination such as phenols, polyaromatic hydrocarbons and possibly pesticides. Huston et al. (2009) put this argument to the test by regularly monitoring atmospheric deposition and rainwater quality in a diverse range of locations (outer suburban, inner suburban and city/heavy traffic/high industrial) in Brisbane. Their results showed that in all locations, the concentration of organic chemicals in tank water was *well below* the Australian Drinking Water Guidelines (ADWG, 2004) limits, and there was generally little difference between locations in inorganic depositions in the rainfall, including heavy metals. However, when rainwater tanks were analysed, up to 15% of the 367 samples from 26 tanks returned lead (Pb) levels exceeding the ADWG (2004) limit of 10µg/L. A prior national survey of 64 tanks in 2004 reported similar findings (Chapman *et al.*, 2008a). However, Huston *et al.* (2009) were able to show that a majority of tanks with excessive lead levels had exposed lead flashing on the roof, and the tank water with low Pb concentrations came from lead-free roofs.

This process of lead contamination from roofing material is shown clearly in Figure 11 where the lead concentration in the tank water and in the bulk (atmospheric) deposition samples are plotted over a 11-month period for one of the (house) locations. The concentration in the rainfall is far less than that in the tank water, which in turn grossly exceeds the guideline value of 10µg/L. The particular home had a tile roof with 0.25m² of unpainted lead flashing. Similar results were found in a CSIRO-run *roof coupon* study in Melbourne, where both glazed and metal roofs produced rainwater Pb levels well in excess of 10µg/L if lead flashing was used to seal the ventilation pipe access (Huston *et al.*, 2009). If lead flashing was absent, Pb concentrations in rainwater were ≤1µg/L.

Given that Pb ingestion has potentially serious health effects associated with neurological development (Goyer, 1993), particularly in children younger than 7 years, it seems prudent to either replace lead flashing with a less toxic material, or at the very least, seal it with a durable protective coating.

Do first flush devices work?

Most of the rainwater tanks fitted under regulatory requirements, including QDC MP4.2 in QLD and BASIX in NSW, have a first flush device fitted by the installer, who is usually the home builder (J. Sullivan, personal communication). These devices are essentially a float-actuated valve, which redirects rainwater to the collection tank only after the first flush reservoir is full – this volume is somewhere between 5 and 25L depending on the design. The devices reset after the rainfall event by draining water from the reservoir via a weeping valve.

Their objective is to divert the first flush of runoff from the roof, which is likely to be contaminated by high levels of zoonotic faecal material, sediment and heavy metals (Thomas and Greene, 1993; Forster, 1996; Mason *et al.*, 1999). Local guidelines (i.e. EnHealth Council, 2004; Chapman *et al.*, 2008b) recommend that the first millimetre or two of runoff from each event be diverted away from the collection tank. For 230m² of connected roof area for the average BASIX-compliant homes in NSW (NSW Department of Planning, 2009), this is equivalent to 230–460L, which is far in excess of the capacity of most diversion devices on the market (about 25L), suggesting that their effectiveness is questionable.

However, while there are numerous studies confirming the first flush behaviour of contaminant concentrations in roof runoff (Thomas and Greene, 1993; Gould and Nissen-Petersen, 1999; He *et al.*, 2001), very few actually measured their effect on the quality of collected rainwater. One exception is the work of Gardner *et al.* (2004), who instrumented three roofs distributed over SEQ and measured roof runoff and event-based water sampling in 0.5 mm increments for subsequent chemical analysis (sediment, heavy metal and faecal coliforms).

An extract from their findings is shown in Figure 12 for runoff from a colourbond roof at the Healthy Home, Gold Coast, for an event in October 2003. The rapid reduction in concentration with increased roof runoff is evident, but even after 5mm the concentrations are well above zero, with faecal coliforms for example in excess of 100 colony-forming units (cfu)/100mL (ADWG, 2004 require zero cfu/100mL for potable use). Because concentration varies with runoff depth, the average concentration of an event is best estimated using a

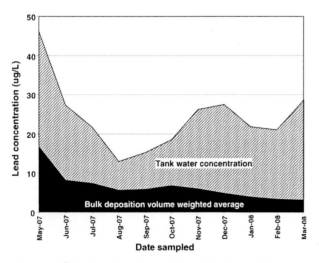

Figure 11 | Comparative lead concentrations in tank water and atmospheric bulk deposition (cumulative volume weighted mean) over time in a domestic dwelling in SEQ
Source: Huston *et al.* (2009)

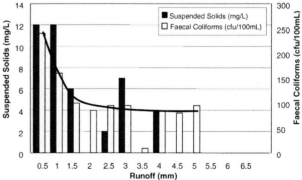

Figure 12 | Decline in contaminant concentrations in runoff from the roof of the Healthy Home during a 5mm rainfall event in October 2003
Source: Gardner *et al.* (2004)

flow volume weighted method to calculate the event mean concentration (EMC), which is commonly used to quantify stormwater quality (Duncan, 1999; Fletcher *et al.*, 2004). For the 5mm event in Figure 12, the EMC for faecal coliform decreased from 102cfu/100mL to 81cfu/100mL if the first 1mm of runoff were discarded. For suspended solids, the corresponding values are 4mg/L (no discard) and 2.7mg/L.

In the Healthy Home study, the water quality of the collected rainwater was regularly measured over a 3.5 year period, and faecal coliform concentrations ranged from <10cfu/100mL to in excess of 450cfu/100mL, clearly demonstrating that even the very 'efficient' first flush device did not produce rainwater of potable standard (Gardner *et al.*, 2004). However, subsequent disinfection using a 40W UV unit did produce water of zero faecal coliforms, as required by the ADWG (2004).

The other aspect of the first flush study was a detailed *hydrological* analysis of the first flush device fitted to the roof of the Healthy Home. These units drained the float reservoir at over 70L/min, making diversion of runoff to the tank a very inefficient process. In fact, the average catch efficiency of the system over 3 years was 62% compared with a predicted 87% if the reservoir leakage rate were reduced to 2L/min, an efficiency that is more consistent with empirically reported values (e.g. Chapman and Salmon, 1996). A detailed hydrology model (Millar *et al.*, 2003) was able to distribute this 'catch loss' into reservoir leakage (29%), filling of the 25L reservoir (7%), and adhesion/evaporation losses on the roof (2.5%). The high leakage from the first flush reservoir was due to a 4mm diameter drainage hole that was resistant to blockage. Most other first flush devices on the market have a capillary bleed valve of ≤2mm diameter, making blockage almost inevitable. Considering the large number of tanks installed under mandated water efficiency regulations (e.g. 43,000 in NSW and 50,000 in QLD), there is no objective information on post-installation performance. Anecdotal information from the NSW study (Sullivan and Wilson, 2009) suggests that drainage valves and filters often become blocked due to lack of maintenance, and pumps may fail or be bypassed via the switching valve, leading to continual mains water use without the homeowner becoming aware of these malfunctions.

Taken overall, first flush devices seem to be a good idea, but are not supported by, admittedly, limited experimental evidence. Considering their expense and propensity to block over time, their installation is not recommended. Rather, other devices such as floating off-takes in the tank are likely to have a more beneficial effect on rainwater quality, at least for those contaminants that are in the particulate phase (Magyar *et al.*, 2007) which tend to settle to the bottom of the tank.

SOCIOLOGICAL ASPECTS: BEHAVIOUR AND ATTITUDES OF TANK OWNERS

Brown *et al.* (2008) introduced the term the 'hydro social contract', where society has passed over the responsibility to government (local or state) to provide safe drinking water and hydraulically efficient sanitation and stormwater services. However, with drought conditions being experienced over much of urban Australia this decade, and a push to diversify water supplies, citizens are being asked to take back some of the responsibility for their water services. Brown *et al.* argue that as we move from a water *supply* city to a water *sensitive* city, there will be much more engagement of the urban community for both behavioural change, that is, water conservation, and responsibility to supply part of their own water.

Owner attitude towards tank maintenance is an important issue. Rainwater tanks were *effectively banned* by local authorities in SEQ up to the mid-1980s because their poor maintenance record allowed mosquito breeding, which was both an amenity and public health problem from arboviruses such as dengue fever.

In SEQ, the drought has led to distribution of over 263,000 Queensland Government rebates under the Queensland Home Waterwise Rebate Scheme (Spiller, 2008) for the retrofitting of rainwater tanks, to which may be added greenfield (i.e. new) developments where rainwater tanks were mandated, and the peri urban community who are not connected to mains water supply. Of the greenfield developments, tanks were either mandated to be internally plumbed due to regulation or estate covenants; or optionally internally plumbed during installation in urban development projects prior to 2007. This diverse range of tank owners (identified as 'retrofitters', 'greenfielders – mandated', 'greenfielders – optional' and 'peri urban', adapted from terms used by Gardiner, 2009) provided the opportunity for social market research to quantify and explain their motivation for tank ownership, planned end uses of the water, maintenance behaviour, problems encountered, and related questions on 'perception, beliefs and concerns about the water shortages and the impact of their personal efforts' (Gardiner *et al.*, 2008).

Gardiner *et al.* (2008) reported on a statistically robust sample of 600 residents in SEQ (in June 2007) that were distributed into three distinct groups: peri urban, retrofitters and greenfielders. The survey was repeated in June 2008 (Gardiner, 2009), focusing on urban tanks, and included retrofitters, greenfielders – mandated and greenfielders – optional. The results of the survey both confirmed and expanded insights gained from the June 2007 survey (Gardiner *et al.*, 2008). Much of the following text is taken from the articles by Gardiner *et al.* (2008) and Gardiner (2009).

The peri urban respondents 'lived in semi rural environments for lifestyle reasons' and 'required the [tank] water to live in the area'. They use large tanks (over 50% with tanks >20kL) and ranked 'the taste and purity of their water as a key issue and consequently their maintenance practices were of a higher standard'. Over 90% of these respondents used their water for internal household uses, including drinking.

The retrofitters tended to be near or at retirement age (nearly half were over 60 years old) and installed their tank to allow them to continue garden (but not lawn) watering during drought water restrictions, and other external uses. Those who obtained government rebates for their tanks believed very strongly that 'the water is their private resource' which can be used as they choose. Few respondents reported community responsibility as a motivator for installing their tank. A small number of them (<13%) connected their tank to internal water uses, for instance for laundry and toilets, which would have reduced demand on mains water supply. However, the majority (75%) practised other water-saving strategies including greywater reuse, installing low flow showers and dual flush toilets. They self-rated their overall water efficiency as 9 (on a scale from 1 – minimum to 10 – maximum). About 20% used their tank water for drinking and cooking purposes.

The greenfielder respondents chose to live in the mandated tank areas 'mainly for socio-geographical reasons, with little regard for the water sensitive urban design context'. The greenfielders – mandated respondents were generally young couples (63% were less than 44 years of age) with children, and with little previous experience with a tank. The tanks were usually plumbed internally to the toilet and washing machine. In most instances, the tank was installed by the builder and was not due to the initiative of the current resident. About 20% were dissatisfied with the rainwater plumbing system installed and/or water quality of the collected water, increasing to >30% dissatisfaction with tank noise.

The greenfielder group also had significantly higher income and educational levels than the peri urban and retrofitter residents, but rated themselves harshly on their water efficiency behaviour. They were the least likely of all groups to feel that they have 'done everything in their control to be water efficient', and yet are the 'most likely to have applied each of the top ten reported household water saving actions' such as shorter showers and use of front loading washing machines. 'Clearly the greenfield families set higher environmental standards for themselves than the retrofitting retirees'.

The greenfielder – mandated group also showed very low activity in tank maintenance (gutters, screens, pipes and pumps), little effort in learning more, with over a third in the 2008 survey 'expressing no confidence in their knowledge or ability' to maintain their rainwater system. They used rainwater for external uses such as garden watering and car washing (>55%). Greater than 60% also used the tank water for lawn watering, presumably reflecting the landscaping of new homes. The use of rainwater for drinking/cooking was rare among the greenfielder group in the 2007 survey (1%), but was about 20% in the greenfielder – mandated group in the 2008 survey.

The greenfielders – optional had attitudes and water use patterns that were very little different from the retrofitters. However, only a small number (<5%) drink their tank water.

Gardiner (2009) then attempted to group the respondents into attitudinal categories rather than on a logistical criterion. Using factor analysis she identified three main groups:

environmentalists, restriction compensators and not really interested (Figure 13).

Not surprisingly, the mandated greenfield tank owners formed the vast majority of the not really interested group (31% of the tank owners). This group tended to be aged under 40 years and were 'more likely to stop using their tank' if problems (e.g. pump failure) arose rather than 'investing time and resources in maintenance'. As the tank and internal plumbing were installed by the builder, the respondents had little apparent ownership and believed it was just a part of the larger council-run reticulated water system. This attitude does not augur well for the future, given that 754,000 new dwellings are expected to be built in SEQ by 2031 (Queensland Department of Infrastructure and Planning, 2009), the majority of which will require some form of alternative water supply, most probably a tank.

At the other end of the behavioural spectrum are the environmentalists (25% of the tank owners), who are motivated by community benefit grounds and voluntarily installed their tanks to replace external water use, which they are likely to continue even when water restrictions are expected to be lifted in November 2009. The majority of this cohort comes from the retrofitter group.

The largest fraction of tanks owners (44%) belong to the restriction compensators, who also come from the retrofitter group. They installed their tanks to allow garden use during drought times and have little interest in connecting tank water to internal fittings such as the toilet. It is uncertain whether most of this cohort will continue to use their tanks once the watering restrictions are lifted and/or expensive maintenance is required, noting that most are retirees. Taken in combination, these two issues make it very uncertain as to how much water planners should depend on this group to reduce demand on the potable water system.

Taken overall, the future of potable water savings will be shaped by a number of pressures – effectively mandating tanks for new dwellings certainly 'hard wires' the technology into the urban water system, but unless the resident has ownership of the catchment area (roof, gutter, downpipes) and maintenance requirements (filters and pumps), the system is likely to fall into disrepair, perhaps even without the knowledge of the homeowner. The need for intervention initiatives would seem inevitable and could range from education activities, to regulations accompanied by home inspections, like those required for swimming pool fences, at the point of sale. Of course, community engagement failure can be partially offset by technological advances, and large, centrally managed community rainwater tanks connected to individual house roofs could mitigate the difficulties of individual rainwater tanks (Pohlner and Wilson, 2009).

The 263,000 retrofitters are likely to become an ever decreasing fraction of homeowners in SEQ as the population expands, so even if the restriction compensators continued to use their rainwater for external purposes, their fractional contribution to potable water savings will become less and less.

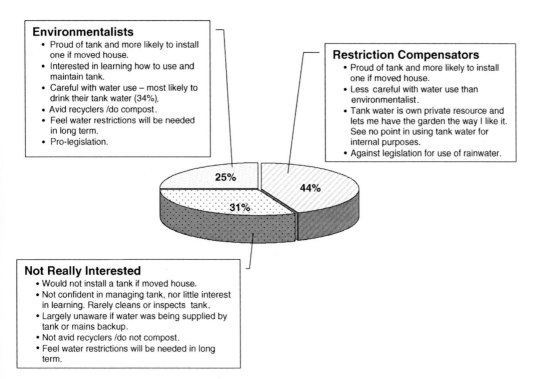

Environmentalists
- Proud of tank and more likely to install one if moved house.
- Interested in learning how to use and maintain tank.
- Careful with water use – most likely to drink their tank water (34%).
- Avid recyclers /do compost.
- Feel water restrictions will be needed in long term.
- Pro-legislation.

Restriction Compensators
- Proud of tank and more likely to install one if moved house.
- Less careful with water use than environmentalist.
- Tank water is own private resource and lets me have the garden the way I like it. See no point in using tank water for internal purposes.
- Against legislation for use of rainwater.

Not Really Interested
- Would not install a tank if moved house.
- Not confident in managing tank, nor little interest in learning. Rarely cleans or inspects tank.
- Largely unaware if water was being supplied by tank or mains backup.
- Not avid recyclers /do not compost.
- Feel water restrictions will be needed in long term.

Figure 13 | Three main attitudinal clusters identified among tank owners in SEQ: environmentalists, restriction compensators and not really interested
Source: Gardiner (2009)

ECONOMICS OF RAINWATER TANKS

How does the financial cost of rainwater tanks compare with traditional water sources and desalination? Water supply decision making in Australia over the past decade has moved very much towards market forces where the true cost of water supplies are made transparent and any cross subsidization is made explicit (COAG, 2004). There is also a general belief that economic consideration should be the dominant criterion in selecting from different water supply options, and that supply and demand imbalances can be rectified by a price signal. Consequently, it is no surprise that the generally accepted water supply benefit from rainwater tanks, which are effectively an Australian cultural icon, should be put through the filter of economic efficiency.

Initially, the economic numbers of rainwater tank purchase, maintenance and energy consumption were proposed by rainwater proponents (e.g. Coombes and Kuczera, 2003b) and generally the numbers were very favourable with costs coming in at less than $1/kL. However, other views were less sanguine, especially from the water supply companies, which argued that rainwater was up to five-fold more expensive per kL than traditional urban water supply. To help bring clarity and objectivity to this issue, the National Water Commission contracted the economic consultants Marsden Jacob Associates to undertake an evaluation of the cost effectiveness

of urban domestic rainwater tanks. Much of the following data are taken from their report (Marsden Jacob Associates, 2007a), but we note that similar reports have been prepared for the Australian Conservation Foundation (Marsden Jacob Associates, 2007b) and the Water Corporation of WA (Marsden Jacob Associates, 2009).

Marsden Jacob Associates (2007a) first constructed a daily water balance model to estimate the water supply (see Figure 8). The next part of the analysis was collation of the cost of installing and operating a rainwater tank. Using survey data from tank suppliers and installers, the average total cost of installing an internally plumbed 5kL tank in a greenfield development was about $3150, although other incidental costs such as a mains water switching device and a first flush diversion system may not have always been included in the survey data. Nonetheless, this (December 2006) figure is consistent with the industry-accepted cost of $4000 per tank used in SEQ for an average new detached dwelling.

In addition, property owners will incur additional expenses for operating and maintaining the tank, which includes energy costs for pumping, installing gutter screens, cleaning gutters, screens and filters, dislodging the tank every 3–5 years and water pump maintenance. Marsden Jacob Associates assumed that collectively this would cost the homeowner $20/year, over a 10-year cycle. It did not include the cost of water pump replacement, which was assumed to occur every 10 years.

Following traditional economic analysis, the discounted cash flow was estimated using net present value analysis, which discounts (i.e. reduces) the costs and benefits over the lifetime of the system. The discount rate assumed in their analysis was 8%, equivalent to the then (December 2006) variable home mortgage interest rate. By combining this analysis with the expected supply volume (kL/year), the levelized cost was calculated, which is the discounted amortized capital and operating costs divided by the expected annual yield.

The results of the levelized cost analysis for indoor and outdoor end uses for Australian capital cities are shown in Table 6 along with the current cost of mains water. The most likely combination is a 5kL tank connected to 200m^2 of roof and the estimated cost ranges from \$2.16/kL in Sydney to \$3.06/kL in Adelaide. As most of the whole of lifecycle costs are fixed, with the tank purchase contributing about 30%, water pump and its replacement about 35%, and installation around 25%, the higher the yield from the tanks, the lower the cost per kL.

Nonetheless, the cost of rainwater is always more expensive than mains water, but is far below the value of five-fold increase over mains supply suggested previously by the water companies. Interestingly, if tanks are used only for external uses and do not require a pump, the levelized cost can fall to as little as \$1.25/kL. For many households with large connected roof areas, the unit cost then falls to within 20% of the top tier price of mains water (data not shown). However, a pump-free tank is likely to apply in only a limited number of households as low water pressure reduces its utility for garden watering.

This analysis assumes that mains water supply will follow a 'business as usual' model, which is clearly not true as future water supplies for large urban areas will be a combination of:

- Sea water desalination – all the coastal capital cities have signed up for at least one large (≥125mL/day) reverse osmosis plant producing water typically costing \$3/kL.

- Water recycling either as potable substitution via dual pipelines or indirect potable reuse into drinking water reservoirs. Indirect potable reuse or dual reticulation costs around \$3.50/kL.
- New dams – particularly in SEQ. New dams such as Traveston in SEQ cost around \$2.25/kL.
- Long distance pipelines that form part of a water grid.

By comparison, water saved/supplied as a result of pressure and leakage and management programmes is very cost effective at <\$0.50kL (Queensland Water Commission, 2008).

The economic tool to assess the cost of those options being added to the water supply system is the long run marginal cost (LRMC), which represents the changed cost if new water sources are brought forward, or delayed. Table 6 shows these figures, which Marsden Jacob Associates obtained from the state price regulator or the water company. With the exception of Brisbane, LRMC is always less than the levelized cost of rainwater tanks. However, as Marsden Jacob Associates observed, source augmentation typically commences with the least expensive option escalating to the higher cost options in the long term. Consequently, LRMC is expected to increase over time as more expensive sources are added to the water supply system.

Given that rainwater tanks reduce the draw down on bulk water supplies, albeit with a much reduced reliability of supply, it could be argued that they delay, or downsize, the implementation of these new water sources, and hence a fairer comparison would be a comparison of their costs (i.e. Table 6) with the cost of these mainstream infrastructure options. In this case, rainwater in new dwellings looks economically attractive for individuals in Brisbane, Sydney and Melbourne but less so for Adelaide and Perth. Given that South Australia has the highest ownership of tanks (48 vs 17% for Australia), it is clear that factors other than economics have been driving installation of rainwater tanks before it became mandated in most states by regulation.

Table 6 | Levelized cost of rainwater tanks supplying water for indoor and outdoor uses in Australian capital cities. Also shown are local prices (2007) for mains water, and the estimated LRMC of water supplemented by new supply sources

| Tank Size | 2kL | | 5kL | | 10kL | | Price of Mains Water | Estimated LRMC |
Roof Area	50m^2	200m^2	50m^2	200m^2	50m^2	200m^2	(\$/kL)	(\$/kL)
Brisbane	5.80	2.99	5.47	2.29	5.86	2.09	0.91–1.20	2.00 +
Sydney	5.05	2.64	4.79	2.16	5.10	2.03	1.26–1.63	1.20–1.50
Melbourne – Yarra Valley	8.40	3.00	9.12	2.63	10.41	2.64	0.81–1.55 +	0.50–0.54
Melbourne – City West	8.40	3.00	9.12	2.63	10.41	2.64	0.81–1.55 +	0.74
Adelaide	9.23	3.57	10.14	3.06	11.59	3.13	0.47–1.09	Approx. 1.09
Perth	6.98	3.51	7.32	3.04	8.34	3.07	0.49–1.59	0.82–1.20

Source: Marsden Jacob Associates (2007)

Taken overall, the Marsden Jacob Associates (2007a) economic analysis of rainwater tanks indicated that on a householder basis, rainwater tanks are less economically attractive than either current mains water supply or the likely future mix of mains supply, as quantified by the LRMC estimate. However, the difference in $/kL is not large if moderate size tanks are connected to large roof areas to supply both internal and external end uses. When compared directly with new urban water supply options such as desalination, recycled water, etc., rainwater supplies seem to be very cost competitive and are likely to increase their financial advantage when stormwater benefits, required under regulation, are considered.

However, to a large extent, state regulation has essentially gazumped the economic argument as QLD, NSW and South Australia have effectively mandated the installation of internally plumbed rainwater tanks in new dwellings (Marsden Jacob Associates, 2009), while Victoria has specified it as an option to solar hot water systems, under its 5-Star Standard building regulations (http://www.makeyourhomegreen.vic.gov.au/resources/documents/14161_BC_5_Star_House_c2.pdf).

In most cases, rebates are no longer available to offset the costs to the householder, except in Victoria, where rebates of up to $1000 are still available under its Water Smart Gardens and Homes Rebate Scheme (http://www.ourwater.vic.gov.au/saving/home/rebates). Of course, there are other factors that motivate people to install rainwater tanks, which include avoiding garden watering restrictions, environmental concern, community mindedness and improved odour and taste, some of which have been discussed earlier in this article.

CONCLUSIONS

The change in rainfall patterns in most of Australia's urban water supply catchments has focused the attention of water planners on the diversity of supply and robustness to climate change. Our present work has shown that large ($\geq$20kL) rainwater tanks are very effective under low rainfall conditions, and of course even more effective under average rainfall years. The advantages are not limited to large tanks as small (5kL) tanks can be substantial suppliers of water (e.g. $\geq$70kL/hh/year), provided they are connected to internal end uses and a large ($\geq$150m^2) area of roof. Both QLD and NSW have effectively mandated tanks for new dwellings, and it appears that they will make a significant contribution to the urban water supply. Of course, empirical observations do not easily allow extrapolation of results in space, time or different operating conditions, and it is for this reason that models that incorporate 100+ years of daily climate data are so useful. Application of the Rainwater TANK model, for example, has demonstrated the considerable gain in water supply (about 30kL/hh/year) if the rainwater is connected to the hot water system, as well as the toilet, laundry and garden tap.

However, balanced against these hydrology gains are issues of carbon footprint and microbiological and chemical safety. As configured in most homes, rainwater pumps are certainly very inefficient and can have an energy intensity (kWh/kL) as high as that from a desalination plant. Their energy consumption will always be greater than current town water supply, raising some doubt as to the assumption that decentralized technology is always more efficient than the big pipes and pumps of centralized systems. Nonetheless, we believe that substantial gains in energy efficiency are possible with some simple engineering system designs, but these are yet to be confirmed and documented.

Because of the ubiquitousness of rainwater tanks in the Australian household and psyche, it is not uncommon for urban households to use their rainwater for drinking and cooking even though disinfection treatment appears to be largely lacking. Our measurements and risk analysis suggest that zoonotic pathogens, especially *Giardia*, are present in tanks at concentrations that will cause unacceptably high incidences of illness in the community. However, epidemiological evidence would suggest otherwise. This issue clearly needs more research but in the interim, disinfection is highly recommended for residents ingesting their tank water.

On the other hand, the chemical composition of rainwater in urban areas is generally well within the levels prescribed by the ADWG (2004). The exception is lead, but the source appears to be lead flashing on roofs and not precipitation. The solution seems self-evident and easy to implement. First flush devices, however, appear to do little to improve the chemical and microbiological quality of the collected rainwater.

Notwithstanding the widespread use and familiarity of rainwater tanks, their continual roll-out in the urban community is causing a change in the hydro social contract, with residents being asked to take more responsibility for their water supply and to learn to steward their water wisely. The social research in this regard is not particularly encouraging as the motivated and technically aware tank owners ('environmentalist' and 'retrofitter') have installed plumbing systems unlikely to contribute much to potable water savings. The greenfielder – mandated tank owners, on the other hand, are essentially disinterested in their system but have the potential to have the most effect because of their growing numbers, from 754,000 new dwellings predicted in SEQ alone by 2031, and the fact that their tanks are plumbed internally to the house. Education outreach activities to engage these tank owners with their own water supply should be a priority.

Finally, tanks are but one solution in the mixture of alternative urban water supplies (including new dams). Financial assessment is therefore a legitimate yardstick and, given the high fixed cost contribution of the whole of lifecycle costs, the higher the amount of water a tank can yield, the lower the cost per kL. Encouragingly, a small tank connected to internal household demands and a large roof area can supply water at a cost (about $2.50/kL) not too dissimilar to the LRMC of new water supplies, and very similar to the cost of climate-independent supplies such as desalination plants and recycling using dual reticulation.

Tanks have a significant role to play in the 21st century urban Australia, but their long-term advantages will be better defined by more research into energy consumption, microbiological safety and social ownership by the mandated householder.

References

ADWG, 2004, *Australian Drinking Water Guidelines*. National Water Quality Management Strategy. National Health and Medical Research Council, Australian Government, ISBN 1864961244. Available at: www.nhmrc.gov.au/publications/subjects/water.htm [accessed August 2009].

Ahmed, W., Huygens, F., Goonetilleke, A. and Gardner, T., 2008, 'Real-time PCR detection of pathogenic microorganisms in roof-harvested rainwater in Southeast Queensland, Australia', *Applied and Environmental Microbiology* 74(17), 5490–5496.

Ahmed, W., Vieritz, A., Gardner, T. and Goonetilleke, A., 2009, 'Health risks from pathogens in roof harvested rainwater in Queensland', *OZWATER'09 From Challenges to Solutions. Melbourne Convention and Exhibition Centre, Melbourne, Victoria, 16–18 March 2009*.

Australian Bureau of Statistics, 2007, 'Environmental issues: people's views and practices', 4602.0 March 2007.

Beal, C., Gardner, T., Sharma, A., Ho, A. and Hood, B., 2009, 'A preliminary analysis of potable water savings from mandated rainwater tanks in new residential properties in South East Queensland', Presented at *Urban Water Security Research Alliance Science Forum, 24–25 August, 2009, Brisbane Australia*. Available at: www.urbanwateralliance.org.au/ [accessed August 2009].

Beal, C., Hood, B., Gardner, T., Lane, J. and Christiansen, C., 2008, 'Energy and water metabolism of a sustainable subdivision in south east Queensland: a reality check', Presented at *Enviro'08*. Melbourne Exhibition and Convention Centre, 5–7 May 2008. The study on the Payne Rd. development which is also marketed as Silva Park.

Brown, R., Keath, N. and Wong, T., 2008, 'Transitioning to water sensitive cities: historical, current and future transition states', *11th International Conference on Urban Drainage*. Edinburgh, Scotland, UK 2008.

Chapman, H., Cartwright, T., Huston, R. and O'Toole, J., 2008a, 'Water quality and health risks from urban rainwater tanks', Research Report No. 42, CRC Water Quality and Management.

Chapman, H., Cartwright, T. and Tripodi, N., 2008b, 'Guidance manual for the design and installation of urban roofwater harvesting systems in Australia (Edition 1)', CRC for Water Quality and Treatment Research Report 39, CRC for Water Quality and Treatment.

Chapman, T. and Salmon, M., 1996, 'Roof runoff data acquisition and analysis', *in 23rd Hydrology and Water Resources Symposium. Inst. Eng. Aust., Hobart, May 1996*.

Chiew, F.H.S., 2006, 'Estimation of rainfall elasticity of streamflow in Australia', *Hydrological Science Journal* 51, 613–625.

Claydon, G., 2008, 'Water, energy & climate change – Queensland perspectives', Presented at the *11th International River Symposium. Brisbane, Australia, 1–4 September 2008*. Available at: www.riversymposium.com/index.php?element=CLAYDONppt [accessed August 2009].

COAG, 2004, *Council of Australian Governments*. Communique 25. June 2004 Canberra. National Water Initiative. Available at: www.coag.gov.au/coag_meeting_outcomes/2004-06-25/index.cfm#nwi [accessed August 2009].

Coombes, P.J. and Kuczera, G., 2003a, 'Analysis of the performance of rainwater tanks in Australian capital cities', Presented at *28th International Hydrology and Water Resources Symposium. The Institution of Engineers, Australia, 10–14 November 2003*, Wollongong, NSW.

Coombes, P.J. and Kuczera, G., 2003b, 'A sensitivity analysis of an investment model used to determine the economic benefits of rainwater tanks', Presented at *28th International Hydrology and Water Resources Symposium. The Institution of Engineers, Australia, 10–14 November 2003*, Wollongong NSW.

Devi, B., 2009, 'State of urban irrigation demand management – a review', Irrigation Matters Series No. 02/09, CRC for Irrigation Futures, July 2009.

Duncan, H.P., 1999, *Urban Stormwater Quality: A Statistical Overview*. Report 99/3. February 1999. CRC for Catchment Hydrology.

enHealth Council, 2004, *Guidance on Use of Rainwater Tanks*. Available at: http://enhealth.nphp.gov.au/council/pubs/documents/rainwater_tanks.pdf [accessed August 2009].

Fletcher, T., Duncan, H., Poelsma, P. and Lloyd, S., 2004, 'Stormwater flow and quality, and the effectiveness of non-proprietary stormwater treatment measures – a review and gap analysis', Technical Report 04/08, CRC for Catchment Hydrology.

Forster, J., 1996, 'Patterns of roof runoff contamination and their potential implications on practice and regulation of treatment and local infiltration', *Water Science Technology* 33, 39–48.

Gardiner, A., 2009, 'Domestic rainwater tanks: usage and maintenance patterns in South East Queensland', *AWA Water Journal* 36(1), 151–156.

Gardiner, A., Skoien, P. and Gardner, T., 2008, 'Decentralised water supplies: South East Queenslanders' Attitudes and experience', *AWA Water* 35(1), 53–58.

Gardner, E.A., Beal, C., Lane, J., Hyde, R., Hamlyn-Harris, D., Skoien, P. and Walton, C., 2008, 'Measuring the metabolism of decentralised urban developments – do they demonstrate increased urban sustainability?', Presented at *IWA World Water Congress. Vienna, September 2008*.

Gardner, E.A., Millar, G.E., Christiansen, C., Vieritz, A.M. and Chapman, H., 2006, 'Energy and water use at a WSUD subdivision in Brisbane, Australia', Presented at *ENVIRO'06 Conference and Exhibition. Australia Water Association, Melbourne Exhibition and Convention Centre, Melbourne, 9–11 May 2006*.

Gardner, T. and Dennien, B., 2007, 'Why has SEQ decided to drink purified recycled water?', in S.J. Khan, R.M. Stuetz, J.M. Anderson (eds) *Proceedings of the 3rd AWA Water Reuse and Recycling Conference. Sydney, 16–18 July, 2007*.

Gardner, T., Millar, G., Baisden, J., 2004, 'Rainwater first flush devices – are they effective?', Presented at *Sustainable Water in the Urban Environment. Australian Water Association, Brisbane, August 2004*.

Gardner, T., Millar, G., Hyde, R., 2003, 'The healthy home: a step towards sustainable suburbs', Published in the *Proceedings of the 2nd National Water Recycling Conference. Australian Water Association and Stormwater Industry Association, Brisbane, September 2003*.

Gould, J., Nissen-Petersen, E., 1999, *Rainwater Catchment Systems for Domestic Water Supply – Design, Construction and Implementation*, London, Intermediate Technology Publications.

Goyer, R.A., 1993, 'Lead toxicity – current concerns', *Environmental Health Perspectives* 100, 177–187.

Hall, M., West, J., Lane, J., de Haas, D., Sherman, B., 2009, *Energy and Greenhouse Gas Emissions for the SEQ Water Strategy*. Urban Water Research Security Alliance. Available at: www.urbanwateralliance.org.au/ [accessed August 2009].

Hassed, C., 2002, 'Longevity: does what goes up always have to come down?', *Australian Family Physician* 31(12), 1116–1118.

He, W., Odenvall Wallinder, I., Leygraf, C., 2001, 'A laboratory study of copper and zinc runoff during first flush and steady state conditions', *Corrosion Science* 43, 127–146.

Hellard, M.E., Sinclair, M.I., Forbes, A.B., Fairley, C.K., 2001, 'A randomised, blinded, controlled trial investigating the gastrointestinal health effects of drinking water quality', *Environmental Health Perspectives* 109(8), 773–777.

Heyworth, J.S., Glonek, G., Maynard, E.J., Baghurst, P.A., Finlay-Jones, J., 2006, 'Consumption of untreated tank rainwater and gastroenteritis among young children in South Australia', *International Journal of Epidemiology* 35, 1051–1058

Hood, B., Gardner, T., Beal, C., Gardiner, R., Walton, C., 2010, 'The Ecovillage at Currumbin – a model for decentralised development', Prepared for *OZWATER'10 Achieving Water Security. Brisbane Convention & Exhibition Centre. Brisbane, 8–10 March, 2010*.

Huston, R., Chan, Y.C., Gardner, T., Shaw, G., Chapman, H., 2009, 'Characterisation of atmospheric deposition as a source of contaminants in urban rainwater tanks', *Water Research* 43, 1630–1640.

Kenway, S.J., Priestley, A., Cook, S., Seo, S., Inman, M., Gregory, A., Hall, M., 2008, 'Energy use in the provision and consumption of urban water in Australia and New Zealand', CSIRO: Water for a Healthy Country National Research Flagship. CSIRO & WSAA 2008.

Loh, M., Coghlan, P., 2003, *Domestic Water Use Study: In Perth, WA, 1998–2001, Western Australia*, Water Corporation.

Magyar, M.I., Mitchell, V.G., Ladson, A.R., Diaper, C., 2007, 'An investigation of rainwater tanks quality and sediment dynamics', *Water Science and Technology* 56(9), 21–28.

Marsden Jacob Associates, 2007a. *The Cost Effectiveness of Rainwater Tanks in Urban Australia*, Commissioned by the Australian Government, National Water Commission, Waterlines series, March 2007.

Marsden Jacob Associates, 2007b, *The Economics of Rainwater Tanks and Alternative Water Supply Options*, Report prepared for the Australian Conservation Foundation, Nature Conservation Council (NSW) and Environment Victoria. 11 April 2007.

Marsden Jacob Associates, 2009, *The Cost Effectiveness of Residential Rainwater Tanks in Perth*, Report prepared for Water Corporation and the Department of Water, Western Australia.

Mason, Y., Ammann, A., Ulrich, A., Sigg, L., 1999, 'Behaviour of heavy metals, nutrients and major components during roof runoff infiltration', *Environmental Science & Technology* 33, 1588–1597.

Millar, G., Bofu, Y., Gardner, T., 2003, 'Rainfall catch efficiency for domestic water supply', In *28th International Hydrology and Water Resources Symposium. Wollongong, 10–14 November 2003*. The Institution of Engineers, Australia.

NSW Department of Planning, 2008, 'BASIX monitoring report water savings for 2007–08', Final Report prepared by Sydney Water for the NSW Department of Planning.

NSW Department of Planning, 2009, 'Single dwelling outcomes 05–08 BASIX building sustainability index', Ongoing Monitoring Program. Available at: www.basix.nsw.gov.au [accessed August 2009].

Pohlner, B., Wilson, P., 2009, 'Tapping the urban catchment. Regional roof water harvesting for reticulated supply', *Prepared for OZWATER'10 Achieving Water Security. Brisbane Convention & Exhibition Centre, Brisbane, 8–10 March, 2010*.

Queensland Department of Infrastructure, 2007, 'South East Queensland Regional Plan 2005–2026', Draft Implementation Guideline No. 7 Water Sensitive Urban Design, Design objectives for urban stormwater management, Queensland Government Office of Urban Management, Department of Infrastructure.

Queensland Department of Infrastructure and Planning, 2008, 'Queensland Development Code MP4.2 (previously part 25) water savings targets', Queensland Department of Infrastructure and Planning. Available at: www.dip.qld.gov.au/docs/temp/mp4_2_water_savings_targets.pdf [accessed August 2009].

Queensland Department of Infrastructure and Planning, 2009, 'South East Queensland Regional Plan 2009–2031', The State of Queensland, Queensland Department of Infrastructure and Planning. Available at: www.dip.qld.gov.au [accessed August 2009]

Queensland Department of Natural Resources and Mines, 2006, South East Queensland Regional Water Supply Strategy. Stage 2 Interim Report. 2nd edn. Department of Natural Resources and Mines QNRM 05497.

Queensland Department of Natural Resources and Water, 2007, *Planning Guidelines for Water Supply and Sewerage*.

Queensland Water Commission, 2008, *Water for Today, Water for Tomorrow*, South East Queensland Water Strategy – Draft Report March 2008.

Retamal, M., Glassmire, J., Abeysuriya, K., Turner, A., White, S., 2009, *The Water–Energy Nexus. Investigation into the Energy Implications of Household Rainwater Systems*, Final Report, CSIRO, Institute for Sustainable Futures.

Simmons, G., Hope, V., Lewis, G., Whitmore, J., Wanzhen, G., 2001, 'Contamination of potable roof-collected rainwater in Auckland, New Zealand', *Water Research* 35, 1518–1524.

Spiller, D., 2008, 'Policy forum: urban water pricing and supply. Water for today, water for tomorrow: establishment and operation of the SEQ Water Grid', *The Australian Economic Review* 41(4), 420–427.

Sullivan, J., Wilson, S., 2009, 'BASIX: The proof is in the water savings', Presented at *OZWATER'09 From Challenges to Solutions. Melbourne Convention and Exhibition Centre, Melbourne, Victoria, 16–18 March 2009*.

Thomas, P.R., Greene, G.R., 1993, 'Rainwater quality from different roof catchments', *Water Science Technology* 28(3–5), 291–299.

Vieritz, A., Gardner, T., Baisden, J., 2007, 'Rainwater TANK model designed for use by urban planners', *Proceedings of Ozwater 2007 Convention & Exhibition*. Australian Water Association, 4–8 March 2007, Sydney. (CD). ISBN 978-0-908255-67-2.

Water Corporation of WA, 2009, *Directions for Our Water Future*. Water Forever Draft Plan, Western Australia, Water Corporation.

Willis, R., Stewart, R., Chen, L., Rutherford, L., 2009, 'Water end use consumption anaylsis study into Gold Coast dual reticulated households: pilot', Presented at *OZWATER'09 From Challenges to Solutions. Melbourne Convention and Exhibition Centre, Melbourne, Victoria, 16–18 March 2009*.

ARCHITECTURAL
SCIENCE
REVIEW

Social networks save energy: optimizing energy consumption in an ecovillage via agent-based simulation

Majd Hawasly[1,a], David Corne[2]* and Sue Roaf[3]

[1]School of Informatics, University of Edinburgh, The Informatics Forum, 10 Crichton Street, Edinburgh, EH8 9AB, UK
[2]School of Mathematical and Computer Sciences, Heriot-Watt University, Riccarton, Edinburgh, EH14 4AS, UK
[3]School of the Built Environment, Heriot-Watt University, Riccarton, Edinburgh, EH14 4AS, UK
[a]This work was done while the first author was at the School of Mathematical and Computer Sciences, Heriot-Watt University.

Energy-conscious communities are continually challenged to optimize electricity usage, maximizing the benefits obtainable from generating systems and minimizing the reliance on the national supply. Achieving an ideal balance is complicated by the fluctuating availability of 'green' supplies and the varying patterns of domestic usage. Optimizing a community's net energy balance depends on the degree to which householders can modify their usage patterns. We consider two questions here: given a collection of realistic preferences and constraints on usage patterns of households, what degree of saving is possible by optimizing 'within' these preferences and constraints?; and, what amounts of energy saving are possible when the community exploits its social network by sharing electrical appliances? These questions are investigated in the context of Riccarton Ecovillage. A model of the ecovillage was implemented using an agent-based modelling toolkit, then simulated under a range of scenarios, automatically exploring the space of usage patterns to find combinations of usage schedules that minimized dependence on the national supply. Our findings are: evolutionary algorithms perform particularly well at this difficult optimization task; modest savings of 5–10% are achievable under standard assumptions, but savings of 35–40% are achievable when exploiting the underlying social network.

Keywords: ABM; agent-based modelling and simulation; ecovillage; energy; evolutionary algorithm; optimization

INTRODUCTION

Any community of interacting individuals is a complex system. In general, such a system of interconnected and interdependent structured components exhibits behaviour that is difficult or impossible to predict when we use simplified models that ignore the temporal and spatial heterogeneities inherent in the system. This is especially the case when the components themselves exhibit non-deterministic stochastic behaviour. Understanding the behaviour of a complex system is a major problem. Even if the structure and behaviour of individual components of a complex system can be captured and described clearly, the behaviour of the complex system also depends on the complicated interaction map of its components, making the whole more than the sum of the parts.

The difficulties in understanding and controlling complex systems are particularly salient in the context of many contemporary challenges, including, in particular, the global need to reduce our reliance on fossil fuels. In addressing these challenges, we often need to predict and/or control the behaviour of systems that we do not yet understand. This can be particularly damaging when it goes wrong. However, the relatively new field of science called complexity science is attempting to develop appropriate methods to handle and understand system complexity. One prominent tool that emerges from complexity science is the use of agent-based modelling (ABM) – also known as individual-based modelling (Hood, 1998; Gimblett, 2002; Edmonds, 2005). For example, if we wish to predict the energy consumption of a community of 1000 people over a year, one way to do this would be to measure the energy consumption of a community of 100 people over six months, and multiply that by 20. This is obviously immensely simplified, and makes several strong assumptions about the relationship between the number of people in a community and that community's energy consumption. Perhaps the crudest simplification in this simplified model is the absence of any factor

*Corresponding author: Email: D.W.Corne@hw.ac.uk

ARCHITECTURAL SCIENCE REVIEW 53 | 2010 | 126–140
doi:10.3763/asre.2009.0108 ©2010 Earthscan ISSN: 0003-8628 (print), 1758-9622 (online) www.earthscan.co.uk/journals/asre   earthscan

other than the number of people and the time period. At the other extreme, one could imagine a sophisticated model of the community whose energy consumption we are aiming to predict. Rather than use simplifying assumptions, such a model encodes distinct behaviours for each of the individuals in the community, realistic time-varying schedules for factors such as sunlight and weather, and reasonable and stochastic rules for interactions between individuals and their responses to external factors. Obtaining predictions from such a model then arises from simulating the model – that is, running the agent-based simulation – and observing and collating the results.

Such a simulation-based model also allows us to explore 'what-if' questions, and can be used as a tool to explore all variety of questions concerning how the components of a complex system – in this case, behavioural policies of households and communities with regard to energy usage – may be designed to achieve specific outcomes. In particular, by using the agent-based simulation within an optimization procedure, we can automatically search through the space of ideal policies in order to optimize the resulting behaviour of the system.

In the context of an ecovillage, which has its own means to generate electricity (its own microgrid), one question that can be explored is how the ecovillage community could maximize the use of its own supply, and minimize its reliance on the national supply – that is, how the village can reduce its net use of the national supply. What makes this a complex challenge is the fluctuating and unpredictable nature of the microgrid, which will be dependent on sunlight and wind, and the difficulty of electricity storage. Meanwhile, individual households tend to have patterns of electricity consumption that vary within predictable bounds (e.g. TV mostly in the evening, washing machine usually in the morning on a Monday, etc.), and preferences and 'comfort zones' around those bounds. For example, a household that tends to use its dishwasher between 8 and 10pm may be easily persuaded to schedule this consumption between 7 and 8:30pm for the benefit of the community, but would not be amenable to shifting this usage to 11am.

The first question that we explore is: given a collection of realistic preferences and constraints on usage patterns for individual households, what degree of energy saving is possible by optimizing 'within' these preferences and constraints? This question is explored using an agent-based simulation model of the planned Riccarton Ecovillage in which differing but realistic preferences and constraints are assumed for each household, and realistic data are used to inform the time-varying level of electricity supply available from the village's own microgrid.

Second, what amounts of energy saving are possible when the community exploits its social network by sharing the usage of electrical appliances? These questions are investigated in the context of the planned experimental Riccarton Ecovillage (20 homes). A model of the Riccarton Ecovillage was implemented using the Repast.Net ABM toolkit, and the

model was simulated under a range of conditions. In particular, optimization methods were wrapped around the simulation model, exploring the space of usage patterns (within given constraints and preferences) to find effective combinations of electricity usage schedules that minimized dependence on the national supply. Our findings are as follows: evolutionary algorithms perform particularly well at this difficult optimization task; and modest savings of 5–10% are achievable under standard assumptions, but savings of 35–40% are achievable in communities that exploit their underlying social network.

The remainder of this article is set out as follows. First, we briefly review the concept of an ecovillage, and describe some details of the planned ecovillage in Riccarton, Edinburgh. Next, we briefly introduce the Repast system – the ABM toolkit used in this study – and then broadly describe how it was used to model the Riccarton Ecovillage. The fourth section explains how we use optimization methods wrapped around the agent-based model (ABM) in order to find sets of usage patterns that combine to maximal overall benefit. This section discusses the two main optimization experiments. Next we present the results, partly from the viewpoint of competing approaches to the optimization task, but largely from the viewpoint of the solutions achieved for the task at hand, comparing the relative benefits available via organizing consumption in the context of a social network. Finally, a concluding discussion is given.

ECOVILLAGES

The concept of ecovillages has emerged in response to natural ecosystem deterioration and climate change. It is regarded as one kind of the broader concept of intentional communities, where people live together in communities that share common beliefs and intentions (Wikipedia, 2009b). Ecovillages are self-sustained, ecologically sustainable intentional communities, where a small group of people (50–500) can live and develop naturally in a full-featured environment that is also ecologically, economically and socially healthy (Gilman, 1991; Kasper, 2008). People living in an ecovillage share the responsibilities of the community, while enjoying the warmth of close relationships and a dense social network.

Ecovillages are usually characterized by the following:

- Harmless integration with nature (Gilman, 1991) through the promotion of recycling behaviour, the avoidance of toxic substances and the exploitation of environment-friendly power sources, using wind turbines, photovoltaic solar systems, geothermal and biomass plants, rather than fossil fuel. Ecovillages have been established to prove that full-featured communities can live and develop with minimum carbon and waste footprints.
- Urban design strategies that lower the environmental impact of the community: buildings in an ecovillage are characterized by a higher degree of insulation and

proper architectural form to achieve the best energy use efficiency. Buildings are usually oriented to be exposed to the highest level of solar radiation. Also, alternative water and sewage processing systems are utilized.
- 'Green' trends in lifestyles, exhibiting more cooperation and less consumerism.

Ecovillages are also ideal examples of real-world complex systems that can be studied and modelled, with the overall aim of understanding how interactions between individuals' behaviour, community policies and the natural environment impact on key issues such as energy usage and carbon footprints.

Riccarton Ecovillage and Living Laboratory

The Riccarton Ecovillage and Living Laboratory (REALL) is a 20-household village that will be built at the main campus of Heriot-Watt University in Riccarton, Edinburgh (Roaf, 2009). The project has emerged as a multidisciplinary initiative by the Energy Academy in the University, to be a whole-system approach to study the 'performance of energy use and supply in buildings' (Energy Academy of Heriot-Watt University, 2009). The project aims to design, build and then thoroughly monitor an inhabited ecovillage. The project is expected to help reach a better understanding of the effects of behaviour adaptation on energy demand, the energy performance of different materials, forms and designs, and to thoroughly investigate various power generation methods on site, renewable and non-renewable. The project aims to provide a unique insight into the reality of how occupied buildings actually work in practice to provide data to underpin emerging standards and recommendations designed to meet the low carbon targets for the economy and greenhouse gas reduction, and to inform decision makers, stakeholders, researchers and people with real findings on the new climate-adapting built environment (Roaf *et al.*, 2009).

The village will comprise five blocks of four houses. All the houses will have the same size, form and orientation, but will differ in their methods of construction and materials. The houses will be occupied by postgraduate students who will participate in researching and monitoring energy performance aspects, including 'thermal, carbon, acoustic, water, waste, climatic and environmental performance, costs and impacts of occupied homes' (John Gilbert Architects, 2008).

The village will have a private microgrid, containing a wind turbine and photovoltaic solar panels for each house. The microgrid should satisfy the energy needs of the village, but it would be linked to the general grid for backup purposes.

MODELLING THE REALL

On modelling complex systems

A complex 'system' is a collection of interconnected and interdependent structured components (Wikipedia, 2009a, c),

often exhibiting some characteristic 'emergent' behaviour (Boccara, 2004). In a complex system, the number of features and components is usually moderate or large, and interactions between the components are usually non-deterministic. From one viewpoint, the 'essence' of a complex system is simply that the outcome of these complex interactions (in other words, the medium- and long-term behaviour of the system itself) tends to defy understanding and prediction by currently known analytic methods.

A classic example of a complex system is the weather. We are all familiar with attempts to predict weather by meteorological centres around the world, but perhaps we are less familiar with the fact that the accuracy of weather predictions tends to be rather poor, and degrades sharply the further in advance the prediction (Stern, 2008). The basis of weather prediction is a model of the atmosphere that treats it as a collection of adjacent air masses, each with dimensions in the order of (typically) 4km. A weather model attempts to simulate the interaction between these masses using physical laws, which, given initial estimates of temperature, pressure, wind speed, wind direction and various other measurements for each mass, determine the states of these parameters after a given length of time (e.g. 5 minutes later). This process is iterated in order to develop predictions over longer time scales. When it comes to weather prediction, the physical laws tend to be well understood, but the quality of the prediction relies crucially on our knowledge of the initial conditions.

This example helps introduce some key aspects of ABMs. It is clear to most of us that as we move ahead in computer processing power, are able to model the atmosphere with finer-grained detail (larger meshes of smaller air masses) and are able to more accurately measure, and hence provide, initial conditions to the models, weather prediction will gradually improve. Few have any argument with this, because it is clear that the weather we see is a result of physical laws, and weather simulation simply models and simulates those laws. The key to appreciating the power of ABMs – where we typically model interacting intentional agents rather than air masses and such – is that much the same can be said of the rules than underpin for example human interaction, or some other aspects of human behaviour that we may wish to model. If we can characterize (e.g. in terms of 'what' and 'how often') the typical interactions that occur between the agents that we wish to model, then an ABM simulation of the system is, in the case of most complex systems, a highly effective, and perhaps the only, way of generating predictions of overall behaviour for that system. The increasing popularity and success of ABMs (Hartmann, 2005), now being explored for many applications (some examples are listed in the section Detailed design of the REALL model), is partly due to the fact that, when well designed, they produce plausible and actionable results – essentially their predictions fit data, and do so better than any available non-ABM models. For example, one broad class of particularly simple ABM models are so-called cellular automata (CA), and CA-based models of the spread of HIV-infected cells within sufferers (in which an 'agent' is a cell) seem to reproduce the complex dynamics of healthy vs infected cell concentration over time that is revealed by observations of patients (dos Santos and Coutinho, 2001; Corne and Frisco, 2008). This match with observed data has to date eluded a variety of mathematical modelling approaches, but is achieved by an ABM with a set of simple but plausible rules for interactions over time between spatially neighbouring agents.

ABMs are a key tool arising from the relatively new field of science called complexity science, which is attempting to develop appropriate methods to handle and understand system complexity (Edmonds, 2005). It involves discovering patterns that recur in complex systems, developing the mathematical foundations of complexity and creating tool sets to facilitate the study: for example, to understand complex data (e.g. using machine learning techniques), to create and evaluate models of complex systems (e.g. using CA and ABM) and to measure the complexity in systems (Shalizi, 2006). Research in complex systems is interdisciplinary, spanning physical, ecological, economical, social and political sciences, in addition to computing.

Simulation and optimization
By enabling simulations of a complex system, an ABM (or similar type of model) is excellent for investigating basic 'what-if's that explore the consequences of the assumptions and starting conditions from which it is developed, but this in itself has limitations for the management of such a complex system. When we have run the model several times and have therefore characterized 'what will happen', it is entirely typical that we would rather something different happened, and our goal is to find out how to set up the initial conditions in such a way that our ideal outcome matches the emergent behaviour of the system. For example, our model of the placement of fire exits may, according to our ABM, mean that the building takes 20 minutes to evacuate; however, we want this to happen in 15 minutes. How do we position the fire exits to achieve this goal? The ABM cannot by itself answer our question. Meanwhile, a naive (but sometimes the only viable) approach is to make inspired guesses of suitable designs and then run the model to see the outcome of these guesses: for example, experiment with different fire exit placements until we happen upon a winning design. But this approach tends to be untenable for two main reasons. First, the number of possible configurations is usually enormous, far too many to explore by repeated simulation. Second, and recalling the essence of complex systems, the better designs may well be counter-intuitive, and unlikely to be among those that would be chosen for our simulation experiments.

ABMs thereby provide a partial solution to the need to identify ways to design aspects of complex systems so that they will meet desired requirements for behaviour, but they cannot do the entire job. Increasingly, this gap is being filled by optimization algorithms. An optimization is simply an iterative (usually) and fully automated process for finding the set of parameters that is 'best' according to a particular measure of quality. In the context of ABMs of complex systems, the measure of quality may typically be the distance between the desired outcome (e.g. 95% of the population of a village become regular users of the recycling bins within 2 years) and the actual outcome of the simulation, perhaps averaged over a number of trials (e.g. for a certain configuration of incentives and policies, the simulation may yield 90% of the population as recyclers within 2 years). An optimization algorithm attempts efficiently to search the space of possible system configurations, aiming to find good solutions reasonably quickly. Optimization of complex problems and/or simulations is gaining increasing interest (Laguna, 1997; Fu, 2002; Olafsson and Kim, 2002; Fu et al., 2005). A number of different optimization algorithms are available, arising from various subfields of mathematics and computer science. For problems with large discrete solution spaces, metaheuristics and random search provide a variety of methods and techniques that are simple to implement and with good convergence attributes. Genetic algorithms are one of the most promising tools, which are efficient, robust against local optima and can scale flexibly according to problem settings.

The REALL model: general considerations
An ABM of the REALL (hereafter, the REALL model) was conceived in order to explore aspects of how communities may best work together to achieve energy savings. In particular, envisioning the REALL community as operating its own microgrid, one aspect of interest is the energy balance, that is, the hour to hour difference between microgrid supply and residents' demand, and how this varies with people's behaviour, how they adapt to new circumstances and the microgrid energy-pricing policy. In the REALL model, this microgrid is assumed to comprise photovoltaic solar panels installed in each house, and one village-wide wind turbine. Electricity supply in the ecovillage is assumed to depend on these renewable sources, reverting to the national supply when necessary. Clearly, the village's microgrid supply will vary considerably according to changing weather, seasons and time of the day. Energy demand, on the other hand, is linked to the behaviour of residents and their ability to adapt and control their consumption habits.

The REALL model therefore requires simulation, at some level, of individuals (inhabitants of the ecovillage) and natural phenomena (weather conditions). This implies the following requirements:

- Realistic time-varying values for natural phenomena should be modelled: particularly wind velocity, solar radiation and temperature, which are all major factors that affect microgrid production.
- The influences of different weather conditions on power generation devices, solar panels and wind turbines should

be identified, taking into consideration the limitations of these devices and their performance characteristics.

- Finally, simulation of each individual household's energy demand through time is needed. To investigate adaptation of behaviour, the consumption habits of households should be modelled realistically.

The simulation of energy demand in an individual household is a key aspect of the REALL model, and works in the following way. We assume that each household contains a typical array of devices that consume energy, and consider only those devices that are typically power-hungry, such as dishwashers, televisions (which may be switched on for several hours) and washing machines. We assign to each household a realistic but different pattern of usage of these appliances. These patterns are assigned at random, but constrained to within plausible ranges. For example, in one household we may assume that the occupants prefer to use the washing machine twice a week, usually on a Wednesday and a Saturday, for 1 hour between 8 and 9am on a Wednesday and between 1 and 5pm on a Saturday; in the same household we may assume a mean amount of TV viewing of 5 hours per day, starting and ending within a 6pm and 1am window. When the REALL model operates, whether or not a particular device is in use in a particular household at a particular time is decided randomly (by the HouseSchedule agent, see below), but the random decision is biased by the preferences and constraints that have been set for that household. Finally, the main feature of our experiments with the REALL model is the exploitation of social networks, in which households will from time to time share the use of certain resources with other households. To underpin this, in some experiments a random network of links exists between households, which defines a social network in the village (whose density can be varied). Households' behaviour for such includes, for each resource, probabilities that govern sharing that resource from time to time with other households that are linked directly with that household in the social network.

In summary, the REALL model is an energy-focused ABM of the Riccarton Ecovillage, in which the agents (in more detail below) are the individual households. The model is relatively small scale (since REALL comprises only 20 households), and the interactions that will be modelled are relatively simple. The major source of complexity and interaction will be the interplay between energy supply, weather and individual behaviour.

Detailed design of the REALL model

There are now several open-source software libraries in the ABM research community for developing ABMs (Railsback et al., 2006). For the present work, we used Repast (Recursive Porous Agent Simulation Toolkit) (REPAST, 2009), developed at the Argonne National Laboratory – a highly regarded toolkit that has been used for a range of applications ranging through exploration of business strategies

(López-Sánchez et al., 2005), effects of charging for road use (Takama, 2005), simulation of digital markets (López-Sánchez et al., 2005), battlefield simulation (Baker et al., 2005), growth of hydrogen transportation infrastructure (Stephan and Sullivan, 2004), the evolution of house prices (Bossomaier et al., 2007) and many more.

We next describe the REALL model in a moderate level of detail, sufficient for readers to understand how such a model is designed, as well as clarify the underlying assumptions included in our REALL model, and indicate what is simulated within the model and what is not. The description is presented in the style of one of the more well-established methods, called 'Gaia methodology' (Zambonelli et al., 2003), for the design and development of ABMs, and simply amounts to indicating the *roles* of the agents in the model. In the Gaia method (of which only a part was used in the design of REALL), roles are capabilities of agents, and the early design of an ABM includes outlining the required roles; this recipe of roles is then the basis for implementing the ABM (in which each agent may have one or more of the distinct roles). In REALL, a broader understanding of the ABM model itself will emerge from observing this set of roles, listed as follows, falling naturally into themed groups:

- *Roles concerned with climate conditions*
  - *Sun*: A SunSimulator agent plays the role of indicating the expected solar radiation levels for given time and date values. Naturally this agent takes into consideration hour to hour and season to season differences.
  - *Wind*: The role of the WindSimulator agent is to provide realistic values for wind velocity at a fixed elevation, again given specific time and date inputs.
  - *Temperature*: A TemperatureSimulator agent gives the expected ambient temperature associated with given time and date values.
- *Roles concerned with power generation*
  - *Solar panels*: The role of a PVSimulator agent is to compute an amount of generated electricity when provided with given solar radiation, power and ambient temperature levels. The inner workings of this agent are informed by characteristic performance curves and associated loss equations appropriate for the specific photovoltaic module being simulated, and of course takes account of the size of the simulated solar panel.
  - *Wind turbine*: The role of the WindTurbineSimulator agent is to compute an amount of generated electricity when provided with wind speed. The inner workings of this agent are informed by characteristic performance plots associated with the specific turbine device being modelled.
- *Roles associated with energy demand*
  - *Household*: A House agent is responsible for simulating the energy production and consumption of an individual household. It interacts with a PVSimulator agent (each household has its own solar panel) in connection with energy production, and interacts with a HouseSchedule

agent (see below) in connection with the energy consumption of residents of the house.

  ○ *Household preferences*: A HouseSchedule agent has the role of indicating the preferences and habits of residents of an individual house, in connection with their usage patterns for the household's electrical appliances. In particular, the HouseSchedule agent calculates a level of power demand for its house for any given time period.

- *Other roles*
  ○ *Observer*: The Observer agent's role is to coordinate interaction between the other agents.
  ○ *Timer*: A Timer agent is responsible for time-keeping – essentially, a common reference frame that can be queried by any agent.

In short, further aspects of designing an appropriate ABM model amount to designing an appropriate topology of interactions among the various roles, and an appropriate overall control regime (i.e. what happens when in the simulation). Interactions between the roles in the REALL model are illustrated in Figure 1.

With reference to Figure 1, the Observer controls the other major agents (such as House agents), which in turn control others. These 'control' links typically indicate straightforward operations: for example, a house agent will ask its PVSimulator agent to provide the amount of energy that it can supply in the next time step. To do this, the PVSimulator agent needs to make queries to the sun and temperature agents, and so on.

A broad sketch of the operation of the REALL model is therefore as follows. For convenience, we express this mainly in terms of what is being modelled rather than in 'ABM-speak'. First, the Observer initializes the timer, the wind turbine, the weather (sunlight, wind, temperature) and each household in the village. Each household also initializes its solar panel and its HouseSchedule agent. A single time step in the REALL model corresponds to 1 hour of simulated time. In each time unit, the climate agents calculate realistic values for mean temperature, solar radiation levels and wind speed for that time unit. This is done non-deterministically, but within plausible bounds. For example, based on available historical data, the temperature agent knows the normal temperature range for a given time on a given day, and will choose a random temperature within these bounds. Next, the wind turbine and solar panel agents will calculate realistic levels of energy generation given the details supplied by the climate agents and given the characteristics of the devices they are simulating. Independently, each household agent chooses randomly, but within predefined realistic bounds for the individual household, an energy demand for the current time period for each modelled electrical appliance in the household. When a 'social network' is active in the simulation, households also choose, again stochastically, whether or not a device will be shared with another household with which it is directly linked. The entire process repeats over many time steps; in the experiments reported here, experiments typically covered a month of simulated time, with each time step representing 1 hour.

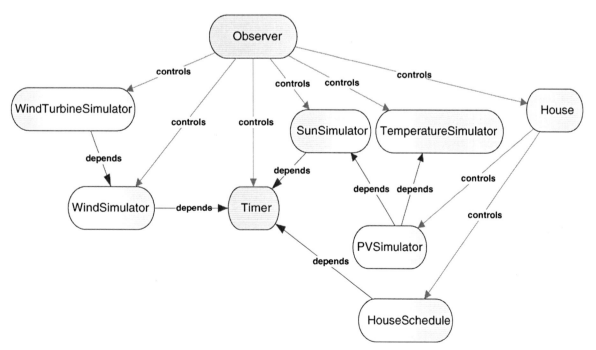

Figure 1 | Roles in the REALL model, their interactions and dependencies

USING THE REALL MODEL IS A TOOL FOR COMPLEXITY-INFORMED MANAGEMENT

Simulation and stochasticity

Management and planning, in any context, depend on the ability to predict the consequences of actions, designs and policies. In restricted scenarios, and especially when we are predicting something that is only a short step into the future, such predictions can be made with confidence and can validly inform management and planning. For example, when a soccer match has been scheduled between the two major soccer teams in London, we can confidently predict a lower bound on the number of spectators, and the police can make sensible provision for their presence; in the run-up to Christmas, postal services in many countries can predict a massive increase in demand, and arrange accordingly for suitable staffing.

This is well known and understood. However, for current purposes it is useful to think of these examples in terms of models, and consider what we are doing when we make a prediction. In the case of the soccer match, we may have historical data that indicate the attendance for this match in previous years. Our predictive model in this case may simply be to fit a straight line to this attendance/year curve, and read off the prediction for the current year from the line. In the case of the postal service, there may be a precisely analogous situation – perhaps this line will show a downward trend, considering the competition for postal services in many countries over recent years, and the growth of email, but nevertheless it will show a trend, and this will lead to a prediction.

However, major difficulties arise as soon as 'complex interactions' are apparent, which undermine the feeling that historical data, or any other such simplified model, will be valid. For example, the soccer match may occur on the same day as an international cricket match elsewhere in London, perhaps both these events are being televised live for the first time, and both local travel and ticket costs may be double last years' levels, at the same time as unprecedented levels of unemployment. In the case of the Christmas post, recent strike action by the postal services, in combination with further increase in competition for postal service provision, whereby alternative providers are able to price their services at unprecedentedly low levels, make us far less confident in simply extrapolating from past data.

In essence, the behaviour of a system becomes difficult or impossible to predict as soon as the system includes interactions between varieties of competing 'forces', especially where we have no basis in prior experience in which the same or a very similar system has operated under the same conditions. The business of complexity science is all about finding ways to arrive at predictions of behaviour in such scenarios, and the way this is done is, in one sense, obvious and as follows: 'if you want to see what will happen – try it and see what happens!'. That is easily said, but it seems to

imply we cannot predict it in advance – instead we wait for the soccer match to happen, or we await the Christmas postal rush, and record the data we are interested in, too late for any management actions. However, the trick in complexity science that gets around this is to see what happens by simulating the system. We build a complex model of the system at the levels of agents, interactions and behaviours (for each of which we can at least make inspired guesses) – rather than a mathematical abstraction based on data that we do not have – and then run the model, thereby simulating the system whose behaviour we are trying to predict.

It is useful to emphasize, at this point, that multiple runs of REALL (or any other ABM with stochastic elements – essentially all useful ABMs) will produce different results. This is entirely analogous to the multiple potential outcomes that arise from, for example, many runs of climate models that attempt to predict future climate parameters. Essentially, any such model has a characteristic probability distribution over the potential outcomes – deploying an ABM helps us gain an understanding of the relative likelihoods of different outcomes rather than enabling us to confidently predict the future in fine detail. However, what we might generally hope for is the ability to confidently predict that certain outcomes are far more likely than others. For example, if we build into the model certain household policies and preferences for sharing resources, and after 10 runs of the model we see energy savings for the community varying from 10% (in the 'worst' run) to 20% (in the 'best'), we can have some confidence in predicting that, to the extent that other aspects of the model are suitably realistic, the given policies and procedures would generally lead to energy savings of 10% or more if implemented by a real-world example of the type of community being modelled.

As a potential tool for managing a real-world complex system, an ABM can be looked upon purely as a prediction tool, in which the model is configured to reflect the current design of the real-world system, and it is then run (several times) to characterize expectations for how the real-world system is likely to behave in the future. However, the development and use of an ABM is more involved, and more useful than this implies. In particular, if and when we find that the real-world system has not developed within the bounds of expectation that our model predicted, we have learnt something. This could be as simple as finding a 'bug' in the model; however, more likely, and more usefully, investigation will find that the disparity is due to aspects of the real-world system that were not thought important enough to include in the model, but which in fact do have a salient effect on behaviour. Perhaps an extreme but instructive example is the case of the London Millennium Bridge, which swayed violently when pedestrians were first able to walk across it in numbers. What was left out of the 'model' in this case was the fact that pedestrians effect unconscious local interactions whereby they gradually synchronize their steps, and in the real-world case this led to setting up a damaging resonance.

Some background on optimization

Earlier in the section Simulation and optimization, we discussed the distinctions between simulation – using an ABM model to see what happens under given starting conditions – and optimization – in which we use an automated method that is 'wrapped around' the simulation, and which attempts to find the starting conditions and configurations for the model that lead to ideal outcomes when the simulation is run. Optimization is in fact the main theme of the experiments we report in this article. Hence we, provide here some brief background material on optimization in general, so as to place into context the optimization methods that are used in the experiments discussed later.

A typical optimization problem can be formulated as follows. Suppose we are given a system, of any kind, which is expressed in the form of a set of parameters (e.g. a set of numbers, each allowed to be between 0 and 1). Any particular realization of these parameters (i.e. specific values for each one) is referred to as a specific configuration of the system. Suppose further that we are given a quality function that, when applied to a configuration, gives us a number that we can take to be the 'quality' of that configuration. 'Optimization' simply refers to a process of trying to find the 'best' configuration – that is, the configuration that yields the best result from the quality function. Further, an optimization algorithm is an automatic method for searching the space of configurations with a view to finding good configurations quickly.

In context, a configuration may be a specific subset of parameters for an ABM model, such as the set of probabilities associated with using specific electrical appliances at certain times of day. The quality function may work as follows: run the ABM model, and return the net use of the national electricity supply over the simulated period. Clearly, we would like this to be minimized, so that the 'best' configuration of parameters is one that yields the lowest demand on the national supply (indeed this may be negative, indicating a surfeit of generation in the ecovillage).

Optimization is a large subfield of each of mathematics and computer science, and there are a wide variety of different families of optimization algorithms (Gray *et al.*, 1997; Garcia *et al.*, 2006; Griva *et al.*, 2009; Weise, 2009), each applicable to different styles of optimization problem. In navigating this space for current purposes, and using a very broad, but nevertheless valid, brush, two salient generalizations can be made. First, it turns out that almost all interesting optimization problems (i.e. those of some practical importance to solve) are 'difficult' in a specific technical sense – this amounts to the fact that no algorithm is known that is guaranteed to find the best answer in reasonable time. The consequence of this is that optimization research is replete with so-called approximate algorithms – these are algorithms that try to find good configurations reasonably quickly, but can never guarantee that they will find the true best result. The second of our salient generalizations is that, when it comes to complex quality functions (essentially, any quality function that is not in itself easily subject to mathematical analysis), the choice of appropriate optimization algorithms narrows down to a single select family known as black box or stochastic search methods. These are, in essence, trial and error methods, but in which the choice of the next configuration to test is guided (in ways that differ between algorithms) by the quality values that have been calculated for previously tried configurations.

Without getting into too much detail, when we perform optimization in the next sections, we test three exemplars of stochastic search algorithms. These are hillclimbing (HC), simulated annealing (SA) and an evolutionary algorithm (EA). In general, when a complex optimization problem has to be solved, stochastic optimization algorithms tend to have different speed/quality trade-offs. HC can typically find good solutions quickly, but then be unable to find further improvement; meanwhile a well-designed EA can typically find better quality solutions than HC, but takes a relatively long time to do so. SA tends to have a speed/quality trade-off somewhere in between these two.

Given any new complex optimization problem, it is always wise to experiment with such a range of optimization algorithms, since the aforementioned rules of thumb can often be violated in practice, depending (in ways that currently defeat the current state of theory in black box optimization) on the details of the quality function. For example, in some cases, but not in most, HC can provide fast and high-quality solutions that are not improved by either SA or an EA. In our optimization tests, we therefore try each of these three methods, in order to characterize their performance on the energy-focused REALL model, and partly to inform the choice of optimization method in further work on variants of this REALL model.

SIMULATION AND OPTIMIZATION EXPERIMENTS FOR REALL

In this section we describe experiments that have been performed with the REALL model, leaving the presentation of results for a later section.

Two sets of experiments were performed. In the first set of experiments, the idea was to examine to what extent energy savings can be made in the ecovillage within the constraints set by the preferences in individual households. In the second, and perhaps most interesting, set of experiments, the idea was to see what levels of savings were possible if an ecovillage exploited the social network of its occupant households (e.g. watching TV with friends), and these experiments explore how potential savings in demand vary with different densities of social linkage.

Before a more detailed explanation, it is useful to note some points common to the two sets of experiments. Each household has a set of preferences that dictate its energy demand behaviour. A household's list of preferences amounts to, for each of up to 10 electrical appliances, an average amount of hours per day using that appliance, and preferred time windows during which that appliance is used. Different, random, but plausible preferences were generated for each household in the REALL model. In all cases, the time step in the simulation, regarding a household's energy consumption, was 1 hour. That is, the HouseSchedule agent repeatedly chooses, given that household's preferences and constraints, the appliances that will be used (and therefore sets that household's energy demands) for the next hour. Finally, simulations in our experiments are restricted to one summer month. This was a pragmatic choice considering the time demands of the simulations, especially when comparing several optimization methods, each of which needs to run the simulation many times.

Optimizing energy balance in the Riccarton Ecovillage

The microgrid of the Riccarton Ecovillage (as modelled) comprises the communal wind turbine and each household's solar panel. The ecovillage could presumably reduce its energy carbon footprint to virtually zero if the generated green electricity is consumed efficiently and no general grid power is imported. The problem, however, is the fluctuation in availability of solar and wind power. An obvious approach in achieving minimal use of grid power would be for residents to adapt their energy consumption behaviour to align with the availability of energy from the microgrid, performing energy-hungry tasks when electricity is normally available and refraining from consumption at other times. In general, this may be rather too much to ask, since individual households may have demand patterns that make such alignment difficult. For example, if work commitments mean that a particular household must be empty during the daylight hours in weekdays, it is inevitable that much of that household's energy demand cannot be supplied by solar power. In this set of experiments, however, we adopt and explore the view that households can be easily persuaded to perturb their natural schedules for using appliances *within* the boundaries set by their own preferences. That is, if a household prefers to use its washing machine on Saturdays between 8am and noon, then that household would be amenable to any suggestion within those constraints (e.g. 8–10am, or 10am–noon) that may emerge from a management process that attempts to optimize energy usage for the village as a whole. The first set of experiments explores this notion by discovering, via optimization, what level of energy savings may be possible in realistic scenarios in which householders shift their schedules within their own constraints and preferences. Note that this is far from straightforward or predictable: we cannot predict, for example, that everyone should shift their usage towards the sunniest part of the day – this would simply lead to too much demand during the sunniest hours and under-utilization (wasted energy or costly storage) of the village microgrid at other times.

Optimizing energy balance: a more precise statement

The optimization problem for the first set of experiments can be described slightly more formally as follows. Given, for each household in the ecovillage,

- P: a list of residents' preferred times and durations for using specific electrical appliances in their household
- C: a list of constraints on times and durations of appliance usage that define what is acceptable or possible for residents and what is not,

find a daily scheduling of consumption events, within the constraints for each household, that minimizes the community's overall need for externally supplied power. In particular, what is optimized are each household's start times and durations for use of their electrical appliances, but ensuring that these times remain within the fixed constraints for that household. In this way, a daily schedule is optimized for each household.

More formally, $P = \{P_1, P_2, \ldots, P_{20}\}$ is the set of preferences for each of the 20 households in the Riccarton Ecovillage, where P_i is the preference list for household i. P_i itself is composed of a set of consumption events, that is, $P_i = \{e_1, e_2, \ldots, e_m\}$, in which the consumption event e_i expresses the household's preferred timeslot and duration for using appliance i. In detail, e_i comprises four parts:

1 *Start time*: the preferred timeslot at which the consumption starts.
2 *Duration*: the preferred number of slots the consumption lasts.
3 *Probability*: the probability that the consumption event will occur. This is used for non-daily used appliances, to overcome the daily structure of the preference list.
4 *Appliance details*: characteristics of the appliance; wattage, usage pattern (continuous vs intermittent) and usage rate.

Meanwhile, whereas the preference lists outline specific start times and durations for each given household, the constraint list, $C = \{C_1, C_2, \ldots, C_{20}\}$, outlines a set of constraints C_i for each household i, indicating how much that household is prepared to operate outside its current habits. A specific household's constraint list indicates the limits within which a consumption event can vary. Each constraint is attached to a consumption event, but not all consumption events necessarily have constraints. There are two types of constraints, start time constraints and duration constraints. A start time constraint defines the maximum accepted value for the attached consumption event's start time field, and the duration constraint defines the minimum accepted value for the duration field.

Estimating the 'performance' of the simulation

As discussed, optimization requires repeatedly running the simulation with different successive configurations, where the choice of the next configuration is guided by the quality of previous configurations (essentially, most stochastic optimization methods work by trying out new configurations that are close to the better-performing pre-viously tested configurations). The quality function is rather crucial to this process. As should be clear, a 'configur-ation' in this set of experiments amounts to a particular daily schedule of consumption events (within the constraints) for each household. The quality function, as noted, is simply a measure of the amount of external energy consumption that is recorded in the simulation, when run with a given configuration.

In some more detail, the quality function of a configur-ation is calculated in the following way. Given a particular configuration to evaluate, the ABM model runs in time steps of 1 hour (simulated). In each such hour, energy con-sumption is calculated for each household (according to the schedule of consumption of events in that household, for that given configuration) and the available energy supply from the microgrid is calculated for that household (its portion of the supply emerging from the wind turbine, plus that emerging in that hour from the household's solar panel). Consequently, for each household, and for each hour of the simulation, we have a difference value – the difference between microgrid supply available to a house-hold and electricity consumption in that household. Each of these difference values are squared, and then they are all summed to arrive at an overall quality value for the configur-ation. The aim is then to minimize this measure.

It is worth considering this issue with care: in both sets of experiments, the quality measure is defined so that we obtain ideal quality by matching the curve of consumption levels over time as closely as possible to the curve of microgrid supply levels over time. Differences – either positive (excess demand, so the national grid must be used to plug the gap) or negative (excess supply, wasted energy gener-ation in the village) – are penalized. This reflects a suitable target for ecovillages that do not have viable means to store, or otherwise capitalize on, excess energy, and was a suitable experimental design issue. However, we remark that it is tri-vially simple to explore alternative quality functions for alternative scenarios in which, for example, REALL was able to usefully store a limited amount of its supply, perhaps at a certain cost, which could itself be incorporated into the quality function.

Notes on statistical confidence

Recalling our discussion in the section Simulation and optimization, since the ABM simulation is stochastic, it is clear that it would not be sensible to evaluate the quality of a configuration on the basis of a single run of the simulation with that configuration. Ideally, we would take as our quality evaluation the mean result from several runs with the same configuration. However, simulations have an appreciable time cost, and we need to minimize the number of repeat runs but at the same time attain a useful level of statistical confidence in the evaluation.

We address this matter in the following way. Whenever a configuration is to be evaluated, we run the simulation five times to obtain a mean quality value and we also note the var-iance of this value over the five runs. If the variance is such that we cannot form 95% confidence in the result (on the basis of a T-test), a further simulation is run, and the mean and variance are recalculated now over the six runs. This is repeated until we have obtained a mean quality value that has suitably high confidence, although we stop at 10 iter-ations irrespective of confidence level.

Exploiting the social network

The second set of experiments was the same as the first set in all respects, but had the additional characteristic of a social interaction network and its exploitation. Ecovillages are communities in which we can naturally expect a high level of social interaction, and we model this in a simple way by defining a network in which each household is a node, and a link between nodes represents a social link between the two households. The aim of this is to investigate to what degree sociability of the community can lead to reduced energy demand. It is assumed that neighbours who are linked with a strong social tie are more likely to share or combine resources. For example, if household A is linked socially to household B, then it is more probable that it would, for instance, invite residents of household B for dinner. Household B would then have less demand for cooking, lighting, TV and heating for that night. If similar types of interaction are actively and regularly carried out in the community, considerable savings may be achieved. The second set of experiments investigates this hypothesis and also explores the effect of modifying the density of the social network.

The density of the social network is characterized by m, which is related to the maximum number of links that an individual household can have. Each household is assigned randomly, at the start of the simulation, a random number of links (between 0 and m) to other households. Notice that the special case of $m = 0$ corresponds to the first set of experiments. During a simulation, sharing worked as follows. Each simulation day, a household can choose to share, or not to share (with probability 0.5), its resources. If the decision is to share, then one linked neighbour on the social network is chosen randomly, and sharing takes place between the original household (the inviter) and the linked household. The sharing is then manifest as a poten-tially only small increase in the inviter's consumption for the shared appliances only, and zero consumption for the invitee household for the same appliances. The increase in consumption of the inviter is a randomly chosen multiplier between 1 and 1.5; this range reflects the cases of devices that do not cause extra consumption when shared (e.g. TV) and others that may be increased (lighting, cooking, etc.). It is worth noting that a boundless variety of sharing 'models' could be implemented; more realistic approaches, for example, would bias the sharing events according to strength values on the links in the social network, and would be informed by available survey data. However, the approach described was deemed sufficient for this experiment.

Finally, while in the first set of experiments we compared the three exemplar black box optimization methods (HC, SA and EA), we used only the best of these (according to results on the first set of experiments) for the social network experiments – this turned out to be the EA.

SIMULATION AND OPTIMIZATION RESULTS

Optimizing energy balance

Each of HC, SA and EA were tested for a variety of algorithm parameter configurations. We do not reproduce a full set of results here, but this is available on request. In this section, we briefly summarize the relative performance of the three optimization methods and focus more on the physical interpretation of the ABM simulation results.

Figure 2 summarizes the performance of HC, SA and EA for this optimization task, after many experiments with varying parameterizations of the algorithms. In this figure, lower is better, but the numbers on the vertical axis can be ignored, to be considered as arbitrary units for current purposes, but is roughly proportional to squaring the amount of energy required from the national supply. A relatively low value indicates a configuration of household schedules that, while each operating within their own comfort zones, amounted overall to an energy consumption curve that was relatively well aligned with the availability of energy from the village's microgrid. The label at the top of each bar indicates the algorithm and the number of iterations for which it was run (which can be taken as directly proportional to the time taken). In this way, the figure also includes a broad summary of the speed/quality trade-offs for the different optimization methods on this problem. Interestingly (but not unusually), the EA is the best quality algorithm, whether at 1000, 5000 or 10,000 iterations. An 'iteration' corresponds to a single run of the ABM simulation on a single configuration. The EA also clearly benefits more than the others (in terms of its ability to find better configurations) when given extra time. The superior solution quality found by the EA is particularly significant when experiments continue for 10,000 iterations; thus, the EA was chosen as the sole optimizer to use in the next set of experiments, and is also the method that led to the solutions we interpret below.

Figures 3 and 4 show visualizations of the preference lists at steps 0 and 5000, respectively, from a 5000 iteration run of the EA. That is, Figure 3 shows a preference list that results from an unoptimized situation, in which households simply follow their natural preferences, without reference to any community-based planning, and Figure 4 represents an ideal situation that may emerge by households attempting to align their electricity consumption in cooperation with and to the benefit of the community as a whole, but still within their own constraints of acceptability.

In Figures 3 and 4, each colour denotes an appliance type. The horizontal axis indicates time of day, while the vertical axis indicates consumption in three different households. The Figure 3 case shows clear trends of consumption in morning (breakfast time) and evening (dinner time) hours. However, presumably influenced by the fact that the dominant source of energy is solar, and the availability of solar energy is concentrated around midday, the output of step 5000 shows more concentration of consumption towards the middle area, with less in the morning and evening. Also, the optimizer enforces a kind of cooperative balance among different households' consumption, taking into

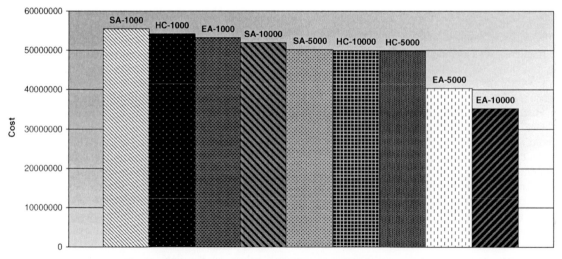

Figure 2 | Algorithm performance comparison for different iteration counts

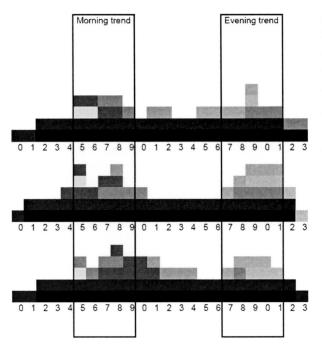

Figure 3 | Visualization of the preference lists for three households – step 0

consideration their constraints, to achieve the least possible degree of dissatisfaction.

A consideration of the energy savings available by optimizing the preference lists in this way is given in the next

section. Recall that this set of experiments is the 'no friends' specialization of the set of experiments that investigate exploitation of the social network.

Optimizing energy balance via exploiting the social network

In this set of experiments, the same objective function was used, and separate optimization runs were done for different levels of social network density. Three values were tested for m (the maximum number of links per household), reflecting different levels of connectivity, in addition to the null case where no social network is incorporated (corresponding to the experiments summarized in the section Optimizing energy balance). Summarized results, following the use of the EA as the optimizer, running for 5000 iterations per experiment, are shown in Figure 5. Again, in this figure the vertical 'cost' axis is in arbitrary units, but can be considered directly related to squared excess reliance on the national supply rather than the village's microgrid.

Figure 5 summarizes the results of several optimization runs for each social network density, and records the best, worst and mean values that emerged from those runs. It is quite clear that introduction of the social network leads to significant improvement in the cost values.

Recalling Figure 2, we note that the results achieved by the 5000-iteration EA were in the region of 40M cost units. This already represents a considerable improvement over configurations where no optimization has been done (i.e. each household simply operates unchanged according to their initial preferences), in which the cost is around 75M units (Hawasly, 2009). In Figure 5, if we simply consider the average results, the exploitation of a low-density social

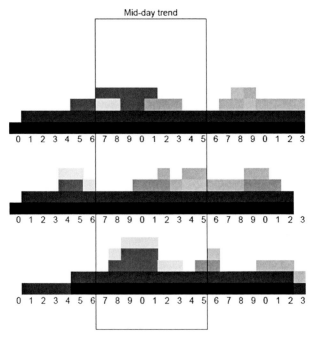

Figure 4 | Visualization of the preference lists for three households – step 5000

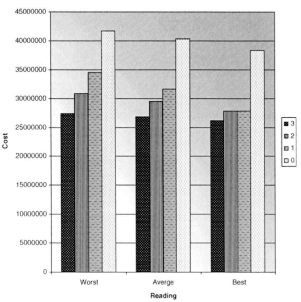

Figure 5 | Comparison of cost for different levels of social network density

network already leads to a sharp improvement (33M cost units), while networks with density level 3 (certainly not unreasonable for an ecovillage community) achieve around 28M cost units.

When we correctly interpret these results in terms of direct amounts of electricity, rather than units of the fitness function – or, equivalently, if we interpret these results correctly in terms of potential financial savings) – we find that the configurations found by optimization using the density 3 social network represent 40% savings over an unoptimized, 'unmanaged' community.

If we consider 5000-iteration optimization only, we note that simply optimizing household schedules without exploiting the social network (the first set of experiments) can lead to ~25% savings, and this increases to 40% with the most dense social network studied (in which each household is friends with roughly 15% of its small community). However, it is worth pointing out that longer iteration runs (the 10,000-iteration EA) were able to find schedules with ~32% savings over the unoptimized case, without exploiting the social network. For pragmatic reasons, such longer runs were not done for the 'exploiting social networks' experiments in this article, but the implication is that better than 40% savings could well be achievable.

CONCLUSIONS

A summary of the model, experiments and results
We have described a relatively simple ABM of the planned Riccarton Ecovillage, in which households' preferences for their daily use of electrical appliances were simulated, in tandem with realistic time-varying availabilities of solar and wind energy. Via optimization, we explored the potential benefits that could be gained in such a community if it adopted a simple and acceptable community management strategy, in which, informed by evidence from simulations, households would be individually requested to lean towards particular times for their regular energy consumption activities. Further, we also explored the potential accrued benefits available if the community exploited its social network by regular resource sharing. Our findings suggest that quite significant savings are achievable via such measures. Simply attempting to establish a mutually acceptable and mutually beneficial schedule of consumption activities, with no assumed resource sharing, can lead to 25% savings in cost (reliance on the national supply), while exploitation of the social network seems capable of raising this to beyond 40%. Meanwhile it is entirely conceivable that more optimization effort could find solutions with appreciably more savings; such requires computational expense, but by no means undue expense.

We find the implications of this, for the design and management of such communities, to be both intriguing and exciting. As discussed, simulation models such as the REALL model allow 'what–if' explorations, but the impact of these explorations can be rather limited without some way of discovering how to organize or manage the community to achieve a specific goal. Via optimization, however, we can automatically explore the space of strategies, and find ones that achieve our targets. As a tool for managing communities, this general approach has been very little explored to date, but the applicability (in the face of no sensible alternatives) and the potential of such an approach seem clear. Naturally, such models can incorporate considerably more complexity than we have shown here; for example, in one thread of continuing research we plan to enhance the REALL model to reflect more real-world complexity by switching from modelling households to modelling people with intentions and beliefs, incorporating more appliances, investigating real households' consumption habits and adaptability, better representing time, and the development of a complex environment where the agents would interact. Such enhancements, among others, allow for a greater range of experiments, and consequently a greater range of implications for design and management strategies for the REALL community. It must be noted of course that such enhancements also carry a computational burden that tends to constrain the amount of optimization that could be done; however, the ever-increasing availability of affordable high-performance computing resources comes to our rescue in this respect. In particular, if we view ABMs as essential management tools for such communities, the wise use of which can promise substantial benefits beyond shorter-sighted approaches, then the requirement of reasonably costly computational resources becomes acceptable.

DISCUSSION

The growing need to build resilience in our societies at a time of rapid social, economic and environmental change with better choices for, and management of, the built environment and the human capacity to deal with change is clear.

This article has shown that new agent-based complex models are now capable of informing choices of technological solutions with the impacts of attitudes, values and behaviours to optimize the energy and environmental benefits of decisions and minimize their costs. It offers the best method to date of ensuring that the best choice is made within a wide range of available adaptive opportunities derived from an extremely complex range of iterations produced from relationships between interacting forces.

Systems such as the REALL model offer a tool to introduce credible 'fresh thinking' with significant potential to engage and educate the public, raise environmental awareness and personal 'buy-in' to the implementation of 'socially viable' solutions in the transformed markets. It may also answer a wide range of questions such as the following:

- At what level are such solutions best fostered at?
- As a result of the outputs of such simulations, would ensuing local community-based changes be best led by governments, dedicated to stimulating economic growth?

- Will local communities find it easier to agree to lower standards of living for their own futures if they can clearly see the clear, equitable benefits using such models?
- Can such models be used to avoid 'collapse' events being the only effective driving force for markets?
- Is it inevitable that the only sustainable future is a simpler one that will work adequately in the approaching eras of scarcity, growing climate impacts and increasingly unaffordable capitalism?
- Are there new paradigms of 'smart development' where man and machines can work side by side to automate, motivate and decarbonize economies while maintaining standards of living and qualities of life?
- People have been shown to be motivated by environmental concerns while also holding strong material concerns, which motivate them to purchase new products and increase their environmental impact. Can the use of tools such as this to 'trade-off' gains and losses clearly demonstrate the effectiveness of solutions to promote goals of long-term sustainability that would appeal to, and be adopted by, local residents?
- Are imposed step changes imposed by society and their politicians, or periodic system collapses, the only way to affect the stringent cuts required by emerging greenhouse gas reduction targets?
- To what extent are people's expectations of quality of life and comfort amenable to modification with information and 'ethical persuasion'?

These tools can be used interactively with real populations to test the water on a case-by-case basis, to explore their core values and what they are willing to sacrifice in the bid to build social and economic resilience in the face of rapid change. Pathways to deep emissions reductions in commercial buildings require not only increased consideration of passive and low-energy architectural principles and renewable energy technologies but also the buy-in of populations in doing so.

Substantial building sector energy and emissions reductions are available through advanced technologies and controls, but even in the very high-tech buildings systems are capable of reaching their full potential only when coupled to behavioural techniques to manage the expectations and perceptions of building users.

There appears to be a pressing need to develop new ways of engaging society to participate in the necessary changes ahead. It is clearly necessary to have a clear and scientifically valid focus on the targets, in time, ahead and the tools in hand to practically achieve them, but radical transformations of the type necessary to meet global reduction targets are unlikely to progress without the engagement of the key stakeholders involved in the built environment in making the decisions to change. Models such as this may well provide a new language to the dialogue that engagement may require as well as ensuring that the best possible solutions are adopted.

References

Baker, T.J.A., Botting, M., Berryman, M.J., Ryan, A., Grisogon, A.M. and Abbott, D., 2005, 'Adaptive battle agents: emergence in artificial life combat models', *Proceedings of the SPIE, Smart Structures, Devices, and Systems II Bellingham, WA*, 574–585.

Boccara, N., 2004, *Modeling Complex Systems*, Berlin, Germany, Springer.

Bossomaier, T., Amri, S. and Thompson, J., 2007, 'Agent-based modelling of house price evolution', *Proceedings of the 2007 IEEE Symposium on Artificial Life (CI-ALife 2007). Honolulu, HI*, 463–467.

Corne, D. and Frisco, P., 2008, 'Dynamics of HIV infection studied with cellular automata and conformon-P systems', *Biosystems* 91(3), 531–544.

dos Santos, R. and Coutinho, S., 2001, 'Dynamics of HIV infection: a cellular automata approach', *Physics Review Letters* 87(16), 168102–1, 4.

Edmonds, B., 2005, 'Simulation and complexity – how they can relate', in V. Feldmann and K. Mhlfeld (eds), *Virtual Worlds of Precision – Computer-based Simulations in the Sciences and Social Sciences*, Berlin-Hamburg-Münster, Lit Verlag, 5–32.

Energy Academy of Heriot-Watt University, 2009, Available at: www.energy.hw.ac.uk/projects/ecovillage.cfm [accessed 28 July 2009].

Fu, M.C., 2002, 'Optimization for simulation: theory vs practice', *INFORMS* 14(3), 192–215.

Fu, M.C., Glover, F.W. and April, J., 2005, 'Simulation optimization: a review, new developments, and applications', *Proceedings of the 2005 Winter Simulation Conference*.

Garcia, J.S.D., Avila, S.L. and Carpe, W.P., 2006, 'Introduction to optimization methods: a brief survey of methods', *IEEE Multidisciplinary Engineering Education Magazine*, 1(2), 1–5.

Gilman, R., 1991, 'The Eco-village Challenge', in CONTEXT, 29, page 10. Available at: www.context.org/ICLIB/IC29/Gilman1.htm

Gimblett, H.R., 2002, 'Integrating geographic information systems and agent-based technologies for modeling and simulating social and ecological phenomena', in H.R. Gimblett (ed), *Integrating Geographic Information Systems and Agent-based Techniques for Simulating Social and Ecological Processes*, Oxford, Oxford University Press.

Gray, P., Hart, W., Painton, L., Phillips, C., Trahan, M. and Wagner, J., 1997, 'A survey of global optimization methods', [online], Sandia National Laboratories. Available at: www.cs.sandia.gov/opt/survey/ [accessed 15 July 2009].

Griva, I., Nash, S.G. and Sofer, A., 2009, *Linear and Nonlinear Optimization*, 2nd edition, PA, SIAM.

Hartmann, S., 2005, 'The world as a process: simulations in the natural and social sciences', PhilSci Archive, archive.pitt.edu/archive/00002412/

Hawasly, M., 2009, 'Optimization of complex systems via simulation', MSc Dissertation, Heriot-Watt University.

Hood, L., 1998, 'Agent based modelling', *Proceedings of the Greenhouse Beyond Kyoto Conference, Bureau of Resource Sciences*.

John Gilbert Architects, 2008, 'Riccarton Ecovillage – feasibility study', Glasgow.

Kasper, D.V.S., 2008, 'Redefining community in the Ecovillage', *Research in Human Ecology* 15(1). Available at: www.humanecologyreview.org/pastissues/her151/kasper.pdf

Laguna, M., 1997, 'Optimization of complex systems with OptQuest', OptQuest for Crystal Ball User Manual, faculty.colorado.edu/laguna/articles/optquest.pdf

López-Sánchez, M., Noria, X., Rodríguez, J.A. and Gilbert, N., 2005, 'Multi-agent based simulation of news digital markets', *International Journal of Computer Science & Applications* 2(1), 7–14.

Olafsson, S. and Kim, J., 2002, 'Simulation optimization', *Proceedings of the 2002 Winter Simulation Conference*.

Railsback, S.F., Lytinen, S.L. and Jackson, S.K., 2006, 'Agent-based simulation platforms: review and development recommendations', *Simulation* 82(9) 609–623.

REPAST, 2009, Available at: http://repast. sourceforge.net/ [accessed February 2009].

Roaf, S., 2009, 'Riccarton Eco-Village: towards zero carbon housing', PowerPoint slides, retrieved from Cifal Findhorn. Available at: http://cifalfind horn.org/docs/TowardsZeroCarbon Hous_Pr.pdf

Roaf, S., Crichton, D. and Nicol, F., 2009, *Adapting Buildings and Cities for Climate Change*, Oxford, Architectural Press.

Shalizi, C.R., 2006, *Complex Systems Science in Biomedicine*, Berlin, Germany, Springer.

Stephan, C. and Sullivan, J., 2004, 'Growth of a hydrogen transportation infra-structure', in C.M. Macal, D. Sallach and M.J. North (eds), *Proceedings of the Agent 2004 Conference on Social Dynamics: Interaction, Reflexivity and Emergence, Chicago, IL*, 731–742, Available at: www.agent2005.anl.gov/ Agent2004.pdf

Stern, H., 2008, 'The accuracy of weather forecasts for Melbourne', *Australia, Meteorological Applications* 15(1), 65–71.

Takama, T., 2005, *Stochastic Agent-Based Modelling for Reality: Dynamic Discrete Choice Analysis with Interaction*, Oxford, UK, University of Oxford. Available at: www.tri.napier.ac. uk/Events/TDM/prestonpaper.pdf

Weise, T., 2009, *Global Optimization Algorithms – Theory and Application*, 2nd edition, E-book. Available at: www.it-weise.de/

Wikipedia, 2009a, 'Complex system', wiki article. Available at: http://en. wikipedia.org/wiki/Complex system [accessed 11 July 2009].

Wikipedia, 2009b, 'Ecovillage', wiki article. Available at: http://en. wikipedia.org/wiki/Ecovillage [accessed July 2009].

Wikipedia, 2009c, 'System', wiki article. Available at: http://en.wikipedia.org/ wiki/System [accessed July 2009].

Zambonelli, F., Jennings, N.R. and Wooldridge, M., 2003, 'Developing multiagent systems: the Gaia methodology', *ACM Transactions on Software Engineering Methodology* 12, 3.